The U.S. Supreme Court's Democratic Spaces

Studies in American Constitutional Heritage
Justin Wert and Kyle Harper, Series Editors

The U.S. Supreme Court's Democratic Spaces

Jocelyn J. Evans and Keith Gåddie

University of Oklahoma : Norman

Library of Congress Cataloging-in-Publication Data

Names: Jones Evans, Jocelyn, author. | Gåddie, Ronald Keith, author.

Title: The U.S. Supreme Court's democratic spaces / Jocelyn Jones Evans and Ronald Keith Gåddie.

Other titles: US Supreme Court's democratic spaces

Description: First. | Norman : University of Oklahoma Press, 2021. | Series: Studies in American constitutional heritage ; 5 | Summary: "Explores the evolution of the U.S. Supreme Court Building and shows how it shapes Washington, D.C., as a space and a place for political action and meaning"—provider by the publisher

Identifiers: LCCN 2021012571 | ISBN 978-0-8061-7601-7 (hardcover) ISBN 978-0-8061-9397-7 (paper)

Subjects: LCSH: Supreme Court Building (Washington, D.C.) | Neoclassicism (Architecture)—Washington (D.C.) | Democracy—United States. | Washing-ton (D.C.)—Buildings, structures, etc. | BISAC: POLITICAL SCIENCE / Ameri-can Government / Judicial Branch | HISTORY / United States / 20th Century

Classification: LCC NA4473.W18 J66 2021 | DDC 720.9753—dc23

LC record available at https:// ccn.loc.gov/2021012571

The paper in this book meets the guidelines for permanence and durability of the Committee on Production Guidelines for Book Longevity of the Council on Library Resources, Inc. ∞

The U.S. Supreme Court's Democratic Spaces is Volume 5 in the Studies in American Constitutional Heritage series

Contents

Acknowledgments

Some books have to marinate for a while before they fully take shape. A decade after 9/11, Capitol Hill had changed. A new, subterranean Capitol Visitor Center directly below the Rotunda welcomed tourists through magnetometers and bag checks. Some things remained the same: professional tour guides still directed traffic through hallowed corridors to major points of interest, including Statuary Hall and the Old Senate Chamber. Others did not: members of Congress and staff no longer accompanied constituents through the building as part of routine daily business. That job had been outsourced due to increased securitization. The final substantive chapter in Jocelyn Evans's book *One Nation Under Siege: Congress, Terrorism, and the Fate of American Democracy* considered the social meaning of the new Capitol Visitor Center and its implications for the broader meaning of the U.S. Capitol Building itself. As that manuscript went to print, we turned our eyes to the broader security of the Capitol Hill landscape, and just across First Street we found the sleepy U.S. Supreme Court Building. Like the Capitol, the building is of neoclassical design, adorned with pediments and friezes, statuary and fountains, and contributed to a fabric of values expressed through architectural forms. But the story of the Supreme Court is not that of the U.S. Capitol, where the "who gets what" of Lasswellian politics takes place. The inhabitants of the Supreme Court Building are charged with the honorable duties of interpreting the meaning of the law, upholding the U.S. Constitution, and protecting the rights of the individual. The court's home is a different creature, built in a different manner and in a different time. Edmund Burke observed to M. de Menonville in a letter of October 1789 that "whenever a separation is made between liberty and justice, neither, in my opinion, is safe" (Burke 1967, 6:42). The courts of the Anglosphere carry in their common law tradition these dual charges: to defend and guarantee the liberty of every person, and also to mete out justice in instances of injurious acts by one person against another. This requires that justice have a home to balance facts, law, and precedent to determine a resolution.

For a decade, we have given the subject of the social meaning of the homes of the Supreme Court careful and patient thought. As time allowed, we accessed correspondence, early imprints, congressional records, planning commission reports, style guides, histories, judicial caseloads, and maps. We left open the possibility of additional chapters and new methodologies because we wanted to fully capture the maturation of the manifestation of the Supreme Court as part of the federal city landscape. We challenged our own preconceived notions of federal courthouse design and style, and ended up with a very different book than the one we set out to write.

A book is a product of all of its contributors. Consequently, we are greatly indebted to several organizations and individuals who provided assistance along this slow and deliberate journey. We received institutional support from the University of West Florida (UWF) and the University of Oklahoma. Fieldwork was made possible through financial support from the University of West Florida. Financial support was provided from the Office of the Vice President for Research, the Office of the Provost at the University of Oklahoma, and the University of Oklahoma Foundation. These resources included subvention funding to support indexing costs and securing permissions to reproduce illustrations and images.

In Washington, D.C., support staff at the Library of Congress gave us access to the Cass Gilbert Papers. Steve Livengood of the U.S. Capitol Historical Society spent several hours walking us through the U.S. Capitol Building, exploring the presence of the Supreme Court in various chambers of the Capitol until the court's permanent home across the street opened in 1935. We also received a warm welcome from the Office of the Senate Historian, and its staff provided copies of historical guides, newspaper clippings, and other rare documentation of the court in the Capitol. Derek Morgan and Elizabeth Barrett of UWF provided Geographic Information System (GIS) services in creating several of the mapping images in the text.

Over the years, we presented drafts of several chapters at meetings of the Southern Political Science Association, the Southwestern Political Science Association, and the Law and Society Association. Fellow panelists provided invaluable feedback, and we offer sincere gratitude to all of the following: Samantha Gassie at Arizona State; Priscilla Machado Zotti at the United States Naval Academy; Paul Foote at Eastern Kentucky University; Ryan Williams at Claremont Graduate University; Joanna Lynn Grisinger at Northwestern University; Joanna Acevedo at the University of Chicago; Robert Yablon at University of Wisconsin–Madison; Kirsten Nussbaumer at Rutgers University; Noga Morag-Levine at Michigan State University; Rachael Belle Houston at the University of Minnesota; Alicia Uribe-McGuire at the University of Illinois at Urbana-Champaign; Lisa Hager at South Dakota State University; Lindsay Rose Russell at the University of Nevada–Las Vegas; Matthew Montgomery at Georgia State University; Robert M. Howard at Georgia State University; Virginia Hettinger at the University of Connecticut; Amy M. McDowell at Old Dominion University; John Charles Morris at Auburn University; Rick L. Travis at Mississippi State University; Jacqueline Sievert at the University at Buffalo; Joshua Boston at Bowling Green State University; and Laura J. Hatcher at Southeast Missouri State University.

Special thanks go to our colleagues at the University of Oklahoma from the Christopher C. Gibbs College of Architecture and the Institute for the American Constitutional Heritage in the College of Arts and Sciences. Stephanie Pilat and Angela Person encouraged us to continue looking seriously at governmental buildings even though serious inquiry took us beyond the comfort zone of our disciplinary training. Justin Wert read complete drafts and provided encouragement and assurance that this treatment of the court in the American consciousness extended beyond current scholarship, made a meaningful contribution, and would spark the interest of those who study judicial history and politics. At OU Press, the two referees, our editor Kent Calder, and the editorial production team helped us hone our idea into a far better and more substantive final product.

Finally, we are indebted to our families and friends, who stuck with us when we filled the mailbox with countless books on American civic architecture, who made it possible for us to conduct fieldwork, who listened to rough attempts to articulate central ideas, and who understand the writer's impulse. Evans grew up around the courthouse. It was part of her family's identity. Having a father with three decades of public service as a state circuit judge made the balance between justice and mercy tangible. It brought home the symbolic significance of donning the heavy black robe and transforming into *Your Honor.* And it actualized equal treatment of all citizens under the law in everyday practice. Gaddie grew up in the construction industry, became an academic, and then spent thirteen years going into state and federal courthouses around the country as an expert witness and litigation consultant, including working several cases that went all the way to the Supreme Court and submitting amici curiae to the high court in several others dealing with America's invisible political architecture, the controversial art of redistricting and gerrymandering. This book is the result of our separate yet complementary formative experiences and the winding road of intellectual inquiry that followed.

Introduction

The U.S. Supreme Court's Democratic Spaces tells the story of the architectural journey of the Supreme Court from a marketplace in Manhattan to its residence on First Street in Washington, D.C. In many ways, we argue, it is a secular temple to the aspirations of democracy under a constitutional system of government. Rituals of American communal justice take place within its hallowed halls, carried out by priests in black robes. It is a space that invites political protest, facilitates conflict resolution, and defines individual rights. Though the building was a late addition to Washington, D.C., its Neoclassical style provided a visually coherent architectural fabric for governmental power in the capital city and a visual identity for American justice writ large. In many communities, this style is echoed in federal court buildings. In others, it is not.

American judicial architecture has democratic manifestations. As the earliest institutions of democratic governance, courts convey the sanctity of the individual. With attention to both civil liberties and civil rights, American judicial procedure embodies the values of unity, freedom, and equality. How does the space in which the process occurs support or frustrate those aims?

This book grew out of a shared interest in public architecture and public institutions that was independently discovered but collectively shared. It is our hope that seriously considering the social meaning of American judicial civic space will yield new appreciation for the ways in which our physical surroundings manifest who we are as a people and what we value as a society. Only then are we positioned to evaluate the merit of civic architecture in our own communities, and only then can we truly appreciate the full reservoir of judicial authority in American society today.

The story of the Supreme Court Building is more than the story of its construction or of its technical architectural elements as a Neoclassical work. It is a story of the evolution of the court and of the succession of its preceding homes in Washington, Philadelphia, and New York that contribute to the shape of both the institution and its modern home. It is also a story of interpretation of the court's home through architectural, democratic, and cultural lenses to imagine all the ways that the court's home might be understood, and how it creates affect in those who come within its walls to visit, to litigate, or to otherwise work. It is the story of how the building shapes Washington as a space and a place for political action and meaning. For those with a deeper interest in the artistic and symbolic elements of civic architecture, examining the court and its homes serves as a vehicle for engaging American political theory through a deep textual reading of notable structures in the built environment and as features of the American democratic enterprise. For those who ponder the future of judicial architecture, we offer additional thoughts that emerge from this multifaceted examination of the court's homes and of federal courthouses in general.

When academics study courts, they do so through disciplinary lenses. Judicial behavior scholars try to make sense of opinion formation, sources of influence, voting coalitions, public opinion, and interbranch relations in a system of separated powers. Communication scholars access the courts through textual analysis of opinions accompanying major rulings. They consider the rhetorical strategies utilized by justices to uphold, challenge, and establish precedent. Democratic theorists and those who study law and society consider the role of the courts in protecting minority rights, upholding the rule of law, and legitimizing state authority. To understand the Supreme Court, we have sought out the crossroads of democratic theory, American political development, and architecture. We draw from previous scholarship across many fields of inquiry to seriously consider the origins and evolution of the social meaning of American federal courts, with particular emphasis on the U.S. Supreme Court Building. The facilities that house the judicial process and administration have significance, in our view, because they structure how we see the law and understand the role of courts in society.

Figure 0.1. Panorama of the west façade of the U.S. Supreme Court Building at dusk. Photograph 2011 by Joe Ravi. Image courtesy of Wikimedia Commons.

Judicial civic space carries symbolic meaning, and that meaning has changed over time with changing architectural styles.

While the literature on the social meaning of judicial civic space is rather limited, a few major works are worthy of note at the outset of this book. With the politicization of judicial appointments to the Supreme Court and the highly controversial foray of the court into questions such as school integration, abortion, gay rights, affirmative action, and electioneering, John Brigham (1987) considers the cultlike aura of final authority surrounding the Supreme Court and its judicial decision making. Its role as the final arbiter in interpreting the Constitution serves as the basis of its institutional authority rather than its unquestionable legal judgment. Consequently, the Constitution has become less the final legal authority in American politics, and more of an institutionalized "cult" of deference to the court itself. The idea of the court as an institution with unchallenged reverence in the American psyche frames our discussion of the built environment of the Supreme Court. We add to Brigham's analysis by focusing on the architectural features and the design patterns that harness reverence for the work of the court.

Barbara A. Perry's treatment of the U.S. Supreme Court focuses on the sanctity and respect with which the court is treated by the American public as a consequence of its public image as the protector of the Constitution. Her 1999 book, *The Priestly Tribe*, illuminates the characteristics of the federal judicial branch differentiating it from the executive and legislative branches of American government. In it, Perry points to specific aspects of judicial behavior, such as fidelity to the rule of law and purposeful inaccessibility to the media, as well as the longevity of judicial tenure and the symbols enshrined in the physical spaces of the courts. Perry's focus is more on the shrouds of judicial behavior than on the symbology of the built spaces housing the court. For that examination, one must turn to more recent work by Judith Resnik and Dennis Curtis (2011), discussed next.

In *Representing Justice*, Resnik and Curtis (2011) take seriously the notion that symbols hold societal meaning. They posit that our understanding of the role of courts in society evolved from centuries of legal adjudication in courts decorated by icons of justice. The authors identify the democratic character of modern courts as bastions of freedom from the arbitrary edicts of kings and the capricious violence of mobs. The authors lay a solid foundation for our work, but they focus more on *specific* symbols of justice and their adaptation over time and across nations as well as the development of modern democratic rights of due process. They also treat the court as a democratic institution, a central feature we accept and incorporate into our argument. Building on this foundation, our work centers on the emergence and role of courts in the American political system, the institutionalization of the U.S. Supreme Court over time, the symbolic meaning of its physical spaces and icons, and the relationship of the court as a situated place to the rest of the governing apparatus and urban fabric of Washington, D.C.

In his most recent work, Brigham (2009) uses an interdisciplinary approach to consider the intersection of law and society. He grapples with the material manifestations of law in the physical world and asks a fundamental question: How does law shape social and legal reality in such a way that the law is then applied to the physical world? His goal for the reader is to develop an ability to see "law in things and things in law." His work unfolded in three parts: (1) theorizing material life, (2) constituting legal spaces, and (3) materializing law. He homes in on the materiality of the law in our understanding of physical space and ownership; human bodies and agency; social inequality and contested sovereignty; and legal constructs, whether architectural or global. This highly philosophical work provides theoretical precedent for thinking about the material dimensions of American courts and the social meaning of the law in material form, giving concrete and tangible expression to inherent beliefs and democratic values.

These scholarly traditions collectively establish the assumptions upon which our work is premised. The Supreme Court, more than any other institution of the American federal government, enjoys a cult-like reverence in the American mind. The folkways and symbology surrounding the court are unique and add to the reverence and mystique of judicial proceedings and decision-making. Though it is shrouded from public view, the court is fundamentally a democratic institution. It has become the protector of individual freedom and defender of the rights of the minority against the capricious will of the majority. And there is a materiality to the court. Its terminology, its physical building, its location in relation to other buildings, its institutionalization over time, and its iconography give material life to the law. It carries social meaning for civic life in that it expresses values concerning the form and function of law in American society. This meaning extends not just to the high court as an individual institution but to all the courts of the federal judiciary.

OUTLINING THE STORY OF THE COURT

In chapter 1, "Democratic Origins in Function and Form," we introduce the concept of the courts as democratic institutions and describe the classical and Enlightenment origins of American democracy and also American democratic architecture as embodied in Greek Revival and Neoclassical styles. We then lay out the planning inflections in the "national city" and how they influence the general development of Washington and also set the stage for the placement of the court's home. The role of a national architectural movement and the desires of a chief justice converged to create one of the last Neoclassical structures erected in Washington, D.C.

In chapter 2, "The American Courthouse," we introduce the concept of *courthouse* and explore its origin in Anglo North America. This exercise in etymology introduces the ubiquitous nature of courthouses in the American experience and sets up an exploration of the transient and tenant nature of the high court and the subsequent twentieth-century creation of a permanent home of its own in the Supreme Court Building.

Chapter 3, "Evolution of the U.S. Supreme Court and Its Homes," explores the historic homes of the Supreme Court, starting with the now long-gone Merchants Exchange Building in New York City. We then study the two historic homes of the court in the republic's second capital, Philadelphia, examining the court's spaces in Independence Hall and Philadelphia City Hall. The relocation of the government to Washington, D.C., takes us into the next two permanent homes of the court inside the U.S. Capitol Building: the Old Supreme Court chambers located in the Capitol basement, and the Old Senate chamber located immediately above the basement chambers on the first floor (the latter chamber served as home to the court for seventy-four years).

Chapter 4, "A Civic Interpretation of the U.S. Supreme Court Building," is our first analysis of the Supreme Court's current home. We apply Charles Goodsell's approach to understanding civic space, originally applied to statehouses and city councils, and extend it to the courthouse. In particular, we explore the "civicness" of the Supreme Court Building in terms of control, public access, purpose, and enclosure. We undertake a detailed study of the perimeter of the space, in terms of both control by the court and communication of purpose. We explore the circulation, civic, audience, operational, and sanctum spaces of the court in terms of relative public access, purpose, denotation and expression, and ritual. This analysis leads to an overall understanding of the court in democratic terms, in terms of both its feature elements and its overall democratic iconography and importance in the American republic.

In chapter 5, "A Cultural Interpretation of the U.S. Supreme Court Building," we change our analytic approach to explore the court's home through three manifestations—material, cognitive, normative—which intersect to create culture. Then, in this cultural context, we use three lenses advanced by Charles Goodsell (2001) in his work *The American Statehouse*—expressive, behavioral, and societal—to explore the intentions and vision of Cass Gilbert's design, with an eye toward his inspirations and influences, and also the resulting metaphors and allegories that arise from the court's newest home. In particular, we explore different temple metaphors of the court (the American Ark, the Temple at Karnak, the Temple of Solomon, the Parthenon) to tease out the nuances of meaning that inform the various metaphors. We also note the extension of these metaphors into the presentation of courts and courthouses in popular culture.

The final substantive chapter, chapter 6, "Establishing the Federal Presence," considers the shift in judicial architecture used for the federal presence at the local level. Architects frequently designed courthouses for local communities in the Federal or Neoclassical style. These buildings sat on the public square of the town and served as the civic heart of the county. They held the public's vital records; they performed the secular rites of marriage and divorce; and they served communal justice by jury trial in the civic temple for all to see. It is worth considering how a national program calling for high design in all new construction of federal courthouses in communities throughout the nation will impact the social meaning of the court to the American public. Do these courthouses speak of accessibility, transparency, and egalitarianism? Or do they appear to be unfamiliar, invasive, inaccessible, extravagant, and threatening? By arguing that there are patterns of democratic architecture, we provide a social critique of undemocratic judicial spaces and call for careful consideration of design choice in building justice for all.

Our analysis ends with an assessment of the social meaning of judicial architecture in the U.S. context. In our conclusion, "The Rule of Law in Space and Place," we consider the late integration of the Supreme Court Building into the cityscape of Washington, D.C., and the implications of this late addition for the imageability of the court in the city (Lynch 1960). Unlike the National Mall, the Capitol, and the White House, the public image of the Supreme Court Building derives its familiarity from serving as a backdrop used by the national media in covering major decisions of the court. The other moments when the court becomes visible to the public occur during the nomination and confirmation process for filling judicial vacancies. The material setting of this process, however, is the hearing room of the Senate Judiciary Committee rather than the Supreme Court Building. The court's public image is mediated by references to political protest and politicization of the judicial confirmation process. In this way, the concluding chapter, by way of synthesis, provides a relational analysis of the court as a spatially fixed place, appended to the Washington, D.C., government apparatus late in the urban development of the city, located in an illogical space relative to the underground public transit system, and mediated by limited media coverage of court happenings. It is a building with significant social meaning in place and space.

1　Democratic Origins in Function and Form

Sixteen massive granite columns support a grand pediment. Behind them, gleaming bronze doors reflect the afternoon sun. A lantern hangs above, to illuminate the portal against the dark. Below, broad stairs climb from the street, flanked by the statues of ancient lawgivers. Emblazoned across the front of the building are the words "Equal Justice under Law," in letters as tall as a human being. Larger-than-life figures adorn the frieze. And behind those doors, atop those steps, beneath those words, nine jurists hold court. This is the home of the United States Supreme Court, a Neoclassical courthouse set on most of a block of land to the east of the U.S. Capitol, a shining white temple standing beneath a blue southern sky.

The Supreme Court Building as described above adorns numerous book covers and accompanies countless stories of the judiciary. Visitors are often surprised to learn that the building is of a very recent vintage, opening its doors in 1935 after three years of construction, and is among the youngest public buildings housing a major national institution.[1] Yet it appears much older, enjoying many of the same elements of its capstone institutional companions, the executive mansion and the Capitol Building constructed at the end of the eighteenth century. The "stone temple" presentation complements the highly proximate Capitol and also a variety of memorial structures around Washington, including the

Lincoln Memorial (completed in 1922) and the Jefferson Memorial (completed in 1943).

Before the Supreme Court took up residence in its "Temple to Justice" during the New Deal, the justices had spent nearly 150 years as either transients or as tenants in the buildings of other institutions. The high court came to this place late, as the great era of Neoclassical construction in public architecture was coming to a close. It had many previous homes, and they shaped both the institution and its final building. The home of the Supreme Court has evolved with the development of its institutional role, the scope of government, and the growth of the capital city. Many local and state courts have had the same experience in American frontier history, serving from temporary or shared spaces, and then moving into permanent, grand homes that were often Greek Revival and Neoclassical structures evoking the temple form. It would be reasonable to assume that these other courthouses took their inspiration from the Supreme Court Building, but that would be a mistaken assumption.

COURTS AS DEMOCRATIC INSTITUTIONS

Courts and courthouses are a central feature of American culture. Courts and the rule of law are a primary component of the expansion of the American nation across the continent. The creation of means to settle disputes and dispense justice through due process is a central feature of the American story. In our culture, we perpetuate this role in both the teaching of landmark cases and the articulation of a culture of rights, as well as through our literature and entertainment, which embrace the courtroom and the courthouse as theatrical venues. Visual media rely on the symbols of the court and justice to convey meaning in stories. The U.S. Supreme Court is the best-known of these stages, serving as the venue for the interpretation of the U.S. Constitution and arbitrating the ongoing struggle between rights, liberties, power, and order in the American experience.

It is fitting that the courts and their homes come to North America in tandem with Anglo settlement and expansion of the United States. Courts are among the earliest spaces of democratic governance. The English shift toward common law around 1100 C.E. and the reliance on precedent beginning in the twelfth and thirteenth centuries introduced equitable standards applied in all cases brought before the court. It aimed to reduce the arbitrary character of judicial decision-making. At the same time, England introduced trial by jury and circuit-riding by judges of the king's court throughout the country. The evolution of the jury system empowered the average citizen and rested the fate of the accused in the hands of collective judgment, marking a significant democratic step (see Resnik and Curtis 2013, 207–8). And the traditions of equipping the jury with the power to determine innocence and the court with the power to overturn a guilty verdict to protect the individual against the mob are both instruments for defending freedom. This new order created a new story source—the courtroom as drama—to accompany the more familiar battlefield of earlier epic tales, and also provided a vehicle for perpetuating the values associated with truth, justice, and reason in place of might making right.

The secularization of the court away from canonical law and toward common law, the inclusion of citizens in the civil and criminal trial process, and the accessibility of the court within local communities marked a major shift toward the modern notion of procedural due process. Transported to the American colonies, these rights became central to the American notion of freedom and equality under the law. As communities built out their town squares, they used county courthouses to express democratic values associated with Neoclassical architecture. The temple motif in small town America is a recurrent feature. Its federal incarnation as a home for the Supreme Court echoed familiar symbols of justice hallowing the rule of law in a democratic society.

The terms "democracy" and "republicanism" require unpacking in the American case, as they are related and often interchanged, yet not the same. "Democracy," for our purposes, is the investment of expansive rights in the people and the presence of processes to allow people to exercise influence and control over institutions. "Republicanism" is a particular form of institutional organization that allows for democratic control of institutions through intermediaries, and is distinct from constitutional, parliamentary monarchies in the absence of a crowned sovereign. Democracy is often confused or conflated with other concepts in our politics, such as freedom and liberalism.[2] So when we assert that the courts are the oldest democratic institution, we do so based on the role of the courts as a safeguard of rights and infusion of the public into the courts through the jury system. In democracy, the expectation is that people enjoy individual dignity, equal protection under the law, and equal due process rights. In this respect, we view courts through a lens consistent with the Enlightenment democratic perspective at the heart of the American political experiment.

BUILDING DEMOCRACY, DEMOCRACY'S BUILDINGS, AND THE ENLIGHTENMENT

American democracy takes inspiration from intellectual conventions of the Enlightenment. Democracy is framed by both Athenian democratic and Roman republican ideals, which are foundational to the classics studied by Enlightenment-era thinkers, including the American Founders, along with their absorption and participation in the rationalist thinking that developed Enlightenment democratic ideals regarding the nature of man. This same era witnessed a return to Greek- and Roman-inspired architecture, which is broadly described as "Neoclassical" but is manifest in the architecture of Great Britain, English-speaking America, and France toward the end of the Enlightenment and draws from both the symbolism and the rationality of form in ancient Greek and Roman architecture.

From these Classical civilizations came the ideal of democracy as process, albeit democracy with qualifications. Participation was open to the *worthy*. From a philosophical standpoint, Classical thought does not readily embrace an egalitarian democracy, either in theory or in practice. It took the Enlightenment to create a broadly embraced substantive democracy.

When we speak of Greek democracy, we mean Athenian democracy, as it is the only Greek *polis* with sufficient historical records to describe. Athens initially used a council (the boule) for administration and vested final power in a constituent assembly called the Ecclesia, which operated as a direct democracy, using a simple-majority vote (see Ober 1996; Wood 1988). Voting was a privilege limited to adult men who had completed military training. Others (including slaves and foreigners) were not granted voting rights, and voting rights could be revoked or purged. Republican Rome held annual elections to select officeholders, and campaigning was common. Three constituencies selected officeholders: the Centuriate Assembly, the Tribal Assembly, and the Plebian Council. Secret ballots were introduced in the last century of the Republic (Ehrenberg 1950; Gargola 1995; Vishnia 1996).

Roman citizenship excluded women, slaves, and the foreign-born living in Rome. As a result, the demos of the Greek polis amounted to perhaps one in ten residents; Rome's *civi republica* was similarly exclusive.

The Enlightenment era articulated the core elements of democracy in the Western world. Sophisticated thinking regarding the nature of humanity and the source, origin, and grants of power would set the trajectory of democracy in North America. The era's great thinkers identified durable concepts that are important to the development of liberal democracy: the social contract; consent of the governed; individual liberty; and the very notions of public sphere and public opinion originate from the Enlightenment. Substantive democratic ideals such as liberty, progress, toleration, fraternity, constitutionalism, and the separation of church and state are central components of classical Enlightenment liberalism. They would serve as powerful influences on the American revolutionaries, starting with Benjamin Franklin and including Thomas Paine, Thomas Jefferson, and James Madison (see Gay 1968; Smith 1990), and laying the foundation for the American "Lockean consensus" of assumed rights to life, liberty, and property articulated in John Locke's 1689 *Two Treatises of Government*. Thomas Hobbes (1651) was the first to advance most of these concepts, writing of individual rights, natural equality, free will, political order as a social construct, the separation of civil society from the state, the role of representation to legitimate political power, consent of the governed, and a notion of liberalism in law that makes permissible anything not explicitly forbidden. Government existed to protect us from one another, to minimize conflict. As a practical matter, courts and other governing institutions were critical to the defense of these concepts, in support of a civil society that would protect natural rights using an unbiased judge.

It was through the Enlightenment that an articulation of arguments was made to diffuse power and reorder institutions. The consequence of the Enlightenment was the separation of the church from the state; the division of judicial, legislative, and executive functions; and the limitation of those institutions through a constitution and the consent of the governed. The American articulations of these reorderings occur in the Declaration of Independence, Jefferson's Virginia Statute for Religious Freedom, Madison's Constitution, and American federalism.

The American experiment was one of empire building in the age of Enlightenment. Everything about our organizing principles and fundamental values as a society must be read through the cultural milieu of the Enlightenment paradigm. The Enlightenment influence also shows up in the construction of public spaces. The late Enlightenment saw a resurrection of Classical architectural styles. The excavation of Greek, Roman, and Egyptian archaeological sites and the histories and pattern books that followed from those excavations influenced architects in England, Germany, Italy, and North America. Two dominant styles emerge: Greek Revival and Neoclassical. These styles take on a leading place in public and monumental construction due to their Classical origin. The shaping of Washington, D.C., from nothing into something reflects the social contract mythos of society emerging from a state of nature. The Neoclassical style of early D.C. architecture transports us from the New World to the birthplace of Western civilization—the Greek polis and the Roman forum.

Greek Revival style became strongly associated with nationalism and civic identity in the United States, Great Britain, and Germany. Architectural pattern books promoted the style, including works such as Asher Benjamin's ([1806] 1816) *American Builder's Companion*, John Haviland's (1818) *Builder's Assistant*, and Minard Lafever's (1835) *Beauties of Modern Architecture*. Jefferson possessed a Greek pattern book and was doubtless influenced by it in some fashion. Greek Revival carries strong philosophical influences, especially those deriving from an American desire to depart from established British styles and forms as part of founding a new and more democratic nation.

In the United States, the introduction of Greek Revival was facilitated by the maturing of the republic at the end of the century and Jefferson's appointment of Benjamin Henry Latrobe as surveyor of public buildings (chief architect of the United States). Latrobe's designs for Washington and also Philadelphia made strong use of classical orders and Greek elements. Jefferson's 1785 design for the Virginia State Capitol building reflects classical Greek elements, even though it is inspired by a Roman temple in France.

The more expansive Neoclassical style came out of France and Italy and drew on both Classical antiquity (Greece and Rome) and Palladian architecture. Neoclassicism also captured American political values of rationality, republicanism, and classic democracy. In the United States, the Federal style (or the National style) was strongly influenced by Robert Adams and pioneered by Latrobe, who was one of North America's first formally trained architects.

In the American imagination, the nation's capital took on the shapes and symbols of government by the people. The Capitol sitting on the Hill, capped with a dome to designate the proper place for political sovereignty in constitutional government; the White House, tucked away without the trappings of aristocratic opulence—accessible but neither central nor palatial; and the U.S. Supreme Court, a temple to justice with a watchful eye on the nation's lawmakers. What seems natural for government buildings to the untrained eye is actually a specific language of scale, form, order, color, siting, and ornamentation. It references the cultural ideas of Greek democracy and Roman republicanism. It reflects the iconic images of the Pantheon and the Parthenon with their simple forms and symmetrical design. The architectural system glorifies the sanctity of scientific rationality and the power of human reason, tenets of classical humanism forged during the intellectual rebirth of the Renaissance and the Enlightenment.

ENVISIONING A PHYSICAL LANDSCAPE
OF AMERICAN FEDERAL POWER

The tapestry of the District of Columbia grew from the pattern envisioned by the French-American military engineer Pierre Charles L'Enfant at the end of the eighteenth century. Yet it would be a full century before the city core would take on the stylistic homogeneity for which it is now known. The Neoclassical style of Washington, D.C., emerged slowly, in fits and starts, and required an architectural renaissance of both style and function to develop the architectural style and aesthetic of Washington into a coherent plan.

One of the most significant architectural feats in American urban development took form in Chicago in anticipation of the 1893 World's Columbian Exposition. Leading architects worked with Daniel Burnham to construct the White City, a promenade of several Neoclassical buildings along a six-hundred-acre stretch of greenspace developed from Frederick Law Olmsted's Jackson Park. Burnham was trained in the Beaux-Arts tradition and was central to the City Beautiful movement. Within a decade, the Senate would commission this elite design community to make recommendations on the development and beautification of the National Mall. The McMillan Plan, released in 1903, laid out a grand vision of monumental urban and landscape design.

This development did not happen in a vacuum. It was not by chance that these forces came together at this particular moment in time. The centennial celebration of the founding of Washington, D.C., provided a theme for the 1900 meeting in the nation's capital of the American

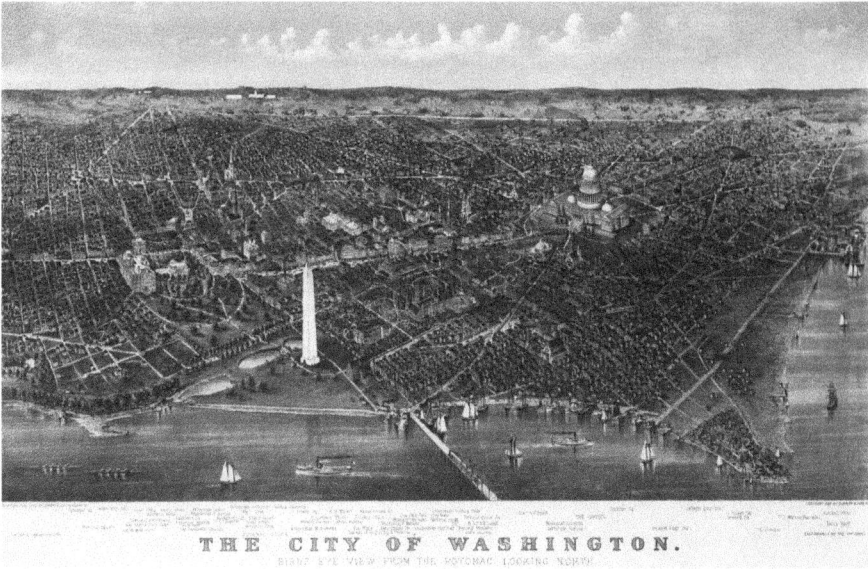

THE CITY OF WASHINGTON.

Figure 1.1. The city of Washington: Bird's-eye view from the Potomac—looking north, ca. 1892. Currier & Ives. Library of Congress, Prints and Photographs Division, LC-USZ62-1235.

Institute of Architects (AIA). Professional architects focused on the state of the city, gave serious attention to federal architecture, and resolved to establish a design commission for capital improvements. The commission that resulted, the Senate Park Commission, assembled in 1901 and brought together architectural giants such as Daniel Burnham, Charles McKim, and Frederick Law Olmsted Jr. with renowned artists such as Augustus Saint-Gaudens, challenging them to make recommendations concerning "the development and improvement of the entire park system of the District of Columbia" (Gall 1913, 5). The U.S. Commission of Fine Arts (CFA) grew out of this effort, established by Congress in 1910. Between 1910 and 1921, prominent figures in the architectural community who designed and erected civic buildings would serve to oversee the transformation of the heart of Washington, D.C. Appointments included Daniel Burnham (1910), Frederick Law Olmsted Jr. (1910), Cass Gilbert (1910), John Russell Pope (1917), and Henry Bacon (1921) (*Congressional Record* 1940, 3158).

Lawmakers drew inspiration from the stunning achievement of the Chicago World's Fair and acknowledged the role of professional architects

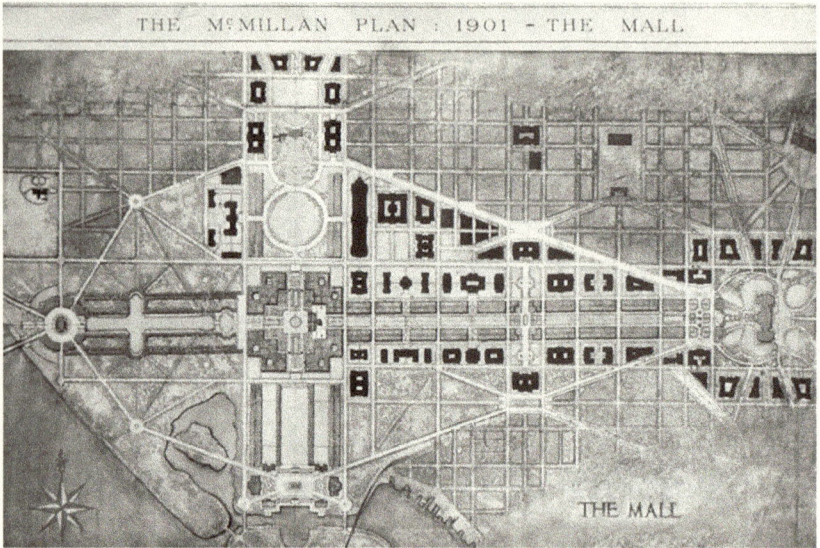

Figure 1.2. The McMillan Plan: 1901—The Mall. "Report of the Senate Committee on the District of Columbia on the Improvement of the Park System of the District of Columbia." U.S. Senate Committee on the District of Columbia. Senate Report No. 166, 57th Congress, 1st Session (Washington, D.C.: Government Printing Office, 1902).

in shaping the future of the national city. The CFA was "to advise the federal government on matters pertaining to the arts and national symbols, and to guide the architectural development of Washington, D.C." (U.S. Commission of Fine Arts n.d.). The City Beautiful movement would transform the capital city and link "the artistic aspirations of the American nation with its nascent role as an economic, political, and cultural leader in the world" (ibid.). Through the value system of the Progressive Era, civic art would lift the civic spirit and enhance the lives of residents and visitors to the national city. The City Beautiful movement would shape the corridors of political power in the New World.

The CFA arrived at three central goals: "to recapture the essential principles of the L'Enfant plan for the Mall; to establish and maintain design standards for this area; and to extend the District of Columbia's park system to protect views and natural areas" (ibid.). The resulting plan presented to the Senate and the American Institute of Architects

Figure 1.3. Plate IX. Senate Park Commission rendering of the Washington Monument Gardens and Mall, looking toward the Capitol, from the original rendering by Charles Graham. Senate Park Commission Report No. 58. Watercolor Photograph by Lee Stalsworth. In Kohler and Scott 2006. https://www.nps.gov /parkhistory/online_books/ncr/designing-capital/plates.html.

proposed major changes. First, the plan removed the Pennsylvania Railway station from the National Mall, where it had sat between the Capitol and the Washington Monument, and advanced the establishment of Union Station for centralized rail traffic in a grand building. The result was a reinstatement of the Mall for open green space from the Capitol to the Washington Monument. Then, the boundary of the Mall would be defined and given coherence with congressional support for the Lincoln Memorial and appropriation for a design competition (American Institute of Architects 1903, 92). As a result, the plan punctuated L'Enfant's visionary layout of the city by reintroducing strong lines and referential meaning.

The first major project to be approved by the commission was the Lincoln Memorial (1922), a masterpiece designed by Henry Bacon, who was appointed to the commission in 1921. By this time, the architectural giants of the City Beautiful movement had served on the CFA and made alliances with the political elite, including President William Howard Taft. In fact, the Taft administration coincided with the appointment of Daniel Burnham, Frederick Law Olmsted Jr., and Cass Gilbert to the commission. Their designs were championed inside the political community even as their favored style began to wane across the country and around the world.

This elite group of design professionals responsible for the American Renaissance in civic and landscape architecture took advantage of opportunities to envision a more cohesive federal city. In Washington, D.C., in 1900, several architects, including Cass Gilbert and Frederick Law Olmsted Jr., presented papers at the annual conference of the AIA articulating visions for the future of the National Mall. They then used advisory appointments to produce "a plan that projected the grand neo-classical design imposed on civic Washington over the next three decades" (Blodgett 1985, 619). Though not a primary goal of the McMillan Plan, the proposal included "the hope that 'at no distant day' a proud new home for the Supreme Court would rise on Capitol Hill" (ibid., 620).

When Taft was appointed to the Supreme Court in 1921 and then served as chief justice until his death in 1930, he was a dedicated champion of the construction of the U.S. Supreme Court Building and commissioned his longtime friend Cass Gilbert to carry out the charge. It would be Gilbert's last major architectural project; he died in 1934. Neither of these giants lived to see the building in use.

Though Congress approved funding for the U.S. Supreme Court Building, many members opposed the idea, and exceptionally few actually lobbied on behalf of the project. Taft describes in 1925 the working conditions of the court while housed in the Old Senate Chamber, as well as his vision for construction of an independent home for the court.

> We have . . . come . . . to a situation where a majority of the Court is strongly in favor of the construction of a separate building for the Court. Most of the Judges are obliged to have their offices and official studies in their own houses or apartments. As Chief Justice, I have no office at the Capitol and must use the Conference Room and Library of the Court to meet any persons who come to see me at the Capitol, either officially or otherwise. Justice Stone is most embarrassed now by the inability to secure a decent room for himself at the Capitol where he can have his Law Clerk and Secretary do his work. I have pleaded with the Committee of the Senate having control of this matter, and have not been able to secure a proper room for him. The records of the Clerk's office are piling up in such a way as to prevent their being housed in an accessible place. The members of the Bar of the Supreme Court have no place to meet

Figure 1.4. The Lincoln Memorial and reflecting pool, ca. 1923. Library of Congress, Prints and Photographs Division, LC-DIG-ds-00173.

or confer except in the crowded offices of the Clerk. The Marshal's office is greatly congested with his employees. The Library of the Court is so crowded that the shelves have to be carried up to the ceiling and the books reached upon step-ladders. The place which has been usually selected by previous promoters of a separate build-ing for the Court is the square corresponding to that of the Con-gressional Library on the north side of East Capitol Street. I hope that no effort will be made to unite other Courts or offices in a building with the Supreme Court. It seems to me that that Court, as the head of the Federal Judiciary, and, in a sense, the head of the Judiciary of the Nation, should be confined to the uses of that Court . . . . I don't know of course what its cost would be, but with the authority of the Court, I write to you to ask your attention to the matter and to know what you think the prospect would be for such legislation. (Warren 1958, 361)

The chief justice was persistent in pursuing the Supreme Court's new home even as his health faded and his faculties started to fail. Cautioned about his health, he had lost a hundred pounds since his presidency and adopted a routine of walking three miles to the Capitol every day. He was concerned about his legacy and, in particular, wanted to ensure both a home for the court and the succession of Charles Evans Hughes as chief if he left the bench. In 1927, Taft writes to his daughter and revisits the court project and his dedication to it.

> Congress is dying. I have not got what I wanted but I did get through the $1,500,000 to buy the Supreme Court lot. I think this fastens the project to the Government so that the building will come. I have had to fight for it from the beginning. My two predecessors were against it and so are four of my colleagues. The others were not enthusiastic but I carried them with me. Then I had to get the support of the House and Senate. I had one supporter who has been urgent not because he was interested in the Court but because he wanted the space we occupy for the Senate. We have been compressed into insufficient and inadequate space for some years, and it was shortsighted of those in our Court to oppose it. They did not look forward or beyond their own service in the Court as to its needs. After the condemnation proceedings are begun, we must then look for adequate appropriations for the building. We hope that Cass Gilbert, who has already drawn plans which seem adequate, will be selected as architect. What I am praying for is that I can live and be on the Court until we can move in. But that is a good deal to hope for. (Warren, 1958, 361–62)

Taft's dream of a home for the court would be realized, but his wish to preside in the new building would not. After a trip to Cinicinnati to attend the funeral of his brother Charles in the winter of 1929, he fell ill and went to Asheville, North Carolina, to recover. He returned to Washington in February 1930, and only resigned after getting assurances from President Hoover that Hughes, and not Harlan Fiske Stone, would become chief justice (Stone would later succeed Hughes to become chief justice in 1941). The former chief justice and president passed away on March 8, 1930, having planted a tree the shade of which he would not enjoy and securing a post for his preferred successor to hold the gavel in the Supreme Court.

Figure 1.5. William H. Taft, ca.
1908. Library of Congress, Prints
and Photographs Division,
LC-USZ62-89437.

Figure 1.6. Cass Gilbert, 1907.
Photograph by Pach Brothers
Firm. Image courtesy of
Wikimedia Commons.

Figure 1.7. Construction of the U.S. Supreme Court Building. Architect of the Capitol. Image courtesy of Flickr.

SITE OF THE BUILDING

Congress had secured a site for Taft's posthumous political act, but it was a site constrained by the consequences of 125 years of development in the District, and then further constrained by the effort to return rationality and coherence to Washington through planning. The McMillan Plan had major ramifications for the U.S. Supreme Court, even though the project was not central to the goals of the commission or even a major consideration during deliberations. The construction of Union Station and its opening in 1907 provided ready access to the National Mall, with its entrance facing the Senate side of the U.S. Capitol Building. The development of Union Station influenced decisions to build a permanent home for the Supreme Court on a tract of land just across the street from the Capitol and adjacent to the Library of Congress Thomas Jefferson Building. The new building would share space with the legislative branch, while L'Enfant's Judiciary Square would go unused.

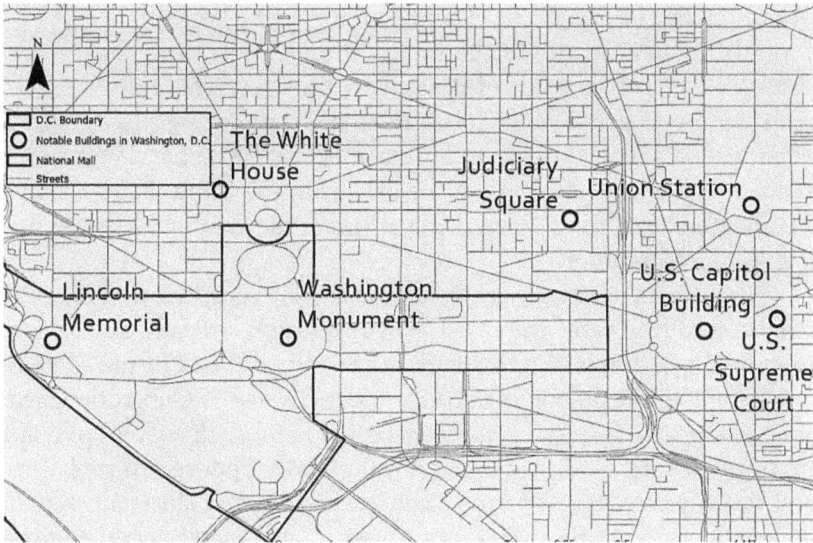

Figure 1.8. Location of U.S. Supreme Court Building in relation to Judiciary Square. Architect of the Capitol.

Consider the architectural landscape of Washington, D.C., at the time of the commissioning of the Supreme Court Building. While the Capitol, the White House, and the Treasury Building were Neoclassical in style, other major civic buildings illustrated the diversity of styles prevalent at the time. The Old Executive Office Building, constructed from 1871 to 1888, is a clear example of the Second Empire style. The Smithsonian Institution Building (the Castle), constructed in 1879, is Renaissance Revival. And several other prominent buildings are demonstrative of the Beaux-Arts tradition, including the Thomas Jefferson Library of Congress Building (1890–97), the Carnegie Library (1901–1903), the Cannon House Office Building (1908), the Russell Senate Office Building (1903–1908), and the General Services Building (1917). In sum, the style was not a forgone conclusion in building the U.S. Supreme Court Building.

Yet within twenty-five years, three temples in the Neoclassical style designed by three prominent architects took shape to reify the American philosophical ideals of unity, freedom, and equality. At one end of the National Mall, Henry Bacon brought to life the vision of the McMillan Plan for a monument to President Lincoln. The Athenian-inspired design stands as a significant example of Stripped Classicism in its early form. It honors Lincoln as the savior of the Union with a sanctuary modeled on the birthplace of democracy. The "severely Doric" memorial is a powerful and serene testament to the enduring and dignified enterprise of a unified representative democracy (Wiseman 1998, 126). It anchors the Mall, expanding the axis from the Capitol beyond the Washington Monument. In so doing, it relates the White House and the Capitol to each other.

Next, Cass Gilbert designed and oversaw the construction and ornamentation of the U.S. Supreme Court Building, a severely Corinthian memorial by comparison. It stands at the opposite end of the Mall as a testament to the pursuit of equality under the law. As Gilbert designed the building and looked for materials suitable for such a grand temple, he traveled Europe. As a conservative ardently opposed to socialism and strongly convinced of American exceptionalism, Gilbert advocated on behalf of the timelessness of the Classical style and against the introduction of the modern skyscraper in the cities of ancient civilization. He watched in awe as leaders fanned the flames of nationalism, but it came with a price. Between the wars, "authoritarian regimes were finding the orderly formal message of classicism—purged of its democratic associations—an appropriate one for their own repressive purposes" (Wiseman 1998, 127). He knew of the developments in urban planning and monumental civic building undertaken by fascist regimes. He gained an audience with Benito Mussolini and imported Italian marble for the majestic columns in the courtroom of the Supreme Court Building at the same time that nationalistic movements were threatening the future of democracy in Europe.

> Like many other worried Americans in the 1920s, Gilbert warmed to the bold energies of Benito Mussolini, whose Fascist promise made him seem, alone among postwar leaders, a bulwark against the collapse of national purpose and morale in Western Europe. In 1924, in his capacity as designer of the world's tallest office building [the Woolworth Building in Manhattan], he wrote to the Italian dictator to warn against building skyscrapers in Rome, as favored by Fascist champions of urban *Futurismo*. They would spoil the city's ancient grandeur, Gilbert argued. Then he took the occasion to tell Mussolini what he thought of him: "I have followed your career with the greatest admiration and I believe in you and what you do. No one has arisen in our time, and especially since the War, whom I

so greatly admire." Three years later he arranged an audience with Mussolini in Rome, found him charming, histrionic, and forceful, and asked for his autograph. At the end of the interview, Mussolini stood and gave him the Fascist salute. Awed by the moment, Gilbert came to attention and returned it. It was, he wrote in a long memo to himself about the visit, "the most dignified, the most natural, the most graceful and the most noble salutation I know." It was Roman, the modern revival of a reassuring ancient form. (Blodgett 1985, 624)

The focus on Neoclassical structures in the national city coincides with an unfortunate obsession with Neoclassical-derived forms in nondemocratic regimes. In the Soviet Union, the first generation of Soviet architecture with its strong Modernist and Bauhaus influences gave way to Monumentalist Neoclassicism evolving toward Stripped Classicism, best represented by the work of Boris Iofan. In fascist Italy, Classical and Palladian forms were similarly stripped to echo the last Roman Empire in the hopes of establishing the next one (see the authoritative compilation in Jones and Pilat 2020). And in Nazi Germany, Adolf Hitler's vision of a new imperial city of Germania was articulated by Albert Speer in grandiose realities such as the Zeppelin Stadium, the Deutsches Stadion, and the Kongresshalle at Nuremburg, and also the Reich Chancellery in Berlin, as well as imagined works such as a hundred-meter-high triumphal arch and a grand Peoples' House with a thousand-foot roof (Scobie 1990; see also Friedrich 2012, 360–63, 366–72). And, much like the imagined and real constructions of the Soviets and fascists, Nazi architecture appropriated Neoclassicism as a vehicle for a nondemocratic ideology of power and authority (Vale 1992, 25–27, 33–36, 36–41).

These authoritarian appropriations create an artistic irony that shrouds the final temple built to accent the National Mall in the first half of the twentieth century. John Russell Pope designed the Jefferson Memorial, an Ionic memorial styled after the Pantheon (see figure 1.9). As a temple to freedom, it opened in 1943 while the Allies continued to fight in two separate theaters of war against the march of authoritarian regimes in search of world empire. The monument strikingly resembles Pope's design for the National Gallery of Art, which opened just two years earlier in 1941 on the Mall (see figure 1.10). It also bears a resemblance to the Classical forms appropriated by Hitler and Speer to envision a new Berlin.

Figure 1.9. The Jefferson Memorial, 2005. Image courtesy of Flickr, https://www
.flickr.com/photos/bootbearwdc/32971256/.

Figure 1.10. South façade of the West Building of the National Gallery of Art.
Photograph 2010 by AgnosticPreachersKid. Image courtesy of Wikimedia Commons.

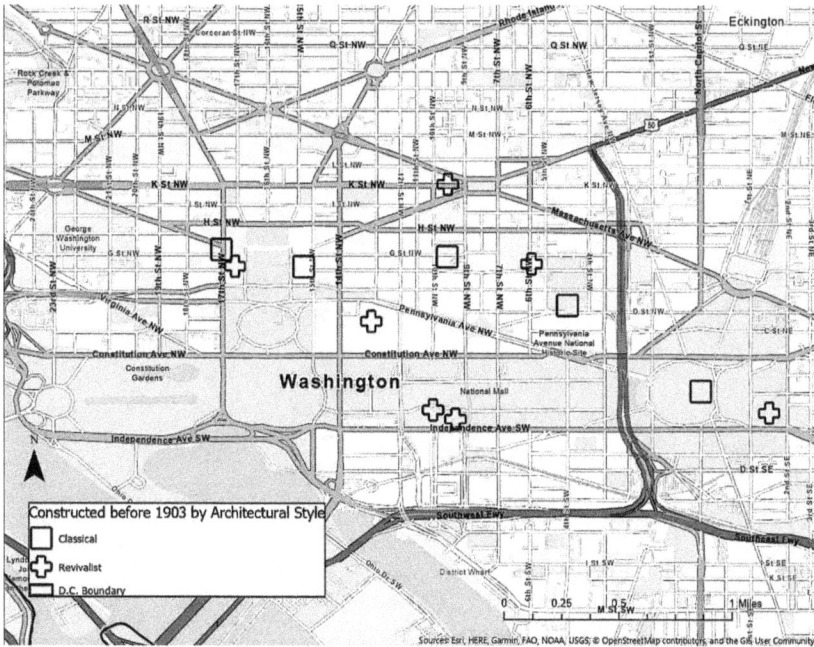

Figure 1.11. Architectural styles on the National Mall before 1903. Compiled and created by the authors.

The cruciform axiality of the McMillan Plan was now complete, but not without critics. By the time construction began of the U.S. Supreme Court Building, the Neoclassical style had fallen out of favor with the American and international architectural community. On the rise was Modernism and the International style. But inside the Beltway of Washington, D.C., political elites continued to grant commissions to designs for Neoclassical structures well into the twentieth century. Several office buildings housing the federal bureaucracy are in the Neoclassical or Stripped Classical style, including the Departments of Agriculture, Interior, State, and Justice Buildings. The Longworth House Office Building, the Rayburn House Office Building, and to some extent the Dirksen Senate Office Building are also Neoclassical. Additions to the D.C. landscape in different stylistic traditions represent aberrations from this theme. While lauded by the design community, new heritage museums on the National Mall, such as the Postmodern National Museum of African American History and Culture and the Modernist

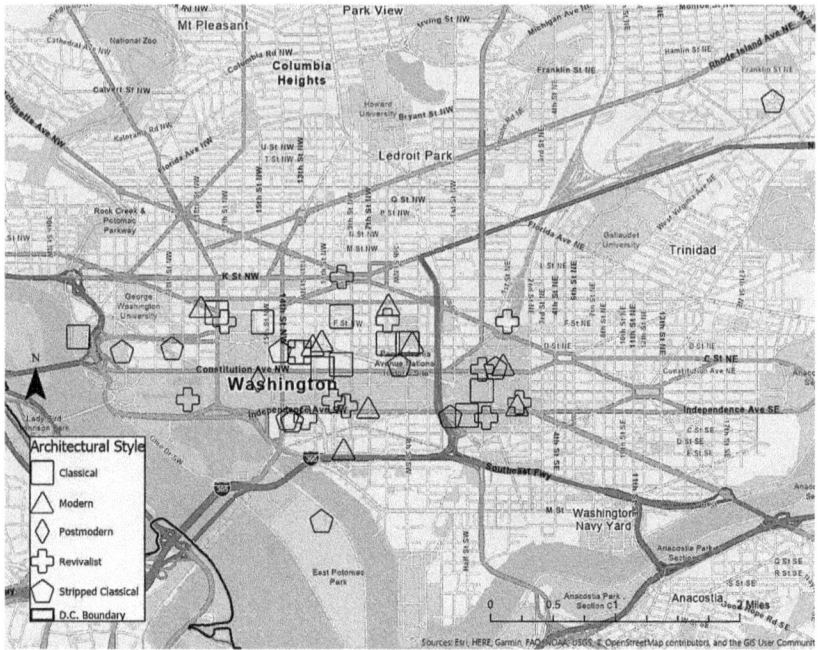

Figure 1.12. Architectural styles on the National Mall after 1903. Compiled and created by the authors.

National Air and Space Museum stand out distinctly from their Neo-classical neighbors (see figures 1.11 and 1.12).

An amalgamation of philosophical, social, political, artistic, economic, and legal influences coalesced to produce the U.S. Supreme Court Building (see table 1.1). Understanding these influences is critical to understanding the social meaning of the U.S. Supreme Court Building as well as the outgrowth of the federal judiciary. The physical manifestation of the court resulted from the strong cultural forces of the period in which it was built. In turn, the court shaped the city and the institution in important ways. We have taken this chapter to lay a foundation for understanding the social meaning of the American federal court as a democratic institution.

The Enlightenment-inspired philosophical underpinnings of the American judiciary illuminate and manifest as several principles informing courthouse design, including due process for conflict resolution, safeguards for the protection of rights, a final check on power, and the

TABLE 1.1. Influences on the U.S. Supreme Court Building

Influences		Chapters
Artistic	• L'Enfant's vision for the national capital with separated spaces and grand avenues	Ch. 3
	• Beaux-Arts influence on Neoclassical civic space	Chs. 1, 4, 6
	• City Beautiful movement and White City	Chs. 1, 4
	• Gilbert's vision for the Supreme Court Building as temple	Ch.5
	• Sculpture and statuary to convey timelines of symbols of justice	Ch. 4
	• Architectural diversity and social meaning of legal space	Ch. 6
Religious	• Religious diversity and democratic pluralism	Ch. 2
	• Primacy of the house in early American life	Ch. 2
	• Evolution of sacred text from religious books to U.S. Constitution	Ch. 5
	• Temple motif with priestly tribe	Ch. 5
Philosophical	• Scientific rationality to uncover universal truth	Ch. 4
	• Justice under law involving due process	Chs. 4, 6
	• Independent judiciary in a system of separated powers	Chs. 4, 6
	• Popular sovereignty with limited government	Chs. 4, 6
Sociopolitical	• Tradition of shared common spaces from meetinghouse (informing Supreme Court in Capitol)	Ch. 2
	• Progressive movement	Ch. 6
	• Expansion of civil rights and liberties	Chs. 6, Concl.
	• Expectations of civic space in terms of accessibility, transparency, and security	Chs. 4, 6, Concl.
Economic	• Expansion of industry and rail informing site selection	Ch. 6
	• Investment in national resources, public works, and infrastructure	Ch. 6
	• Prioritization of and investment in the federal presence	Chs. 4, 5, 6
	• Great Depression and recovery (FDR's court-packing plan)	Chs. 4, 6
Legal	• Expansion of caseload	Ch. 3
	• Institutionalization of the federal judiciary	Chs. 3, 6
	• Routinized processes; expansion of calendar	Ch. 3
	• Spatial differentiation (perimeter, circulation, civic, sanctum)	Chs. 3, 4
	• Judicial decision-making requiring sanctum space	Ch. 4
	• Principle of stare decisis (codification of precedent)	Ch. 5
	• Theater of justice	Ch. 5
	• Balance between transparency and secrecy of judicial proceedings	Chs. 3, 4, 5

SOURCE: Compiled by the authors.

pursuit of equity in the name of human dignity. A brief consideration of the origins of classicism and its architectural rebirth in the Neoclassical style gives visual expression and physical manifestation to philosophical ideals and contextualizes the use of the temple motif in grand civic building. And by considering the specific siting of the U.S. federal government in Washington, D.C., we see the blank canvas on which urban planners and architects crafted a city on a hill, emboldened by the political elite.

The national city would take two centuries to fully develop, and the Supreme Court would wait for its home for much of that time. Max Weber's observation in the concluding paragraph of his 1918 essay "Politik als Beruf" (Politics as a Vocation) has direct bearing on the creation of both this institution and the home we analyze herein: "Politics is a strong and slow boring of hard boards. It takes both passion and perspective. Certainly all historical experience confirms the truth—that man would not have attained the possible unless time and again he had reached out for the impossible" ([1918] 2004, 93).

Eventually, sociopolitical, economic, and political forces converged to prioritize the federal presence and make government accessible to the people and their representatives. By the early twentieth century, the Supreme Court faced an imposing docket, a full calendar, and cramped quarters in the Old Senate Chamber of the U.S. Capitol Building. With its many champions, most certainly Taft in the case of the Supreme Court, the physical presence of Washington, D.C., took on great symbolic meaning across a broad vista of the city. The U.S. Supreme Court Building articulates democratic space within this particular milieu.

2   The American Courthouse

Courthouses exist in every American community. They are some of the oldest structures to be found in American political development. And they facilitate the everyday processes of law and order at the local, state, and federal levels of government. Yet homes of the court in the American context carry a unique history and a particular independence from other arms of the state. To understand the Supreme Court's home, we must start with the ubiquitous nature of courthouses in the American experience. So we start this story with a little exercise in etymology: what is a "courthouse" and where does the term come from?

ETYMOLOGY OF "COURTHOUSE"

The term "courthouse" derives from the two root words "court" and "house." The origin of "court" is from the Latin words *cōrtem*, *cohors*, and *cohort*, meaning "yard," "enclosure," or "retinu" (see Chantrell 2002, 124; Klein 1966, 363). The Latin term *hortus*, meaning "garden" or "an enclosed place," is also related. "Court "is the result of *co-* (together) and the stem *hort* (Barnhart 1988, 228). The Middle English and Old French terms *court* and *curt* as well as the Italian, Spanish, and Portuguese term *corte* developed from these Latin roots (see Klein 1966, 363).

Before 1200, *curt* referred to a "princely residence or household" (Barnhart 1988, 228). The French word also related to the Latin term *curia*, used to describe an assembly, council, or court of justice in medieval times (*American Heritage Dictionary* 2001, 445). In this context, a court consisted of a group assembled to assist a ruler at a certain time "for social, political, or judicial purposes." The Curia Regis dates back to the Norman Conquest (1066). This royal court or "King's Court" survived through the thirteenth century and served as the foundation for the development of British courts of law (Morris 1929).

"COURT"

Simpson and Weiner (1989) suggest a number of meanings for "court." While the term can mean any building(s) in a courtyard, a yard surrounded by houses, a place for tennis, or a royal residence, these do not appear to be the references used by early Americans. More closely related is the use of "court" to describe the collective reference to a sovereign and his councilors and the proceedings of this assembly (ibid., 1057). This body might gather not only for administrative purposes but also to receive special delegations or host stately receptions (ibid.). This royal assembly evolved into the "courts" of parliament and of justice. From here we arrive at the courts of law and legal administration as the term is frequently used today.

In the legal sense, the term can also refer to a collective body of judges in any jurisdiction, division, and level of government (Simpson and Weiner 1989, 1057). The location in which judicial administration occurs can be called a court. And the proceedings of legal administration can be described by the term, such as the act of settling a case "out of court" or the event of a session of "court" (ibid.).

Beyond political meanings, the term "court" historically has also referred to assemblies of company members, such as boards, executive councils, and general membership. This usage dates to the early sixteenth century. A related usage refers to the collective members of a friendly society, such as a lodge of the Knights of Columbus or the Foresters (Simpson and Weiner 1989, 1058).

The term was used to designate legislatures in Massachusetts and New Hampshire both before and after the American Revolutionary War. As early as 1628, the Charter of Charles I to the Massachusetts Bay Colony identified four assemblies to be called "the four great and general courts" (ibid.; Massachusetts 1814, 9). Dictionaries of the late 1860s retained this usage of the term to denote the two houses of New England state legislatures (Simpson and Weiner 1989, 1058).

"HOUSE"

The origin of the word "house" is Germanic. Consequently, it has cognates with Old Frisian, Old Saxon, Middle Dutch, Old High German, and Old Icelandic (Barnhart 1988, 493). As a noun, it stems from the Dutch *huis* and the German *Haus*. As a verb, "to enclose" or "to hide" stems from the Dutch *huizen* and the German *hausen*. From the German developed the Old English terms *hūs* (noun) and *hūsian* (verb) (Chantrell 2002, 257; see also Klein 1966, 746). In theater, the term "playhouse" dates back to the seventeenth century (Chantrell 2002, 257).

The term "house" is used to describe a number of contexts. Beyond the traditional meaning suggesting "a building for human habitation. . . . the ordinary dwelling-place of a family" (Simpson and Weiner 1989, 435), the term once referred to portions of a building used as common space, the kitchen, or for work (ibid., 436). Similarly "household" captures the collective residents in a dwelling place (ibid., 437). Gothic references to the term, such as -*hūs* found in the compound *gudhūs*, denote a temple (literally "the house of God") and mean in this sense a shelter or dwelling place for a god (Klein 1966, 746). This gives the term meaning as a worship place, a church (Simpson and Weiner 1989, 436).

Finally, and most related to the etymology of "courthouse," "house" sometimes refers to a number of deliberative assemblies—ecclesiastical, legislative, academic, or municipal (Simpson and Weiner 1989, 436). Take, for example, the U.S. House of Representatives, the British House of Commons and House of Lords, the upper and lower houses of the Convocation of Canterbury, and Prague's Municipal House. The first use of "House of Representatives" in the American context dates to 1692, when it was used to describe the Massachusetts colonial legislative assembly (Barnhart 1988, 493).

"COURTHOUSE"

Barnett (1988) dates the term "courthouse" to the late fifteenth century ("probably about 1475") but gives no attention to the origins of the term or its early meaning. Neither Klein (1966) nor Chantrell (2002) mentions "courthouse." The richest description is provided by Simpson and Weiner (1989). Its simple meaning is "a building in which courts of law are held," but its historical development reveals a rich heritage important to this analysis. The first reference to the term dates to 1483 in *Catholicon Anglicum*, where it appears as "Cowrthouse" (Herrtage and Wheatley [1882] 1997, 79). Outside of the United States, the only other reference to "courthouse" as a judicial building is to the Wigtown-shire Courthouse in the late nineteenth century (Simpson and Weiner 1989), a structure built on the site of the shire's townhouse—the site of the famous trial of Margaret McLachlan and Margaret Wilson, Cove-nanters who refused to declare an oath to recognize the King of England as the head of the church and were drowned in 1865. To this day, the lowest courts in the Scottish judicial system are sheriff courts, and the buildings housing these courts are sheriff courthouses.

This apparent linguistic connection between local judicial archi-tecture in America and Scotland points to a shared community heritage with deep roots in Covenant theology (see Mullan 2000). The growth of Puritanism from the late sixteenth century through the seventeenth shaped early colonial development in the New World as well as the political landscape of the Old World. In referring to Scottish divines (theologians), Mullan suggests that "certainly they had a direct bearing on the creation of colonial religious cultures, notably in the emerging Atlantic states of the later American republic" (ibid., 6).

Understanding the etymology of the term "courthouse" provides the foundation for an examination of the development of these civic structures in colonial America in the seventeenth and eighteenth centu-ries. Next we trace the architectural heritage of courthouses as mainstays of local governance and conclude the analysis with an examination of the utilization of these facilities and implications for understanding the place of courthouses in American society today. This general foundation is critical to understanding the home of America's best-known and most-powerful court.

THE EVOLUTION OF LOCAL CIVIC ARCHITECTURE

Recognizing the etymology of the term "courthouse," we now must con-sider the development of communal life in colonial America and the civic architecture that facilitated it. Doing so helps us understand both the evolution of courthouses and the inflections that drive their design and artistry. Martha McNamara, in her work on early Massachusetts courthouses (2004, 5), draws attention to the limited scholarship by historians on "the physical spaces that accommodated and defined professional work" in early American life. Although various motivations led to settlement across the British colonies in the New World, the urban planning of the seventeenth and the eighteenth centuries followed a similar pattern. In early Anglo America, such as seventeenth-century Connecticut, "the universe for most people was the town in which they lived" (Mann 1984, 448). The typical community was a town of fewer than a thousand people, where residential structures encircled the town center. The mutual interdependence of these community residents "gave the first towns a powerful cohesiveness" (ibid.). And the value of buildings and lots was often higher the closer their proximity to the court.

Early legal proceedings stemmed from this milieu and often included voluntary arbitration. This localized focus of public life accentuated the importance of early civic structures and the role of religious and secular authority (Mann 1984, 449). They became the physical embodiment of the social capital of colonial communal life. Mann (1986, 1429) argues that "the cohesiveness of communities in the seventeenth century, fostered by the necessity of living together in a physical and spiritual wilderness, gave adequate assurance that parties would abide by the awards of the arbitrators they had chosen." The insular nature of early colonial towns reinforced legal authority and emphasized the town center as a place of community and conflict resolution. The meetinghouse of the seventeenth century thus serves as a necessary starting point for our examination of the evolution of American judicial architecture.

THE MEETINGHOUSE AS A CORPORATE HOUSE

For early New England colonists, the meetinghouse served as a town center, linking individuals to the community and standing as the physical place of social interaction and the symbolic representation of the settlement (Wood 1986, 56). Colonists conceived of this space as a communal house. Trumbull (1902, 25) notes that one of the initial activities of the town of Northampton was to build a meetinghouse, "a house for the towne." In fact, communities lacking sufficient resources to construct a meetinghouse often held their meetings in homes or barns (Sweeney 1993, 68). This practice was familiar to the Puritans who had been worshiping in private since the mid-1500s. Elevating the status and role of the laity, Puritans held "conventicles" (meetings in the home) for which they suffered ecclesiastical sanction (Ryken 1990, 118).

Towns with adequate means to construct meetinghouses modeled these public spaces after their domestic architecture—extending the metaphor even further. For example, in housing ideologies of the New England and Chesapeake Bay colonies, regional construction preferences serve as "tangible physical expression" of the differing worldviews of the Puritans and the Anglicans (Ameri 1997, 6). The Puritans of New England built meetinghouses that reflected their humble wood-frame, clapboarded domestic dwellings. By contrast, the Anglicans of the Chesapeake Bay region built their meetinghouses of brick and stone that mirrored the parishes of England (ibid., 12). This diversity stands as useful evidence of early American architecture as a vehicle for expressing the sovereignty of the individual, the importance of local identity, and the shared values of the community. Ameri (1997, 13) observed: "If the selection of one house type and building material over the other is significant, it is because wood or brick . . . formed linguistic paradigms in the shared architectural vocabulary of the early settlers. As such, they allowed the colonists to think, express, and live their differences in material form through the selection of one house form or material instead of and in opposition to the other."

Once public space is provided, it is used, and by many different publics. For over a hundred years, public spaces such as these provided a venue for religious and secular town meetings, including sessions of the courts (Donnelly 1968, 107; Trumbull 1902, 25). The life of the town centered in the meetinghouse; it appears that town records were sometimes stored beneath the pulpit (Labaree 1962). Reading this story in the American context, where church-state debates center on both legal-institutional and physical segregation, the role of the religious meetinghouse as a place for secular function can seem confounding. But it is more understandable if one accepts that the meetinghouse did not serve as a *sanctuary* but merely as a place where the church as a body would gather. The Congregationalists had a unique understanding of the physical representation of the body of Christ. The meetinghouse building was not sacred in and of itself; it was not a "house of God." Rather it was "a house of the publicly congregated faithful" (Sweeney 1993, 60). This orientation to the architectural space of worship persisted well into the mid-eighteenth century (ibid., 64).

In denying the sanctity of any particular building, the Puritans of the seventeenth century could easily conclude that the meetinghouse was an appropriate and logical site for judicial proceedings (McNamara 2004, 21; Walsh 1980: 84). And they were not unique in drawing this conclusion. Lounsbury (2006, 3, 8) suggests that this belief structure with its mistrust of "sacralization of space and objects" extended to Quakers, Calvinists, Mennonites, and Baptists as well. Puritans as well as those of similar communitarian faiths called their communal structures meetinghouses "in an effort to divert attention from the physical space to the spiritual activities that were the true core of church worship" (Ryken 1990, 117). Over the next century, the construction of new meetinghouses prompted reevaluation of the purpose of these structures and facilitated a separation of religious and secular activities. Sweeney (1993) notes that settlements such as Lebanon, Connecticut, established new meetinghouses "for divine service and the worship of God from time to time forever and for no other use" (ibid., 64).

New England meetinghouses and the villages they serve represent a formative break in the design of public buildings and public spaces compared to their English and European precedents—villages of New England did not owe their urban design to their English predecessors (Wood 1986, 63). Nor did the New England meetinghouses completely owe their functionality to medieval markets or town halls (Sweeney 1993, 68), though they hold some design features in common. In both instances, the structures were sited centrally in the settlement. Land grants made by the Massachusetts Bay Colony's General Court to groups of Puritan families wishing to settle in the New World were often given in square tracts laid out "around a central village green" in relation to the meetinghouse, the parish house, and the school (Labaree 1962, 166). The structures were plain and rectangular and were relatively indistinguishable from other ordinary houses as a building type (Donnelly 1968, 95). Walsh (1980, 85) notes that the Puritans enjoyed the opportunity to articulate a collective space in congruence with their belief structure, "a space whose very nomenclature would be mundane." The Protestant Plain Style, an architectural form originating with the Puritans, avoided cruciform floor plans, stained glass, and statuary, opting instead for square or rectangular utilitarian spaces (ibid., 86). The orientation of the early meetinghouse buildings along the short axis rather than the long axis further reflected domestic architecture and differentiated them as an architectural form. Donnelly (1968, 108) concludes that "in order to meet a new communal need, the Puritans devised a new type of public building in which elements of parish church and market hall were used as each community found appropriate."

The New England meetinghouse of the seventeenth century was used for different purposes than the meetinghouse of the eighteenth century, and this evolution deserves attention as part of the heritage of the American courthouse tradition. By the late 1700s, certain rituals, including those related to marriage, moved from the home into the meetinghouse. Functions previously served by magistrates shifted to ministers, and secular business increasingly moved from the meeting-house to newly built public townhouses (Sweeney 1993, 60, 66).

The landscape in colonial Virginia was similar to that of New England with regard to the intermingling of religious and secular activities and authority. The governor of the colony held responsibilities designated for the bishop of the Anglican Church in England. He oversaw letters of ordination, employment of clergy, marriage licenses, and wills (Upton 1997, 5). The legislature held similar oversight authority. At the county level, courts enforced the moral law, managed the list of taxable parishioners, and sometimes collected tithes to the church. Some secular functions, such as caring for the indigent, educating orphans, and maintaining vital statistics, fell to the church. The organization of public life was built around the term "parish," which endured into the southern low country well into the eighteenth century. Due to these localized activities, Upton (1997, 6) argues that for practical purposes, the colonial churches of Virginia were really "congregational, or more properly parochial. Activities centered in the parish, the affairs of which were conducted by the vestry."

Architecture of these spaces followed distinct building practices. While the Congregational meetinghouses of the northern colonies demonstrated an austerity consistent with Puritanical ideologies, the Anglican meetinghouses of the Southern colonies carried ornamentation consonant with gentry plantations (Lounsbury 2006, 4). Construction of townhouses offered an opportunity for a collective built environment less reflective of common religious identity. Lounsbury (ibid.) notes that at times "there was a dichotomy between sacred and profane spaces. In eighteenth-century Philadelphia, wealthy Quaker merchants built exceedingly handsome townhouses stocked with fashionable furnishings."

Early townhouses date back to the mid-seventeenth century. The first townhouse of Salem was built around 1636, and the first townhouse in Boston was built in 1657. Similar structures in Milford and Windsor,

Connecticut, as well as Charlestown, Massachusetts, date back to this period (Sweeney 1993, 69). Nonetheless, the construction of New England townhouses increased dramatically throughout the next century. Sweeney (ibid., 78) estimates that "at least sixty New England towns had their town meetings in town houses, courthouses, or schoolhouses by the 1790s." Some have argued that the proliferation of townhouses in the 1700s and early 1800s throughout New England marked a number of developments, including "the changing character of local politics and the rising tide of religious dissent, as well as the growing physical and mental separation between church and state." Even physical comfort influenced the choice of siting for civil dialogue. Most meetinghouses lacked stoves or fireplaces, whereas schoolhouses and taverns provided warmth during the cold winter months (Sweeney 1993, 60, 68).

Others suggest that the spread of townhouses in the first half of the eighteenth century constituted a response to growing economic commercialization. The spread of information, currency, and trade required physical and conceptual differentiation of professions and activities. Townhouses provided differentiated space and thus a specialized venue for court sessions (McNamara 2004, 22).

Particularly in these spaces, the vestiges of the English market hall could be seen. The early townhouse of Boston, according to McNamara (2004, 14), "brought together the worlds of New England merchants and Puritan divines by providing space for a mix of government, judicial, social, and economic functions." It served a variety of purposes, housing "colonial government, courts, markets, militia, and shopkeepers" (ibid.). Though Sweeney (1993, 72) identifies four main types of townhouses, he suggests that all of these structures, regardless of appearance, served to accommodate local government affairs, including sessions of the county court. They often provided two floors, a first-floor hall for town meetings or commercial activities and a second-floor array of chambers for assemblies and courts to meet and hold session (ibid.). As the primary civic structure of every town, this space housed the exchange of information—both formal and informal—of import to the local community (McNamara 2004, 18).

THE COURTHOUSE AS A PROFESSIONALIZED CIVIC SPACE

A confluence of factors led to the establishment of several county courthouses throughout the colonies. In the 150 years before the republic, magistrates held sessions of the court in meetinghouses, schoolhouses, and townhouses, as well as in public houses and taverns. With increasing differentiation between religious space and secular space and drinking space; population growth; and the routinization of local politics, townships awoke to the need for buildings devoted to law, law enforcement, and governing. McNamara (2004, 3) suggests that this realization stemmed in part from the professionalization of both the legal field and the architectural community, noting that "courthouses and newly built prisons were brought together to create a landscape of justice." Through this explanatory lens, lawyers played a large role in reshaping court rituals away from "pomp and parade" and toward ritualized *proceedings* through which the legal community could perform their craft, highlight their "professional demeanor and legal acumen," and thereby enhance their legitimacy in the public eye (ibid.).

Anthropological examinations of colonial America by legal historians underscored the diversity of legal cultures of this period. It was a time in flux and involved distinctive northern and southern cultures (Hartog 1981; Hoffer 1992; see also Ross 1993, 32). Unlike the emphasis of contemporary legal culture on separation of power, distinction in the areas of the law, and differentiation of legal professionals from the average public, the premodern legal culture of colonial America emphasized "fusion" and "amalgamation," according to Ross (1993, 34–35), who noted that "by asking us to meld together different spheres of society (law, religion, politics) and disparate elements of the legal system (institutions, rules, values, perceptions), the concept of legal culture pulls us into the premodern legal world." It was a culture that melded European customs; it applied differentiated norms based on race, gender, occupation, and class; it lacked clearly defined institutional responsibilities; and it relied on disparate sources of legitimacy (ibid., 36).

Nevertheless, the county courthouse was a secular censor of communal conduct. Morgan (1986, 440) points out that "Virginians of the Tidewater learned what obligations they owed to superiors and inferiors and what constituted the norms of social conduct," and the jury, as the representative body of the freemen of the community, "upheld the moral and religious laws of the community."

These new courthouses were functional but elegant. Upton (1997) describes with rich detail the design and function of eighteenth-century courthouses in Virginia. The axial layout directed visitors from one end into the courtroom and toward the long, raised bench at the other end.

County magistrates were ordered according to their seniority, with the most senior in the center. With a curved rear wall and sometimes an oval window above the bench, these county courthouses made reference to the Capitol in Williamsburg and ultimately to the tribunes where magistrates presided in Roman basilicas (ibid., 205–6). The congregation who gathered to observe court sessions had to stand—a further differentiation through physical space between officers of the court and the general public (ibid., 206). Features such as the oval window above the bench hinted at the Episcopal building style of the period, one including rounded features for doors, windows, and vestibules. Puritans and their descendants derided these features as peculiar and ostentatious (Lounsbury 2006, 7). Courthouse exteriors in colonial Virginia were relatively plain, with little attention to façade or elevation, according to Upton (1997, 214).

The New England courtroom, by contrast, mimicked the Puritan meetinghouse in important ways. While the judicial bench remained elevated, seats for justices formed a U shape centering on the width of the room while also running the length of each side to encircle the proceedings (McNamara 2004, 24). In both arrangements, courtrooms denoted hierarchy and seniority through furnishings—with the chief justice sitting in the center in the "grait chair" (ibid., 52). Similar arrangements subsequently appear in the seating of the Massachusetts and Maine Senate chambers.

By the end of the eighteenth century, courthouses were appearing across the New England landscape. McNamara (2004, 56) notes that "between 1780 and 1830, every county in Massachusetts, including the District of Maine, acquired a new courthouse." These buildings constructed for the function-specific administration of justice provided differentiated interior space, including deliberation rooms for juries (ibid., 41). Housing juries in one discrete place kept the court from having to financially support the boarding of jurors in taverns and provided the court with stricter control over jurors' interaction with the public at large (ibid., 52). The space facilitated not only trial proceedings but also the management of court and county affairs by the justices and the clerk of the court (ibid., 42–43). These spaces, combined with function-specific jailhouses or houses of correction (as well as the jailer's house), provided a judicial complex in many town centers. A spatial network of judicial buildings physically differentiated the activities of law enforcement (trial and punishment) from other religious, civic, or commercial activities (ibid., 48–49). It was a bounded space for one specific purpose, and this made it a very different type of civic space than that provided by the meetinghouse and townhouse (ibid., 57).

An equally important development at the turn of the nineteenth century was the architectural move from a short axial plan to a long axial plan. Lounsbury (2006) argues that this shift transcended denominational differences and even influenced secular design. While previous scholarship drew attention to this shift in New England, the explanations centered on parochial developments following independence. Lounsbury (2006, 12) observes that just as the meetinghouse as a building type existed across the nation before the turn of the century, so the transformation of this built form occurred in New England, the Mid-Atlantic, and the South.

This evolution of local civic architecture is important for legal historians and judicial scholars for a number of reasons. First, it illustrates the communal religious underpinnings of judicial proceedings in early colonial America. Across the thirteen colonies, Puritan and Anglican tradition and authority infused court space with both domestic and symbolic trappings. Second, it highlights the gradual shift in venue of court proceedings. With early court sessions held in meetinghouses, townhouses, and taverns, judicial legitimacy rested with the reputation, status, and behavior of individual magistrates as agents of community justice. These activities were intertwined with religious and commercial affairs, further complicating the perceived legitimacy of the court (McNamara 2004, 7). It would be a mistake to associate the new courthouses of the late eighteenth and early nineteenth centuries with the American Revolutionary War, political independence, and emerging statehood. As McNamara (ibid., 57) recounts: "The impetus for the physical rebuilding of the legal system was not political in origin. The Massachusetts Constitution of 1780 required complete separation of powers among the three branches of government, but it introduced very few changes in the judicial system, and none that would have required new forms of architecture or new planning strategies for courtrooms. The constitution created no new courts and discontinued none of the existing courts."

It is reasonable to question Allan Greenberg's (2006) assumption concerning the timing of the linguistic turn in secular architecture (which he implies coincided with the American Revolution). It is also reasonable to *affirm* his assumption concerning the uniqueness of the linguistic pattern to American architecture. On the one hand, there was great diversity in the religious ideologies undergirding communal space, the basic patterns and ornamentation given to these structures, and the relationship between religious and legal authority exercised inside of these civic buildings. On the other hand, there was great uniformity in the development of these town centers, the language used to describe them, and the types of activities they housed. They were physical houses for communal bodies, and they were as diverse as the groups of settlers who chose to call the Anglo-American "New World" their home. In this sense, Greenberg's (2006) observation is particularly astute, that a common philosophical orientation to power and authority (both religious and political) took root throughout the colonies and manifested itself in the language of American vernacular architecture.

Greenberg, a South African, argues that American civic architecture reflects the ethos of American government that the foundation—the "basic building block"—is the individual citizen, and therefore is fundamentally democratic. American civic architecture's fundamental structure informing all other built environments is therefore the citizen's home (Greenberg 2006, 32). The public spaces that resulted from this revolutionary ethos embodied the spirit of democracy, a modest character, a pragmatism, and a regional diversity fit for the new nation (ibid., 34–37). As Greenberg observes in extending this case, the American architectural school of the seventeenth and eighteenth centuries is a remarkable departure from the European patterns of the Renaissance and the early Enlightenment. "The history of American architecture, unlike that of centuries before it, is not written as a great symphonic expression of power in cathedrals and palaces, of God and God's kings on earth. Rather it is a song composed of small houses that may be seen as the expression of diffused power, of the dignity and the authority of the American citizen in a republic. It is in this sense that the citizen's house is indeed the equivalent of a royal palace" (ibid., 68).

This is the physical manifestation of an emerging democratic zeitgeist. Greenberg reflects on Tocqueville's understanding of democracy in America, suggesting that it is more than a philosophical notion or form of government. The democratic state of mind, Greenberg argues, directly impacted the architecture of the young republic—infusing the built environment with a unique character specific to American identity (ibid., 26). This architecture included the home, the village, the township, the city, and the countryside, and it influenced institutions of education, worship, and governance (ibid.).

TABLE 2.1. The evolution from meetinghouses to courthouses

Meetinghouses 1600s	Townhouses Mid 1600s–1800s	Courthouses Mid 1700s–present
Viewed as communal house	First built in 1600s, but limited evidence Grew from 1700 to 1780	Largely introduced in second half of eighteenth century
Modeled after domestic architecture	Early examples include Boston (1657), Salem (1636), Milford (1645), Charleston (1657), Windsor (1670s)	Formed a "landscape of justice"
Housed town records	Housed town records	Housed town records
Provided venue for religious and secular town meetings	Provided neutral meeting space	Ritualized proceedings
	Accommodated religious difference	Provided secular censorship of communal conduct
	Facilitated government business	Differentiated legal profession
	Attracted county courts	

SOURCE: Compiled by the authors.

It is evident that meetinghouses and townhouses served as models for courthouses (see table 2.1). These spaces constituted a derivation of medieval European town or market halls with separate space for governmental functions and commercial activities. They articulated a fundamental understanding of the town as the center or locus of power rather than the county or colony. Finally, these spaces served multiple functions, providing necessary rooms for assemblies of the public, the courts, and committees.

These structures appeared across the thirteen colonies, originating in New England but spreading through the Mid-Atlantic and Southern territories. A collection of early American imprints illustrates the presence of courthouses, often called "court-houses," throughout the eighteenth

Table 2.2. References to "court-house" in early America

Location	Example (year)
Connecticut	Advertisement for store located east of the Court-House (1773)
Delaware	Speech at the Court-House marking the incorporation of the city of Newcastle (1724)
Georgia	Fixing and establishing court-houses (1784)
Maryland	Sons of Liberty meeting at the Court-House (1766)
Massachusetts	Rebellion at and occupation of the Court-House at Northampton (1786)
New Hampshire	Hymns and spiritual songs printed by office near the Court-House (1795)
New Jersey	Address to the Federal Republicans concerning slate of nominees for upcoming election (by committee appointed at the Court-House) (1778)
New York	Meeting of a Court of Common Pleas at the court-house (1790)
North Carolina	Meeting at the court-house (1774)
Pennsylvania	Advertisement for public sale at the court-house (1795)
Rhode Island	A course of experiments on display at the Court-House (1752)
South Carolina	Sermon preached after destruction of province court-house by fire (1748)
Virginia	Organization of troops at court-house (1780)

Source: "Early American Imprints, Series I: Evans, 1639–1800." Accessed at https://www.readex.com/content/early-american-imprints-series-i-evans-1639-1800.

century and across colonial America. We uncovered numerous references to "courthouse" or "court house" or "court-house" in these imprints. There could be more ("Early American Imprints, Series I: Evans, 1639–1800"). Table 2.2 provides a sampling of the references to "court-house" in this collection by date and location.

This collection of all known imprints from the period provides strong evidence that courthouses predated the American Revolution

By the HONORABLE
The Lieutenant

GOVERNOUR

And Commander in Chief
In and over His Majesties Province of the
Massachusetts-Bay in *New-England*,
The COUNCIL & REPRESENTATIVES, in
General Court Assembled within the same.

THIS Court being *Affectionately Sensible of the Singular Providence
of GOD in the Early Discovery of a most horrid & detestable
Conspiracy to Assassinate the Royal Person of our most Gracious
Sovereign Lord the* KING ; *whom God has eminently Spirited
to Expose Himself in the defence of the* Protestant Interest :
*And upon whose Life the Safety and Welfare of His Majesties Dominions
do so intirely depend : And at the same time to make an* Insurrection
within His Majesties Kingdoms; in Conjunction with an intended Invasion
*by His Enemies from abroad : The Intelligences whereof are lately Arrived to
these Parts : And as we have a just Detestation and Abhorrence of so
Villanous & Barbarous a Design* ; *So we Account it our Duty to Acknowledge
with all Humble Thankfulness, the Special and Signal Mercy & Goodness
of GOD in Detecting, and Preventing of the same from taking Effect.*

AND do Therefore Appoint and Order; That *Thursday* the Eighteenth
of *June* next, be set apart as a Day of Publick *THANKSGIVING*
throughout this Province : And hereby Recommend it to the several
Ministers and Congregations within the same, to Offer up Solemn and
Hearty *PRAISES* unto Almighty God, for so great Deliverance,
and Preservation of His Majesty and His Kingdoms. And therewith to
Conjoyn their *Sincere* and *Fervent* Supplications, That GOD of His in-
finite *Mercy,* would continue His Gracious Providence towards His *Majesty,* Preserve His *Life,* Prosper His *Government,* Detect and Frustrate all
the Attempts of *False* and *Traiterous* Conspirators, and *Succeed* His *Arms,*
both by *Sea* and *Land.* And all Servile Labour is hereby forbidden
upon the said Day.

Given at the Court-House in BOSTON, May 30th. 1696.
In the Eighth Year of His Majesties Reign.

Isaac Addington Secr.

Figure 2.1. Pronouncement of a "Day of Publick Thanksgiving," offered
at the Court-House. "Province of the Massachusetts-Bay," 1698. Early American Imprints, Series I, Evans, 1639–1800, no. 39329. https://www.readex.com
/products/early-american-imprints-series-i-evans-1639-1800.

THE AMERICAN COURTHOUSE 47

The Proceedings of the Sons of Liberty, *March* 1, 1766.

THE SONS OF LIBERTY of Baltimore County and *Anne-Arundel* County, met at the Court-House of the City of *Annapolis*, the firſt Day of *March* 1766.

On Motion made by a Son of Liberty, to appoint a Moderator and Secretary, the Reverend *Andrew Lendrum* was choſen Moderator, and Mr. *William Paca* Secretary.

Mr. *Joſeph Nicholſon*, ſignifying to the Sons of Liberty, that he had an Addreſs from the Sons of Liberty of *Kent* County, was introduced to the Sons of Liberty in Aſſembly met as aforeſaid, and delivered the following Addreſs; Indorſed thus,

Figure 2.2. "The Proceedings of the Sons of Liberty, March 1, 1766." Early American Imprints, Series I, Evans, 1639–1800, no. 41656. https://www.readex.com/products/early-american-imprints-series-i-evans-1639-1800.

and stemmed from the Puritans' use of meetinghouses as the basic organizational structure of society. The earliest documented courthouses date to the late seventeenth century and early eighteenth century. Elizabeth Hawes Ryland (1940, 110) notes the gifting of two acres of land by Henry Fox and Richard Littlepage in 1702 to King William County for the express purpose of a courthouse. This Virginia county constructed a new courthouse in 1722, a facility that opened in 1725 and remains to this day the United States' oldest courthouse in continuous use (ibid., 111; see also "King William County"). Table 2.2 and figures 2.1 and 2.2 offer other illustrative examples, including the declaration of a day of thanksgiving from seventeenth-century Massachusetts and an early meeting of the Sons of Liberty in Maryland.

The courthouse was a central feature of the county, often serving as a major landmark for orienting visitors to local establishments and thereby establishing a powerful sense of reference. It represented the place and role of government in local daily life. The public used this civic site for demonstrations (such as sermons, exhibits, parades, entertainment, elections, and trials) and local meetings (including religious, partisan, and civic gatherings). Courthouses provided a site for organizing members of the community for military engagement, for dissemination of information, and for protest.

Tracing the evolution of colonial vernacular architecture illustrates the importance of *meetinghouses* as the basic community structure of early settlers. With only enough resources for one meeting place, the colonists used civic architecture for both religious and secular purposes. The development of the *townhouse* reflects a transition away from this model due to population growth, religious diversification, routinized local governance, growing economic commercialization, and expanding economic resources for public facilities. This differentiated space accommodated the activities of the court and proved useful. Ultimately, American colonists built *courthouses* and *jailhouses* for judicial administration. These facilities shared an architectural heritage, but they also represented parochial preferences. Virginia courthouses referenced Episcopal buildings and Roman basilicas. New England courthouses referenced Puritan meetinghouses. Crucial to this analysis, courthouses predate the American Revolutionary War by nearly a century. They were not a response to political resistance to the Crown in the late eighteenth century. Rather, they were a corollary of religious architecture (derived from revolutionary religious ideas and local economic circumstance) and a means for differentiation of civic space.

CONCLUSIONS

Courthouses emerged as a central feature of the civic landscape in towns across colonial America. They evolved from seventeenth-century meetinghouses and eighteenth-century townhouses, and their appearance coincided with major shifts in commercial development, population growth, religious diversification, and legal professionalization. This new legal landscape represented a different and new understanding of civic space. Law was the purview of a few highly trained elites. The practice of law was a retrained activity occurring within the confines of a judicial space (McNamara 2004, 53).

As the republic grew and spread across the continent, counties, states, and the national government all built courthouses. Courts and their homes became institutionalized as the centers of civic and political activity. Yet in Washington, the highest court remained unhoused until the 1930s. In a planned capital, the eventual construction of the Supreme Court Building therefore presented a unique opportunity to create a new civic space, and to do so as an evolutionary inflection in an otherwise-planned political space. This would have consequences for both the court and the capital. In the chapters that follow, we explore the shaping of the court's spaces and its institutional development; analyze the meaning and interpretation of the court's spaces from several perspectives; and consider how the inflection of the court as a free-standing architectural entity creates, finally, a courthouse square for all of the republic.

3 Evolution of the U.S. Supreme Court and Its Homes

The origin of the American republic is characterized by intent to create a governing place. Article I, Section 8, Clause 17 of the United States Constitution developed in Philadelphia in 1787 called for the creation of a capital district ("District [not exceeding ten miles square] as may, by cession of particular states, and the acceptance of Congress, become the seat of government of the United States"). In 1790, Congress passed the Residence Act ("An Act for establishing the temporary and permanent seat of the Government of the United States," 1 Stat. 130), which provided for the placement of the temporary capital in Philadelphia, and a permanent capital along the Potomac River. The task of designing the capital would fall to a Frenchman named Pierre Charles L'Enfant.

Pierre Charles L'Enfant was born in Paris and studied at the Royal Academy in the Louvre. With the outbreak of the American Revolution, L'Enfant enlisted to fight with the American revolutionaries and served with the Continentals as a military engineer on George Washington's staff. After the war, he started a civil engineering firm in New York City and was an ally and friend of Alexander Hamilton. One of his major projects was the 1788 redesign of New York City's city hall at 26 Wall Street to serve the national government as Federal Hall. The building, which was initially constructed in 1703, represented after its redesign an early version of the Federal style, which fused Georgian styles with aspects of Neoclassicism. (The building now standing at 26 Wall Street was built as the U.S. Customs House and completed in 1842. It is one of the most distinctive examples of early Greek revival architecture in the United States.)

The new Federal District was specified in the Residence Act of 1790, and L'Enfant was tapped by George Washington in February 1791 to lay out the city. By August, he had developed both a written plan and a map of the proposed city, inspired in part by the gardens of Versailles. The grid design with broad diagonal avenues derives from his original plan. However, L'Enfant did not implement his plan. He was dismissed by Washington, and Andrew Ellicott revised the plan in 1792, including the removal of one prominent square. However, key elements survived, including his proposed placement of the notable institutions of government.

The Supreme Court would find itself with no independent home of its own in Washington, D.C., until the mid-twentieth century. Instead, much as the court had done in New York and Philadelphia, it would make do in either shared or repurposed spaces.

THE COURT IN SPACE AND PLACE

In this chapter we examine five U.S. Supreme Court homes in New York, Philadelphia, and Washington to understand the evolving physical space of the Supreme Court, the values projected by these changing spaces, and the institutional evolution of the court. We do so by looking at two separate "layers" of the court in space and place. First, we examine the physical environs of the court itself. Then, we consider the growing autonomy of the court and its differentiation from other courts as it becomes institutionalized as a political body. This precedes our discussion of the coincidental emergence of the highly ritualized and politically central modern court after it moved across First Street from repurposed space in the U.S. Capitol and into its twentieth-century "temple."

In the process, we encounter some interesting questions. To what extent did the early homes of the Supreme Court provide the range of spaces necessary to conduct business as a legitimate third branch of the federal government? Can we understand institutionalization of judicial power in spatial terms? Does the provision of a range of spaces for judicial activity reflect the recognition of the court as a legitimate branch of government?

THINKING ABOUT DEMOCRATIC SPACE

Architecture is not a static thing. It is a design system. It changes the physical environment and modifies the behavior of living beings. Architectural design, when done right, resolves problems and conflicts that the physical environment presents. It crafts purposeful solutions. It serves the user. And, in the process, architecture and the larger built environment articulate values. To understand the built environment, we must have a mechanism for classifying its features. And we must understand how those features interact. Doing so helps us understand the effectiveness and dynamic of the solution posed by architecture. We must both understand the features of the built environment and how they relate to one another. A path has a beginning and an end; a wall has two sides; and a window in a wall looks out onto some external scene.

The connective tissue of the built environment affects our movement and potentially alters our behavior (see Goodsell 2001). The assumed conflict resolved by "good" patterns of civic spaces in a democracy is that of reconciling the effective operation of government with democratic access and control. This includes the creation and support of connected relationships between the sovereign people (the masses) and those whom they elect to serve in the black box of government (governing elites). We therefore need to have a sense of the values underpinning civic spaces and the functions they serve to understand democratic architecture.

In this exercise, we make use of two primary perspectives on the social meaning of the built environment. The first comes from Nelson Goodman (1985), and particularly his understanding of the unique character of the artistic qualities of architecture. Second, we make use of his concept of "referential meaning" in built design. Goodman's contributions to the field of art theory and aesthetics, and particularly his piece "How Buildings Mean," suggest the types of references contributing to the meaning of works of architecture. Architectural work is unique as an art form in terms of scale. As Goodman (1985, 642–43) observes:

> A building or park or city is not only bigger spatially and temporally than a musical performance or painting—it is bigger even than we are. We cannot take it all in from a single point of view; we must move around and within it to grasp the whole. Moreover, the architectural work is normally fixed in place. Unlike a painting that may

FIGURE 3.1. Goodman's Typology of Referential Meaning

Denotation	+ Expression	+ Exemplification	+ Mediated References	= Meaning
Literally "What?"	Symbolically "What?"	Symbolically "How?"	Contextually "Why?" "What then?"	

SOURCE: Authors' conceptual model of Goodman (1985).

be reframed and rehung or a concerto that may be heard in different halls, the architectural work is firmly set in a physical and cultural environment that alters slowly. In architecture as in few other arts, a work usually has a practical function, such as protecting and facilitating certain activities, that is no less important than and often dominates its aesthetic function. The relationship between these two functions ranges from independence to mutual reinforcement and to outright contention, and can be highly complex.

Buildings constitute architectural art when they signify, mean, refer, or symbolize—not only because of design intention but also because of function (Goodman 1985). Four separate types of referential meaning are found in built design. Together, these four types of references (denotation, expression, exemplification, and mediated reference) give shape to the overall meaning of the physical space (see figure 3.1).

The first type of referent Goodman identifies is *denotation*. Here Goodman asks literally "What?" What does the building or designed space depict? What narration appears on the walls? What artwork is in the space, and what does it symbolize? To get at denoted meaning, we should ask these types of questions. Is there text? What is it? What is written to explain the memorial's intention? How might the building or space be read literally? What is the direct message communicated by the space? What is a straightforward reading of it? The second type of referential meaning Goodman suggests is *expression*. Here he asks symbolically "What?" What is the metaphor invoked by the building or space? What does it symbolize? What symbolic or metaphorical attributes characterize the architectural work? The third type of meaning is *exemplification*. Here he asks symbolically "How?" To what features does the design call attention? How does the architect use form, space, and material to convey an idea? How is that symbol accomplished in this design? The final type of meaning is *mediated reference*. Finally,

Goodman asks, "Why is this building or space significant?" Is it part of a larger social process or movement? Why was it necessary? After its construction, what happened there? Since its construction, with what has the building or space become associated? "As Goodman notes, 'A building may mean in ways unrelated to being an architectural work— may become through association a symbol for sanctuary, or for a reign of terror, or for graft'" (quoted in Vale 1992: 3).

The other approach we take is to make use of Goodsell's (1988, 1998) understanding of the concept of civic space. Primarily and notionally applied to parliamentary spaces and capitol buildings, Goodsell's work focuses on types of civic space and ways to identify uniquely civic space from other types of space. Goodsell's approach is to consider public buildings and grounds and the physical setting of institutions therein, which allows us to consider particularly the connection between architecture and democratic political institutions.

In his seminal work on statehouses, Goodsell identified six types of space in public buildings, which might be broadly considered "civic spaces." These types of spaces are differentiated by function, form, and location. According to Goodsell, in all statehouses space is differentiated. All parts of public buildings are not to be treated the same. The buildings and grounds of political institutions have several distinct purposes. This spatial differentiation within governmental space has to do with resolving the dilemma of protecting versus exposing the governing elite in a democratic society. Six classes of spatial area in this regard exist:

1. Highly exclusive places in which boundary control excludes non-elite persons entirely. These elite preserves are *sanctums*, which are the purview of the elite official.
2. Support areas that are of little or no value for democratic scrutiny of the governing elite. Termed *operational space*, they include staff work areas, storage space, and equipment rooms.
3. Spaces where officials regularly receive visitors individually or in small groups on an invitation or appointment basis. Such offices or reception areas are termed *audience space*. They are predominantly elite defined and elite controlled, and will often reflect the authority and values of those elites controlling the space.
4. *Ritualized* civic spaces are rooms in which formal meetings are held by governing bodies. Examples are legislative chambers, courtrooms, and hearing rooms. These are usually spaces where formal charges of authority are exercised.

5. Lobbies, vestibules, corridors, open stairs, the rotunda, and public restaurants and restrooms in the statehouse are termed *circulation space*.
6. Then there are exterior steps, walkways, and grounds encircling the building, considered *perimeter space* (Goodsell 1988, 1998).

In this chapter, we consider and evaluate the emergence of these six types of spaces in the homes of the Supreme Court prior to its movement in 1935 to the U.S. Supreme Court Building.

INSTITUTIONAL EVOLUTION OF THE HIGH COURT

Here our study focuses on the geospatial evolution of the U.S. Supreme Court and the evolution of the physical home of the court and the social meaning of its civic spaces. The court did not physically evolve in a vacuum, independent of other forces. Government itself grew, evolved, and moved. We examine the growth over time of federal appropriations and staffing to support the court, and also note the larger implications of this history for understanding the role of the court in American political life. We will begin with a visit to the early, temporary governing communities of the republic in New York City and Philadelphia, and an examination of the court's homes in those temporary capitals. We then focus on the court in Washingtn, D.C.

THE COURT IN TEMPORARY CAPITALS

The early history of American government is the search for a stable home. The Confederation Congress kept its seat in Philadelphia but had to take flight at various times to surrounding environs in Pennsylvania to avoid British troops. Between 1781 and 1785, the government would also flee from domestic mobs in Philadelphia and take up residence in Princeton and Trenton, New Jersey, and in Annapolis, Maryland, before settling in New York City in 1785. The government stayed in New York through the First Congress of the United States. The seat of power returned to Philadelphia on a temporary basis in 1790, until by statute the capital would move to the planned city of Washington by December 1800.

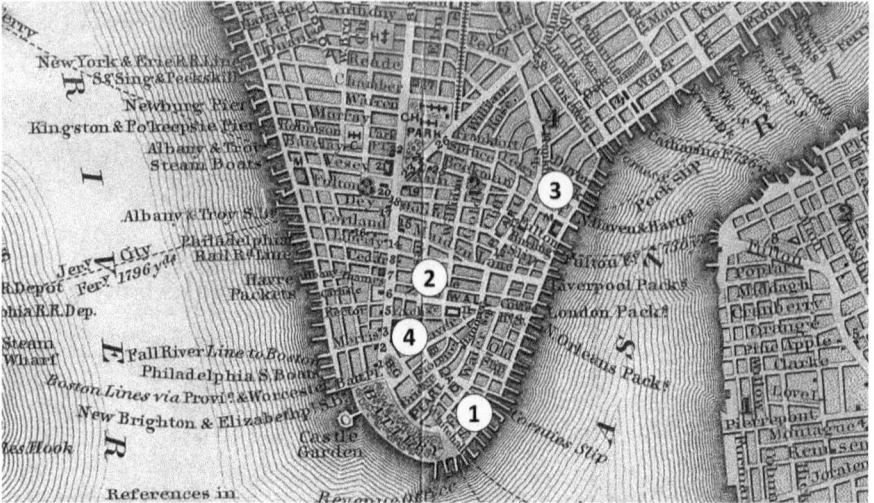

Figure 3.2. 1847 map of Lower Manhattan, annotated to show the physical setting of the U.S. Capitol in New York, including (1) The Royal Exchange; (2) Federal Hall; (3) Osgood House; and (4) Macomb House. Image courtesy of Wikimedia Commons.

New York City: The Merchants Exchange Building

The first capital city of the United States government was New York City (see figure 3.2, which illustrates the physical placement of institutions in eighteenth-century Manhattan). Having hosted the Stamp Act Congress, New York City became the home of the Confederation Congress under the U.S. Articles of Confederation beginning in 1785, and the home of the Congress under the U.S. Constitution for its first two sessions from 1789 to 1790.

New York City did not remain the capital for very long, but it did provide a precedent for future homes of the federal government. The buildings occupied by the three branches were separated by physical distance (see figure 3.2). The Supreme Court shared its space due to its small size and limited workload. Before the Constitution structurally separated the federal government into three distinct branches with different institutional powers, the president and Congress worked from this single location. However, upon ratification of the Constitution, the powers were geographically separated as well.

Figure 3.3. Drawing of the Old Royal Exchange building in New York City. From Lamb 1881, 2:634. Image courtesy of Wikimedia Commons.

President Washington lived in and worked from Osgood House, a mansion rented for the purpose, from 1789 until February of 1790. He then moved to Macomb House, located closer to Federal Hall, but he only resided there for approximately six months before moving with the capital to Philadelphia. The Congress met in Federal Hall at 26 Wall Street. (Federal Hall was built in 1700 as the City Hall of New York, and also housed the Confederation Congress. Charles L'Enfant enlarged the space in 1788 to accommodate the new bicameral Congress.)

The Supreme Court's first home was the former Royal Exchange House of New York City, located at the corner of Broad and Water Streets (see figure 3.3). The marketplace had been originally built in 1675 as a one-story marketplace and then rebuilt in 1752 with an open-air marketplace on the ground floor, and with an enclosed upper floor. Renamed the Merchants' Exchange Building with the Revolution, it served as home to the Chamber of Commerce of the City of New York; the New York State Legislature during the national government's occupation of Federal Hall; and also the Federal District Court of New York.

Institutional Development

The Judiciary Act of 1789 provided specifics concerning the judicial branch of the new federal government that were lacking from Article III of the U.S. Constitution. It called for six justices to serve as the Supreme Court, and it created three circuits, with each circuit providing two of the justices. The first session of the Supreme Court began on February 1, 1790. However, the court lacked the necessary four justices to constitute a quorum and was forced to postpone business until the following day. In its entirety, the term lasted ten days, ending on February 10, 1790. The court considered no cases during the term but did admit a few dozen attorneys to the federal bar (Hodak 2011). It was during this inaugural session that the court appointed the court crier and the clerk. The Supreme Court met for one more session in the Royal Exchange, from August 2 to August 3, 1790, before moving to Philadelphia.

The upper floor was used by the Supreme Court for its inaugural sitting in February 1790, and also for a brief August session before joining the rest of the national government in Pennsylvania. For the duration of the court's tenure in the enclosed upstairs of the marketplace, the butchers were evacuated from the market "so as to spare the court 'interruption from the noise of carts'" (Hodak 2011).

Precise dimensions and descriptions of the upper floor of the Exchange are not known, but the total upstairs area appears to have been less than 1,500 square feet. The interior constitution of the chamber is not known. As viewed in exterior drawings, it was likely well lit, with ample exterior illumination. In this respect, it reflected the traditional medieval use of a meetinghouse-above-market that combined different community functions.

The Exchange was demolished in 1799 to be replaced by a subsequent structure, which burned in 1835. The Exchange sat across the street from the earliest incarnation of Fraunces Tavern, which served as home to the departments of War, State, and Treasury during the Articles of Confederation government.

Two Homes in Philadelphia

The Supreme Court joined the relocation of the national government to Philadelphia in 1790. There, for the next decade, the court occupied two different quarters in the same city block on Chestnut Street and

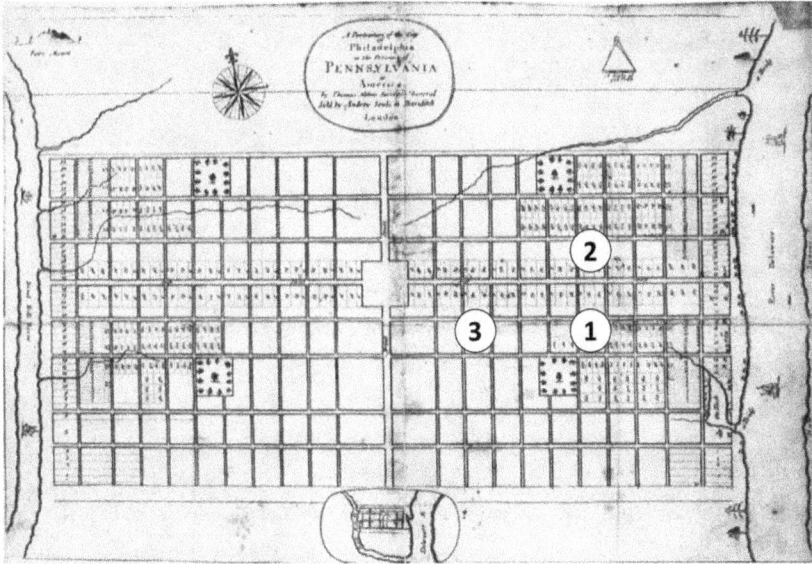

Figure 3.4. *A Portraiture of the City of Philadelphia*, 1683. Created by Thomas Holme to be the first map for Philadelphia. Image annotated to show (1) Philadelphia City Hall, the County Courthouse, and Independence Hall; (2) Masters-Penn House; and (3) the Presidential Palace. Image courtesy of Wikimedia Commons.

always within a few paces of the building used by Congress. As indicated in Figure 3.4, Independence Hall, the county courthouse (subsequently called Congress House), the Old City Hall (where the court eventually sat), and the Masters-Penn House, which served as the executive mansion and was later called "The President's House," were all located within a brisk one–city block walk.

Justices met for two days in February of 1791 in Independence Hall, but there were no cases on the docket for the Supreme Court to consider. Independence Hall (also known as the Pennsylvania State House), connected two separate wings, the county courthouse wing and the city hall wing (National Register of Historic Places 1988; see figure 3.5.) Upon completion of the westerly wing later in 1791, the court met for its August session in the new Philadelphia City Hall.

The Congress met in the Philadelphia County Courthouse (also called the Philadelphia County Building). The county courthouse served as an executive municipal complex, with the mayor's court on the first

Figure 3.5. Detail of north elevation of Pennsylvania State House (Independence Hall), from 1752 map of Philadelphia, Pennsylvania. Image courtesy of Wikimedia Commons.

floor and the mayor's office and council chamber on the second floor. The Philadelphia institutional setting provided separate facilities for the legislative and judicial branches, but these were borrowed spaces for both governing bodies. In this context, however, judicial deliberations transpired in a space conflated with municipal executive office. The federal executive branch operated out of a mansion several blocks away, which was also home to President George Washington and President John Adams before construction of the White House in Washington, D.C.

The room housing the Supreme Court in Philadelphia was 40 feet by 40 feet, and it still exists. Today, the court's room is restored to look as it did when housing the U.S. Supreme Court. The bench is raised, and there are six chairs for the five associate justices and one chief justice of the Supreme Court.

One observation to note before moving to the D.C. homes of the court is that the prior two buildings were simple two-story structures adorned with a cupola. Allen notes, "Most American public buildings in the late eighteenth century were based on domestic forms and details.

Figure 3.6. Supreme Court Room, Independence Hall, Philadelphia, Pennsylvania. Library of Congress, Prints and Photographs Division, LC-DIG-det-4a11772.

A cupola was often the only feature that distinguished a public building from a private residence" (2001, 13).

The first location of the Supreme Court was in the old Pennsylvania State House, more popularly known by the name Independence Hall and scene of the signing of the Declaration of Independence and site of the 1787 U.S. Constitutional Convention. Proposed in 1729 and built as funds were available between 1732 and 1751, it was designed by the architects Andrew Hamilton and Edmund Woolley and built by Woolley. Until the end of the nineteenth century, the red brick Georgian structure served as the home to the Pennsylvania legislature.

The public is generally familiar with the Assembly Room, with its green table coverings, high-back wooden chairs, and twin fireplaces. It was there that the Continental Congress and the Constitutional Convention met. Across the vestibule opposite the Assembly Room was the courtroom of the Pennsylvania Supreme Court. The U.S. Supreme Court initially used the Pennsylvania Supreme Court Chamber after the move to Philadelphia from New York City (see figures 3.6 and 3.7). The court met in these chambers for two days in February and

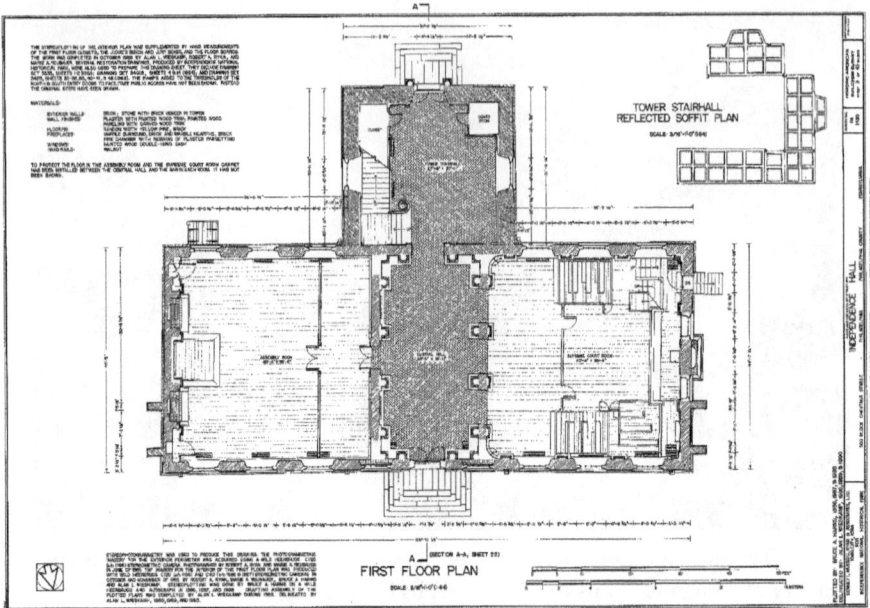

Figure 3.7. Pennsylvania Supreme Court Chamber as home to the U.S. Supreme Court. The court's chamber in Independence Hall is in the west end of the building, on the first floor (lower-right corner). Historic American Buildings Survey, documentation compiled after 1933. Independence Hall Complex, Independence Hall, 500 Chestnut Street, Philadelphia, Pennsylvania. Library of Congress, Prints and Photographs Division, HABS PA,51-PHILA,6- (sheet 9 of 45).

then adjourned from their session (stairs at the rear of the courtroom led to the Long Gallery on the second floor of the hall).

Independence Hall would eventually be turned over to the city of Philadelphia. The seat of the Supreme Court in the hall would subsequently house the "Mayor's Court." The Assembly Room was converted to a courtroom as well, and later in the nineteenth century the second floor was leased to the national government for the use of the district and circuit courts. When the court reconvened in August 1791, it met in what is now known as the Old City Hall, at the corner of 5th and Chestnut, immediately east of Independence Hall (see figure 3.8). The Hall was intended to replace the previous city hall. However, on its completion in August, the Supreme Court immediately moved into quarters there, and would sit in session at the corner of 5th and Chestnut until leaving Philadelphia after the February 1800 session.

Figure 3.8. Old City Hall (Philadelphia), 2011. Photograph by Antoine Taveneaux. Philadelphia Old City Hall was the home of the U.S. Supreme Court from 1791, when construction was completed, until 1800, when the nation's capital moved to Washington, D.C. Accessed November 18, 2020, https://enacademic.com/dic .nsf/enwiki/9684775.

The courtroom features light on three sides, including a large bay containing four windows, located to the south (see figure 3.9). The court's bench is located in the bay, elevated on a riser about 30 inches above the courtroom floor. The bench is roughly shoulder height when approached. As shown in figure 3.9, the courtroom also features a jury box, a witness dock, and seating for the attorney appearing before the court. Located at the north end of the courtroom is a gallery from which the public can view proceedings. The room is finished in white and taupe, with very little dark wood.

Each of the first three homes of the U.S. Supreme Court provided adequate judicial spaces. These were contemporary courtrooms of the time in terms of layout and space, but they were rarely used because of the peculiar character of the court at that time. The 1789 Judiciary Act required that the six justices of the Supreme Court preside twice

Figure 3.9. The U.S. Supreme Court meeting space in Old City Hall. National Park Service photograph. "Visiting Old City Hall," Independence National Historical Park. Accessed November 18, 2020, https://www.nps.gov/inde/planyourvisit/old cityhall.htm.

a year over federal circuit courts. This act of "riding circuit" was grueling at a time before the country had a well-maintained turnpike system, let alone railroads. The speed of travel was limited to that of the horse or the sail. The justices were often exhausted, and the time demands and physical wear contributed to turnover on the bench.

To the Federal City

James Sterling Young's (1966) account of the early Washington establishment highlights the driving symbolism of L'Enfant's plan. In designing the federal city, L'Enfant sought to "create a community divided into separate and discrete units" and to make the community accessible to the outside constituents it aimed to serve (ibid., 3). He used spatial distance to create three urban centers, one for the executive branch, one for the legislative branch, and one for the judicial branch. This distance would situate the branches so as to frustrate collusion and avoid mutual confrontation (ibid., 4). As shown previously in figure 1.8, L'Enfant's vision for the federal city incorporated and determined locations of the three branches of government within the district.

L'Enfant's plan for the location of the Supreme Court is particularly separate. As he summarizes, "Placed roughly equidistant from the presidential and congressional centers, the site for the Court is provided no avenues to render it accessible to either of its coordinate centers within the community or to the outlying society. In a community in which outside communication is planned to figure so prominently, it would seem that this segment is an anomaly" (Young 1966, 6).

The capitol building, termed the "Congress House," was to serve as a home for the legislature. The President's House was intended to be a suitably inspiring palace designed to impress foreign dignitaries. These structures were the subject of much thought and attention, much like the institutions they housed. The judiciary received far less attention. Clearly the intention of L'Enfant was to provide some sort of home for the Supreme Court. According to a National Parks Service building survey on Judiciary Square,

> On his grand plan for the city, Pierre L'Enfant chose this area on a slight rise between the President's House and Capitol as the site for the federal judiciary, thereby placing the three branches of government—executive, legislative, and judiciary—in geographic relationship. L'Enfant marked this site encompassing the area of three large city blocks to indicate intended plantings or buildings. Two avenues were planned to emanate from the rounded south end of the appropriation; that to the west was to provide an impressive vista to the planned monument to George Washington at the apex of the Mall and the grounds of the President's House. (U.S. National Park Service 1993, 2)

When Ellicott replaced L'Enfant, he preserved this element of the plan for Washington, indicating two buildings for the federal judiciary in his 1792 engraving of the design for the capital city (ibid.). However, though the urban designers commissioned for the city suggested their intent for the space, the financial appropriators did not prioritize the space. Over the ensuing decades, city commissioners adapted the space to provide for a city jail in 1802 and a city hall in 1820. From that point

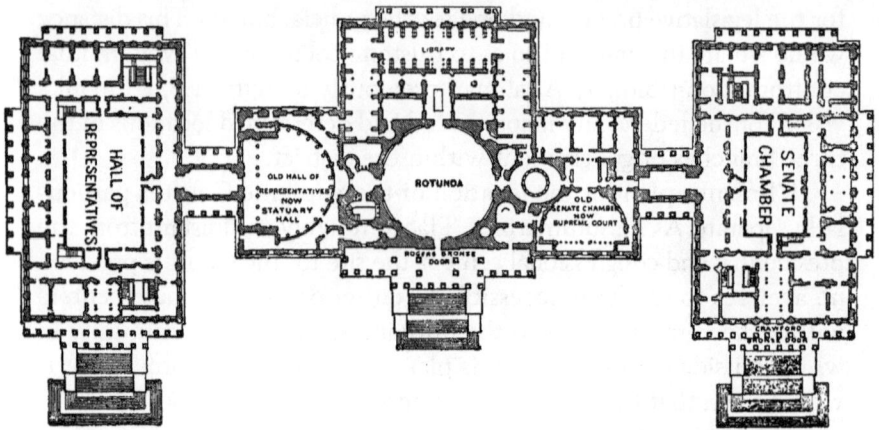

Figure 3.10. The original Senate Chamber and Committee Rooms. From Shaw 1900, 22:681. Image courtesy of Flickr, https://www.flickr.com/photos/internetarchive bookimages/14597782457.

forward, Judiciary Square served as a municipal center for the city of Washington, D.C. L'Enfant's plan thus failed to materialize (ibid., 2–3).

Congress did not prioritize construction of a facility for the Supreme Court at the site L'Enfant envisioned or at any other site for that matter. Judiciary Square was located on the shore of the Tiber Creek swamp. Clearing the site and constructing a building on it seemed unjustifiable given the limited personnel and business of the court in the early 1800s (Young 1966, 76). The result was that the judiciary had no home when the government transferred from Philadelphia to Washington, D.C. Within a week of its first scheduled session in the new capital city, the court gained access to space in the U.S. Capitol Building.

The Supreme Court in the Old Chamber

For the first several years in Washington, D.C., the Supreme Court worked out of committee rooms on the west side of the ground floor in the Capitol. These are now designated S-146 and S-146A, and are off a corridor behind the old, original Senate chamber (see figures 3.10 and 3.11). At times, construction in the Capitol displaced the court, forcing justices to conduct business in private residences or taverns. The original Senate chamber was partitioned and rebuilt between 1808 and 1810 to provide additional space for the upper house of Congress. With renovation

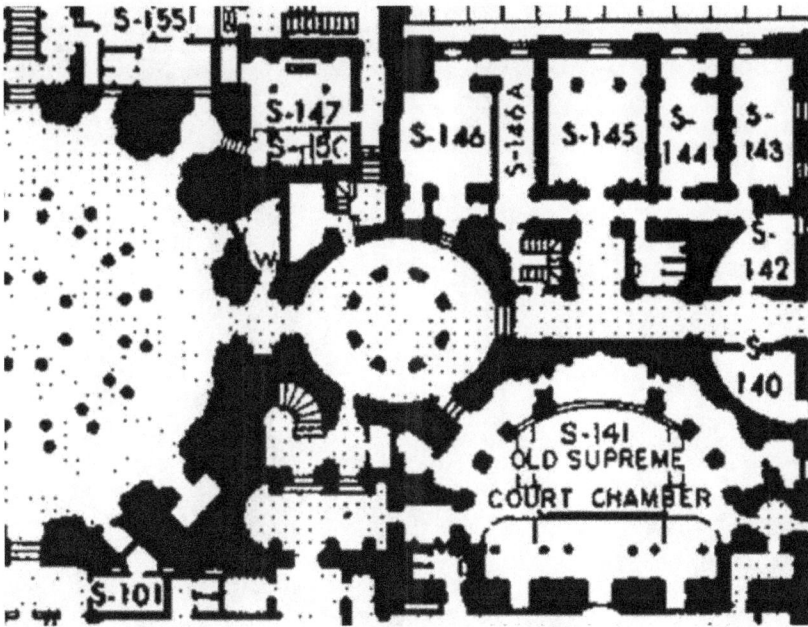

Figure 3.11. Detail from the first (ground) floor plan of the United States Capitol, as it appeared in June 1997, in the *Official Congressional Directory, 105th Congress 1997–1998* (1997), 548. The detail shows the meeting spaces of the Supreme Court in the Senate committee rooms. Image courtesy of Wikimedia Commons.

of the original Senate chamber, the architect Benjamin Latrobe created a space on the ground floor directly underneath the new Senate chamber—a space designed to meet the needs of the public sessions of the court (ibid.).

The old chamber was 75 feet wide and 50 feet deep, with a curved rear wall and a low vaulted ceiling. Figure 3.12 provides an image of the original chamber, which had limited space for spectators to view the court's proceedings. The curvature of the room reinforces a feeling of intimacy, perhaps symbolically giving meaning to the private nature of the court's deliberations, the limited reach of judicial power, and the attention given to individual claims even in a system of majority rule.

Young (1966, 76) draws from diaries of the period to describe the operation of the court at the time.

> The Court made itself inconspicuous and served justice in the basement of the Capitol. "It is by no means a large or handsome apartment; and the lowness of the ceiling, and the circumstance of its

Figure 3.12. "Old Supreme Court Chamber." Architect of the Capitol. Accessed November 18, 2020, https://www.aoc.gov/capitol-buildings-old-supreme-court-chamber.

being under ground, give a certain cellar-like aspect, which . . . tends to create . . . the impression of justice being done in a corner . . . while the business of legislation is carried on with . . . pride, pomp, and circumstance." . . . The proceedings of the Court attracted, on the whole, only slight attention in the capital except when lawyers of wide repute were arguing cases, and "the moment they sat down, the whole audience arose, and broke up, as if the court had adjourn'd."

Let's consider the placement of this space within the overall U.S. Capitol Building and also the chamber's internal character, which reveals important referential meaning. Compared to the main-floor location of the assembly halls of the Congress, the Old Supreme Court Chamber was located in the basement. It was physically and thus symbolically below the work of the Congress. The room provided very limited space for an audience, reinforcing the idea that the work of the court was insignificant and of little interest. A small room to the north of the chamber likely served as a robing room for the justices, and they sometimes also lunched together in this space. The Old Supreme Court Chamber provided limited operational space or sanctum space, forcing the justices to use makeshift accommodations for their deliberations. Young (1966) suggests that much of this work took place in their boardinghouse, where they lived together until the mid-1840s.

SUPREME COURT ACTED AS A CLOISTERED BROTHERHOOD

The members of the Supreme Court lived and dined together in the same boardinghouse until the mid-nineteenth century. And thereafter, they lived together in two separate residences for some time (Young 1966, 77; see Busey 1898, 315). Together they constituted a sort of fraternal brotherhood, similar to many of the boardinghouse alliances within the congressional community. According to Justice Joseph Story, "The Judges here live with perfect harmony . . . in the most frank and unaffected intimacy," wrote Justice Story. "We are all united as one. . . . We moot every question as we proceed, and . . . a very accurate opinion, in a few hours" (quoted in Young 1966, 76–77; see Story 1851, 1:215–17).

The court's responsibilities further separated them from the Washington community. Circuit riding kept them away for most months of the year, and the scheduled sessions of the court were no more than two months annually for much of the nineteenth century. Young (ibid., 77) notes that the unanimity of their decisions, their secrecy concerning deliberation and activity outside of public sessions of the court, and their reclusive social habits provide us with little information on this period of court history. It appears that this cloistering behavior was intentional. Justice Story reflected in his personal papers, "I scarcely go to any places of pleasure or fashion . . . [and] have separated myself from all political meetings and associations. . . . since I am no longer a political man" (Young 1966; see also Story 1851, 1:215–17).

What is significant about the social distance between the court and Congress is that it was a matter of choice rather than convenience. The executive community was spatially distant from the legislative community, a condition that frustrated communication and coordination. This was purposeful, but it also reflected the natural disposition of these two groups to maintain mutual distance. In the case of the legislative and judicial communities, there was no spatial distance. Though separate in function, these bodies could have interacted with great ease.

Social segregation between these two groups, who lived and worked in shared physical space, was a matter of purposeful choice. As Young (1966, 79) notes, "The maintenance of social distance vis-à-vis members of the 'political' branches accorded with both the recognized proprieties of judicial conduct and, presumably, the interest of the judiciary in maintaining its own independence."

INTO THE OLD SENATE CHAMBER

In what is now the restored Senate Chamber, the Capitol housed the Supreme Court from 1861 to 1935. Although the chamber was more spacious and dignified than the basement one, there was no dining room (the justices lunched in the robing room), and no individual office space for the justices and their staff (the justices often worked at home). When the court moved upstairs in 1861, the old courtroom became the law library for both Congress and the court.

Latrobe styled the chamber for the Senate in the fashion of a Classical amphitheater. It served as home to the Senate from 1810 to 1859 (with a brief relocation due to the fire of 1814 during the British march on Washington). When the Senate outgrew the chamber and moved to its current home in the U.S. Capitol Building, the Supreme Court moved into the space from the Old Supreme Court Chamber. It held its public sessions in this space until moving into the U.S. Supreme Court Building in 1935.

Young notes that the House and Senate chambers served a multitude of purposes in the first few decades of the nineteenth century. The design choice of an amphitheater for the Senate chamber is significant. The ancient amphitheater was the place of public entertainment. With theater seating in a gallery around the floor, the space provided a forum for public observance of oration and debate, and the House chamber often served as a concert venue and a place to host village sermons. Young (1966, 72) notes:

> For diversion, members had only to walk down to the Tiber for good fishing and duck-shooting or step into the woods immediately east of the Capitol for a morning's hunt before Congress convened at eleven or twelve o'clock. . . . Public lectures were occasionally to be heard in the Hall of Representatives, when the House might

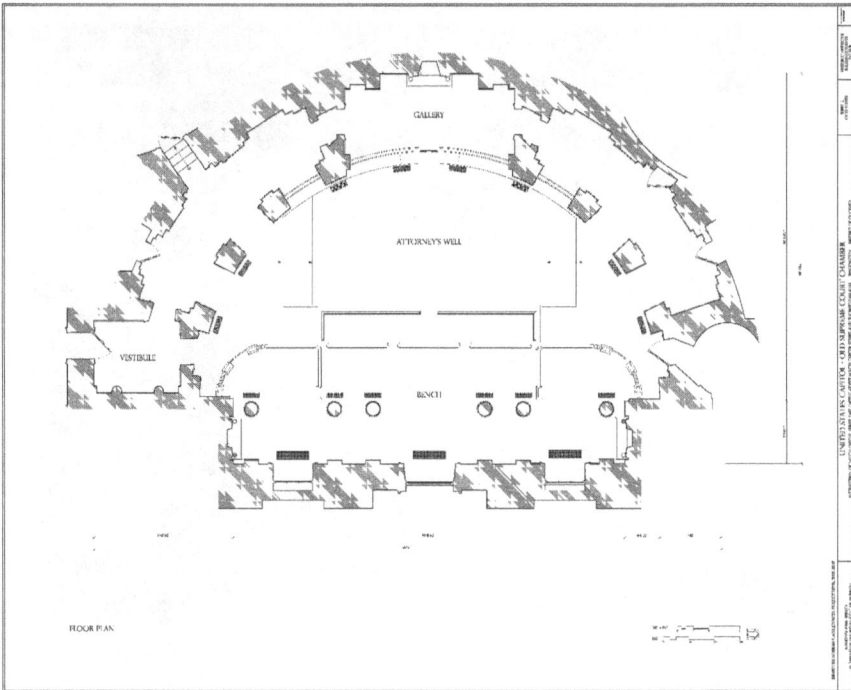

Figure 3.13. Floor plan: U.S. Capitol, Old Supreme Court Chamber, Intersection of North, South, and East Capitol Streets and Capitol Mall, Washington, D.C. Henty Latrobe, designer. Documentation compiled after 1933. Library of Congress, Prints and Photographs Division, HABS DC-38-B.

adjourn to offer the podium to an important constituent or an interesting personality who happened to be passing through Washington.

So thoroughly was the community life of the congressional contingent centered upon itself that their work activities, the daily debates, became one of the principal diversions for legislative society. Senate and House chambers were the settlement's theaters, the galleries serving as the "lounging place of both sexes, where acquaintance is as easily made as at public amusements" (see Smith 1906, 95).

In contrast to the Old Supreme Court Chamber, this interior space was more public and less intimate. Yet modifications to the interior design of the space included removal of the balcony, thus limiting the size of the audience welcomed by the court (see "The Old Senate Chamber,

Figure 3.14. "Supreme Court Chamber," ca. 1930. U.S. Capitol Visitor Center. Accessed November 18, 2020, https://www.visitthecapitol.gov/exhibitions/timeline/image/supreme-court-chamber-ca-1930.

1810–1859"). Additionally, the new space provided little in the way of sanctum space or operational space to justices. Very little space was allocated to them for privately deliberating as a group, housing staff or law clerks, or working outside of the public eye.

Figure 3.13 presents a floor plan of the Old Senate Chamber before renovations to house the court were made. The public gallery encircles the chamber floor. Prior to renovation, the dais for the president of the Senate served as the focal point of the room for spectators.

Very few pictures remain of the Old Senate Chamber when it housed the Supreme Court. Figure 3.14 captures the installation of the long bench to seat the nine justices of the court. We also see one major modification to the chamber when used by the court. We noted above that when the Senate occupied the space, the curved west wall of the chamber featured an elevated balcony, the "Ladies Gallery." This feature is notably absent in this photograph. The restoration of the chamber to

Figure 3.15. The Supreme Court in session in the Old Senate Chambers. Photograph 1937 by Eric Salomon. Image courtesy of Wikimedia Commons.

its senatorial configuration included the return of the Ladies Gallery. (Figure 3.15 is one of the few photographs taken while the court was in session because of the prohibition on cameras in the chamber.)

As the Supreme Court captured and held institutional space, a variety of symbols accompanied this institutionalization. Many were artifacts of necessity, or of previous choices of décor before the court took up occupancy, or were simply a nod to the practicality of the court and its function. Take, for example, the curtains at the rear of the two Capitol courtrooms. These exist out of necessity, to provide shade from exterior light. The pillars at the back of the two Capitol courtrooms provided a practical function—holding up the ceiling in the Old Supreme Court Chamber and holding up the press gallery in the Old Senate Chamber. The curtains and pillars continue into the modern court's current, lavish 6,500-square-foot courtroom. They are not necessary. The rear of the courtroom backs up to the robing rooms and a hallway, behind which is the chief justice's chambers. But the curtains and the imagery of "pulling back the veil" has been a consistent fixture in the courtroom and continues to this day. This sort of symbolism serves to elevate the perceived importance of the institution and its work.

A continuation of previous symbolism is the placement of the eagle and shield over the center of the bench in the Old Senate Chamber. The eagle and shield are symbolic of authority, strength, and freedom; they are found in the Great Seal of the United States. And, in the context of this space, their placement would have been over the chair and table used by the president of the Senate (the vice president) in the old chamber. Latrobe chose the piece specifically for this space. It stood as "a symbol of the strength and unity of the young American republic" ("The Old Senate Chamber, 1810–1859"). According to the history of the U.S. Senate, William Barton contributed to the design of the eagle and stated, "The Eagle displayed is the Symbol of supreme Power & Authority, and signifies the Congress" (88). As such, it was intended to speak of the strength of congressional power. The continuation of this symbol into court's chamber was likely done without thought—the only major modification, beyond the layout of the furnishings, was the removal of the Ladies Gallery. But, the continuity of the symbol of the Union, in the midst of a battle for its survival that had been precipitated in part by the court itself, cannot be discounted.

The "audience space" of the court has evolved, both in terms of size and the treatment of "special audiences." The early, "borrowed" spaces in New York and Philadelphia had the audience space defined by the existing courtrooms and reflected the design of courtrooms that are quite familiar to modern Americans: a bench elevated about 24–30 inches higher than the rest of the courtroom; a jury box off to one side; a witness stand or box, depending on the age of the courtroom; tables for the lawyers; and a bar separating the public from the proceedings.

Once the Supreme Court took up permanent residence, audience space specialization started to unfold. In the Old Supreme Court Chamber in the Capitol, the important members of the audience were given access to front-row seating directed away from the justices and toward the oration of the lawyers. Later, in the Old Senate Chamber, the claimants occupied the desks of the senators, and the audience sat in the gallery. The press often occupied space above the courtroom, in the gallery. This strange accommodation reinforced the sense that the judiciary was a temporary body, a poor fit, granted space as an afterthought on terms created by the legislative branch. But it also started the tradition of segmented seating for different publics, something that will be brought to full fruition in the court's modern home.

TABLE 3.1. Civic spaces in U.S. Supreme Court homes, 1790–1934

	Sanctums	Operational Space	Audience Space	Civic Space	Circulation Space	Perimeter
New York						
Exchange House	No	No	No	Yes	No	Yes
Philadelphia						
Independence Hall	No	No	No	Yes	Limited	Yes
Old City Hall	No	No	No	Yes	Limited	Yes
Washington, D.C.						
Old Supreme Court Chamber	Limited	No	No	Yes	Limited	No
Old Senate Chamber	Limited	Limited	No	Yes	Limited	No
Supreme Court	Yes	Yes	Yes	Yes	Yes	Yes

SOURCE: Compiled by the authors.

GROWING CIVIC SPACE AND THE END OF THE CLOISTERED COURT

Examination of the five temporary homes of the U.S. Supreme Court before its relocation to a permanent home in 1935 reveals an evolving physical space housing the administration of justice by the high court. If we consider Goodsell's six classes of space, what we see is the piecemeal emergence of the court as a fully formed institutional actor with space that is completsely defined and controlled by the court. As indicated in table 3.1, the earliest incarnations of court space were designed to accommodate its formal civic and ritual function: the Supreme Court needed a courtroom. But the court generally lacks most of the other intermediate spaces or operational spaces Goodsell identified. It enjoyed some benefit of these spaces in the Capitol, but did not enjoy the full benefit of all classes of space until it moved into its own building in 1935.

In New York, while the court met for just a few days in the Merchants' Exchange, efforts were made to secure the perimeter space by shutting down commerce in the downstairs market and also closing the streets to traffic. But no other administrative, audience, or sanctum space was available to the court.

During its decade in Philadelphia, the court (and also Congress) enjoyed civic space in both Independence Hall and their subsequent home, the Old City Hall. Limited circulation space was available in both homes, in the form of a public lobby outside the courtroom. And there was a perimeter, an exterior of the building that was enjoyed by the court and was accessible to the public. But any permanent sanctum for the justices, dedicated administrative workspace, or audience space was absent.

On arriving in Washington, D.C., the Supreme Court continues its tradition of finding civic space and making do. Initially the court finds spare rooms in the Capitol (the aforementioned rooms S-146 and S-146A), but it performed most of its other Washington business in the boardinghouses where the justices roomed while in town. However, with the carving out of permanent and dedicated civic space in Latrobe's reconstructions of the Senate Chamber, the court does capture some form of sanctum (the robing room) and also has the benefit of limited circulation space in the lobby and rotunda outside the chamber. The court also acquired some operational and audience space after 1861 through the creation of the law library in the Old Supreme Court Chamber and also a more substantial robing room and conference space. However, it is not until the court moves into its own building (taken up in the next chapter) that we see the court obtain the full complement of civic spaces ordinarily enjoyed for decades by the Congress and the executive.

INSTITUTIONALIZATION: THE CONSEQUENCES OF A COURT IN PLACE

In this last section, we consider the growing autonomy of the Supreme Court from its inception to the present day and its differentiation from other courts as it becomes institutionalized as a political body. The court in place has an impact on the development of the court as an institution. It sheds light on the physical context projecting values on the court's proceedings. It reveals the character of civic space and referential meaning housing the court for the better part of its history.

We consider three separate measures of institutionalization: the early growth of federal personnel in the Washington establishment, the size of the annual caseload handled by the court, and the days spent in session by the court. These measures reveal a picture of relative institutionalization that complements the evolution of the court's place in space. Though we hesitate to draw causal inferences, it is clear that there is a correlation between the institutionalization of the court's resources and behavior and the space it was given in which to operate.

Personnel

A look at James Young's (1966) data on the growth of the executive, legislative, and judicial branches of the U.S. federal government over the first few decades of the American republic is informative. Here we see a huge discrepancy between the size of personnel within the executive and legislative branches and the size of personnel in the high court. Forty years after the first session of the Supreme Court, it still operated with the same number of support staff (one clerk) and only one additional justice. By contrast, the executive branch more than doubled in size. The legislative branch, save for the Senate, did as well. Between 1802 and 1829, the staff supporting the executive branch nearly tripled, from 132 to 318, with the greatest gains in Treasury (+137) and State (+22). Congress nearly doubled its staff from 152 to 299, with the House more than doubling staff support (+119). Clerk and library staff also nearly doubled. Meanwhile, the Supreme Court chugged along with seven justices and one clerk. The president (two professional staff) and the vice president (one) similarly had little growth in personal staffing.

It is worth noting that both of these institutions had space in which to grow. With representation in Congress based on a formula tied to population and statehood, the institution grew commensurate with expansion of the nation. And construction and expansion of the U.S. Capitol Building clearly was a priority to the Congress. It took decades to complete and was stymied by the war with Britain, but it provided dedicated space to the House and the Senate for conducting legislative business. Executive growth lacks any clear constitutional basis, unlike in the Congress through apportionment. The Constitution provided much detail for the electoral college, but little by way of defining the size of the executive apparatus supporting the president. The language of Article II does imply a military reporting to the president as commander in chief, a cabinet with secretaries reporting to the president, and diplomats representing the office abroad. And as legislation grew the executive branch out of necessity, so, too, did the supporting bureaucracy grow. The court, on the other hand, was at the mercy of Congress. It depended on legislative resolution for its structure and personnel. And

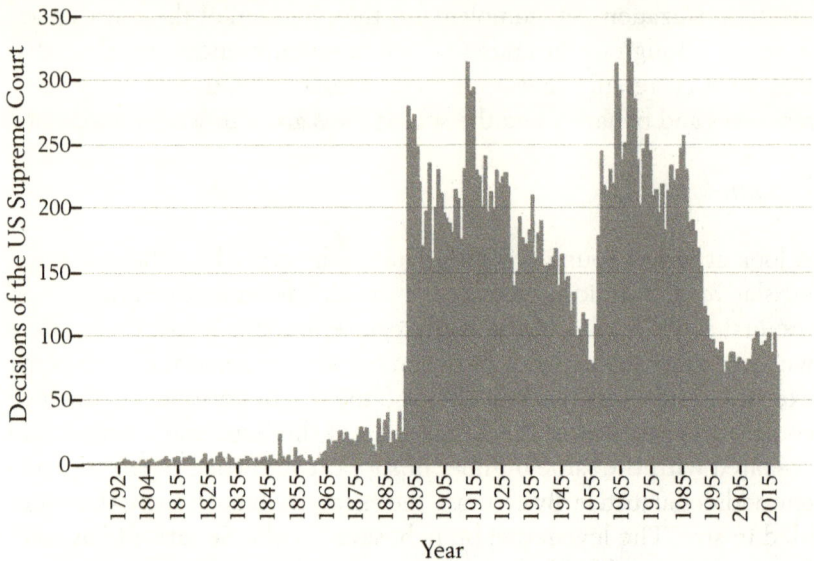

Figure 3.16. Decisions of the Supreme Court, 1792–2017. Compiled by the authors.

Congress did not prioritize construction of an independent physical space for the court. Young (1966) suggests this was likely because of its small size. It is hard to say whether the court was small in number because it lacked space, or it lacked its own space because it was small in number. Either way, this measure of institutionalization further contextualizes the marginalization of the court to temporary facilities unequipped to meet its functional needs and poorly designed to symbolize its role in the American political system.

Case Load

From 1800 to the early 1860s, the Supreme Court averaged 4 to 6 cases, rarely hearing more than 7 cases in a year. The striking exception is in 1850, when the court heard 23 cases (see figure 3.16). Between 1892 and 1893, the court's docket skyrocketed from 76 cases to 277 cases. Throughout the first quarter of the twentieth century, the court continued to hear approximately 200 cases per year, but the number dropped in the late 1920s and continued a decline until the late 1950s and early 1960s. In 1967, the court issued opinions on a record number of cases—a total of 330 in a single year. But this record was not too far afield from the average caseload of the period. The court regularly heard between 200 and 300 cases per year. In 1987, the court reversed its course. With William Rehnquist appointed as the chief justice in 1986, the court reduced its caseload significantly. By 1994, it was deciding fewer than 100 cases a year with rare exception.

Why is this relevant to the physical spaces of the court? Young notes that there were very few cases brought to the Supreme Court in the early period of American political development. With little to do, the court could use borrowed spaces for the few days out of the year it was in session. At the same time that the U.S. Senate is outgrowing its space in the mid-nineteenth century, the Supreme Court is hearing more and more cases involving constitutional questions. It moves into the Old Senate Chamber at the same time that it increases its caseload. And by the turn of the century, it is considering hundreds of cases a year. This reality makes it easier to justify the construction of a separate governmental building to accommodate the U.S. Supreme Court. Important factors are no doubt responsible for this change in caseload.

Congress established the circuit courts of appeals in 1891. The high court had reviewed over 1,600 cases in 1890, a crushing workload that taxed the resource-thin institution. With this expansion of the federal judiciary, Congress also removed the requirement that Supreme Court justices ride the circuit to hear cases brought on appeal. This change in judicial responsibility brought about an immediate reduction in workload. It relieved justices from the onerous travel required by circuit riding. Congress also gave the court control of its docket, with appeals now heard by the circuit courts of appeal.

At the same time, the justices became place bound. Whereas circuit riding had kept them apart for many months of the year, the new structure of the federal judiciary gave them the ability to remain in D.C. to conduct business together. The ultimate outcome was an increase in the number of cases decided by the court on an annual basis and collective institutional activity spanning more months of the calendar year.

The record of the Supreme Court's days in session from 1790 to the present day reveals the true impact of physical setting and administrative responsibilities on the rhythm of the court's proceedings (see figure 3.17). In the late eighteenth century, the court had very few cases (no more than two cases per year) and met only for short periods of time, twice annually, and only in either February, April, or August. This

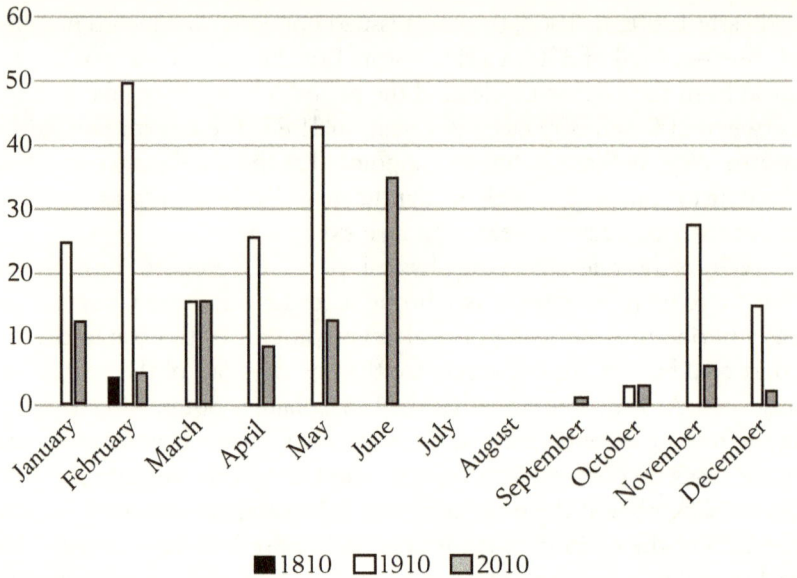

■1810 ☐1910 ▨2010

Figure 3.17. Decisions issued by the U.S. Supreme Court by month, 1810, 1910, and 2010. Compiled by the authors.

schedule derived from the Judiciary Act of 1789, which established two sessions per year for the Supreme Court. The court shifted to an annual term in 1802, and it shifted the time of year for the start of the session three times during the nineteenth century. The current practice of beginning the session on the second Monday in October dates to 1916.

What we see over time is the gradual expansion of the judicial work calendar from two sessions in February and August each year to a continuous term spanning nearly all twelve months of the year. We now consider the Supreme Court term to begin in October and end in late June or early July. This is the period during which the court hears oral arguments and issues opinions on cases. It is important to recognize, however, that this is a relatively modern development.

A PLACE-BASED UNDERSTANDING OF JUDICIAL INSTITUTIONALIZATION

The early Washington community was one of relative isolation, with the legislative and executive branches somewhat isolated from each other.

As the party system emerged and then fell into fragmentation with the demise of the Federalists, the political communities and lawmakers' alliances were built less around partisan ties and more around boarding-house ties. Young (1966) speaks in passing of the role of the judiciary in this physical setting and political climate, but his lack of any significant attention to this branch is revealing. In the early development of the federal government and a nascent Washington establishment, the justices' time spent riding circuit and the lack of any sustained physical presence limited the meaningful relevance of the judicial branch to federal politics of the early period.

Some exploration of judicial symbolism speaks to the perceived ideal values of the judiciary. Judith Resnik and Dennis Curtis (2011) provide a thorough and multicultural examination of the ways in which justice has been symbolically represented. Some of the dominant symbols (such as a blindfolded lady justice) appear in the ornamental adornment of the modern U.S. Supreme Court Building. However, the focus of Resnick and Curtis is not on the evolution of judicial architecture housing the Supreme Court and the meaning this might hold for understanding the role of the court in American political life.

These seminal works on American institutional political development do not consider qualitative measures of the physical homes of the court or the social meaning of these civic spaces. They do not consider the implications of these spaces for judicial power vis-à-vis the other branches, or the dependent relationship between the physical spaces of judicial politics and American psychological understanding and interpretation of federal judicial power. And we readily concede that this book does not complete the circle on these relationships. But, in history, in popular culture, and in our discussion of political development, we know that spaces hold referential meaning. We know from the study of political architecture that this meaning is layered. Tracing the development of the physical embodiment of the court in time and space holds value for understanding how we view the court as an institution and its behavior as a legitimate organ of political power. It opens the door to a deeper reading of our institutional political development.

The early lack of a home has implications for the Supreme Court as an institution. The judicial branch lacked a clear sense of community separate from the legislative branch during the early period of American political development. The physical space provided to the court was an afterthought. The size of the personnel of the judicial branch was minuscule compared to the congressional community. For nearly a century and a half, the members of the court found themselves operating in a location embedded within the legislative domain. Consequently, they were fairly reclusive as individuals and as a small group. Their proceedings were public when meeting in Washington, D.C., and because of the limited activities in D.C. and remote location of the national city from cultural centers such as Boston or Philadelphia, sessions of Congress and the court took on the role of theatrical spectacle. This can be seen in the physical furnishings of the Old Supreme Court Chamber. It is interesting to think about the ways in which the purpose of the public meetings of the court (oral argument more so than issuing opinions) still involves theater. The banter between justices sometimes appears to be theatrical, but the limitations on the public (no video, photography, or noise of any kind, combined with a relatively small audience space) seem to suggest that this procedural activity has become more functional and less theatrical. We do note that with the emergence of a modern, well-housed court and a robust and sophisticated system of clerk recruitment, the court has grown its own deep, cloistered, sophisticated community.

So what do we make of the move to a permanent home in 1935? In the following pages we explore the social meaning of the U.S. Supreme Court Building. But we can state, unequivocally, that the new building served to remove the court from its cloister within the Capitol. It gave it legitimacy in the form of a prominent architectural work designed to meet the needs of a judicial branch with distinctive responsibilities.

But L'Enfant's vision was lost. Judiciary Square did not become its home. Nor did any site equidistant from the White House and Capitol. The site chosen for the court was across the street from the Capitol. Why does this matter? If L'Enfant's plan was to geographically reflect the principle of separation of powers, then the court's proximity to the Capitol provides cognitive dissonance. It is separate yet still connected. It waits while physically facing the nation's lawmakers to hear constitutional controversies as they arise. It is reactive rather than proactive, responding to the institutions on which it depends for resources and enforcement. Finally, if L'Enfant intended to convey institutional significance through spatial separation and placement, the permanent home of the court conveys relative insignificance and dependency.

It is within this context that we see justices of the Supreme Court holding on tightly to institutional norms that shroud its deliberations in secrecy, that convey group solidarity even in dissent. The court continues to gradually give way, in tiny steps, its cloistered tradition. They are more public now than in the past. But other than the occasional narrative, such as Bob Woodward and Scott Armstrong's (1979) *Brethren: Inside the Supreme Court,* we know little about the inner workings of the court or of how they use their space and how it shapes them. It is as if the justices have compensated for the court's relative insignificance by pulling closer together and limiting information about deliberation and images of proceedings from public dissemination.

4 A Civic Interpretation of the U.S. Supreme Court Building

The architect Cass Gilbert and the artisans he commissioned to design the U.S. Supreme Court Building adorned the space using symbolism to emphasize the importance of the law and the significant role of the judicial branch in American democratic government. James Earle Fraser's statues *Contemplation of Justice* and *Authority of Law* flank the grand approach to the building. The West Pediment above the front entrance, designed by Robert Aitken, presents nine allegorical references to liberty, justice, and order. The temple's portico leads visitors through Classically inspired bronze doors that chronologically trace the evolution of justice in the West. The East Pediment balances this symbolism with an additional thirteen allegorical references from the Eastern tradition. The four friezes of the great courtroom infuse the inner space of the building with referential meaning as well.

In chapter 3, we introduced a framework for considering civic space (Goodsell 1988, 1998) and showed how the changes in homes for the Supreme Court were accompanied by increased spatial complexity. From here we turn to a closer analysis of the role of public space in a democratic society as well as the unique character of civic space as a type of public space in which democratic politics, sometimes in the form of representative governance, takes place. Here we interrogate the overall design of the Supreme Court Building in light of the civic space framework and the thematic representations embodied within the architecture of this monumental space.

TOWARD A THEORETICAL UNDERSTANDING OF CIVIC SPACE

Charles Goodsell observed that the term "public space" is utilized by many academic fields to depict an arena of communal activity. Democratic theorists, urban theorists, and political scientists all examine the idea of public space and encourage its utilization. Across the academic literature, certain common depictions of public space emerge. "The features in common are the openness of public space, its importance to democratic life, and perceptions of its degeneration under conditions of modernity" (Goodsell 2003, 361). Hannah Arendt suggests that public space is important because it constitutes the "space of appearance." Arendt (1958, 198–99) describes the polis as the space "where I appear to others as others appear to me, where men exist not merely like other living or inanimate things, but to make their appearance explicitly." This space is indispensable because it provides a public vehicle for political speech and action. Collective engagement for purposes of political persuasion forms the substance of democratic power (Arendt 1972). Similarly, Habermas suggests that the "public sphere" mediates between civil society and the state (see Goodsell 2003, 362).[1] A space for the expression of this power, for the activity of deliberation and the provision of popular consent, is essential to legitimize the institutions of democratic government (Habermas 1964).

Whether for political action or for communication, public space provides a realm for people to exercise their citizenship. It also provides an opportunity for the physical (and perhaps virtual) expression of power (Edelman 1995). This depiction of state power can serve to reinforce the authority of the state or reassure the protection of the citizen. Political regimes make use of "myths, rites, and other symbolic forms" to shape the opinion and behavior of mass publics (Edelman 1985, 4). These spectacles often form the backdrop for public space. As Goodsell (2003, 365) points out, "The very monumentality of significant public buildings itself exudes a sense of clarity, order, timelessness, and predictability with respect to the authority of the government" (see also Edelman 1995).

One such space is the courthouse. The physical space of the judiciary might symbolize state legitimacy (through the rule of law) or oppression (through the power of authority; see Edelman 1995). Some have suggested that "to know courts is to love them, because to know them is to be exposed to a series of legitimizing messages focused on the symbols of justice, judicial objectivity, and impartiality" (Gibson, Caldeira, and Baird 1998, 345). The physical presence of a courthouse might suggest the rule of law, the possibility for justice, the responsibilities of citizenship, the role of the judiciary in a system of separated powers, the objectivity of judges, or the right to trial by jury. However, a courthouse might also suggest intolerance for criminalized behavior, the severity of the law, separation from loved ones, or the fickleness of the public will as expressed through juries.

A few scholars have examined the physical expression of political power through courthouse spaces. Thomas Markus (1993), for example, suggests that courthouses denote the power of judges through the use of benches. Yet they also equalize the power of judges through common spaces such as locker rooms and cafeterias. Housed in the same space, members of the judicial branch share power and serve collectively as arbiters of justice (ibid.).

These spaces express not only power relationships but also the enduring quality of the institution itself. In his analysis of judicial institutions, John Brigham (1987) notes the mortal and immortal character of the Supreme Court. At times, the court is defined by the justices who sit on the bench, whether in terms of the dominant political view of the chief justice or that of the majority coalition. Nonetheless, the court as an institution is more than the individuals who compose it. Brigham (1987, 15–16) notes: "Like other cultural phenomena, institutions are able to transcend changes in membership. This is the quality that gives them their 'Naturalness,' and it is a characteristic of institutions that suggested to Aristotle the analogy of rivers and fountains that have a 'constant identity' even as the flow changes the composition of the thing."[2] American judicial architecture through the mid-twentieth century often invoked sacred symbolism through the use of pyramidal and temple design features (Kammen 1992). Architects of modern American courthouses, however, have largely rejected the Classical Greco-Roman temple design in favor of modernist forms (we return to this topic in chapter 6). According to Brigham (1994), this trend runs parallel to changing conceptions of the role of the court from the conference of sacred judgment to the bureaucracy of conflict resolution.

TABLE 4.1. Delimiting civic space

	Private / Individual	Public / State
Inaccessible	*Castle doctrine:* homes, offices, depositories (banks)	*Elite Sanctums:* offices, caucus space, conference rooms
Accessible	*Commercial:* retail, showrooms, reception, congregation, entertainment	*Civic:* courts, councils, legislative assembly, civic assembly (plaza)

SOURCE: Created by the authors, based on Goodsell (1988, 13).

THE SPECIFIC CHARACTER OF CIVIC SPACE

To examine the symbolic references used in judicial architecture, we first describe the specific theoretical lens framing this analysis of judicial civic space. In a book-length treatment, *The Social Meaning of Civic Space*, Goodsell (1988) articulates a conceptually precise definition of civic space as a subset of public space. He notes four distinct dimensions one must consider to truly appreciate the "civic-ness" of a particular place. Civic space is distinguished from other architectural space with regard to: "(1) ownership or control, (2) accessibility to outsiders, (3) purpose or use, and (4) degree of enclosure" (ibid., 10). According to Goodsell, civic spaces are "(1) state owned, (2) publicly accessible, (3) ceremonial, and (4) enclosed" (ibid., 12). We replicate the figure he uses to illustrate this differentiation as table 4.1.

   While certain state-owned spaces are used for the performance of government activity, they are relatively inaccessible to the public. Government offices or conference rooms house government elites and administrators and facilitate interaction within the institution or between institutional elites but are not generally available to the public. In addition, some state-owned spaces are accessible to the public, but they are used for utilitarian purposes and provide little service to the performance of government activity. These would include the circulating hallways and public amenities (restrooms, snack bars) in government buildings. The civic space of most interest to Goodsell and to our analysis is state-owned space that is accessible to the public and that is utilized for ceremonial purposes. In this work, we turn to the character of the judicial civic space provided by the U.S. Supreme Court Building.

Goodsell's focus is on the civic space provided by American city council chambers (1988) and statehouses (1998, 2001). He suggests that spatial conflict is manifest in these particular arenas in several ways (1998). Through the spatial arrangement of furniture, these chambers ideologically separate members. Through the spatial arrangement of the floor plan, these buildings separate constitutional powers. Through the spatial arrangement of offices, these statehouses distinguish those with power from those without power (Goodsell 1988, 7). Inherent in democratic politics is the need for both security and transparency, or, as Goodsell (ibid., 7) suggests, the need "to protect and expose elite space in the statehouse." Security is required because it is a prerequisite to the functioning of representative government. Transparency allows the people to observe the functioning of their government and to challenge acts of misrepresentation. Herein resides the challenge of balance.

In chapter 3, we introduced Goodsell's conceptual framework for space in statehouses and extended it to previous homes of the Supreme Court. The classifications of space, and how stakeholders related to space (see table 4.2), provided a foundation for interpreting the changing relationship between the court and other institutions and the court and the public. We invoke this classification scheme as it applies to the Supreme Court's current home and encourage readers to consider carefully the information in table 4.2 going forward.

Because of the prestige associated with the office and the tradition of seclusion shrouding the Supreme Court, the distinctions between these classes are all the more clear in this context. The following few paragraphs briefly sketch the contours of the Supreme Court Building in terms of classes of civic space to illustrate this point.

While only a few political elites enjoy sanctum space at the state legislative level, the nine justices of the Supreme Court have office suites that are entirely removed from access by the public. Perhaps the most private space in all of American politics is also in the Supreme Court Building. The Conference Room is furnished with a table surrounded by nine chairs. No staff are allowed in this room while the justices confer over cases on their docket.

The operational spaces of the U.S. Supreme Court are also closed to the public. The offices of the clerk, the police, the curator, the marshal, and several others lack general access. However, the Supreme Court Building does offer some space for receiving guests. The East Conference Room and the West Conference Room, both located on the first floor, are used by justices to host small gatherings and conduct interviews with

TABLE 4.2. Classes of civic space and the U.S. Supreme Court Building

Class	Description	Supreme Court Space
Sanctums	Highly exclusive places in which boundary control excludes nonelite persons entirely. Goodsell calls these elite preserves "sanctums."	Justices' Offices Justices' Conference Room Robing Room Justices' Library Reading Room Justices' Dining Room
Operational	Support areas that are of little or no value for democratic scrutiny of the governing elite. Termed "operational spaces," they include staff work areas, storage spaces, and equipment rooms.	Office of the Clerk of the Court Counselor to the Chief Justice Police Headquarters Public Information Office Press Room Curator's Office Personnel Office Marshal's Office Solicitor General's Office
Audience	Spaces where officials regularly receive visitors individually or in small groups on an invitation or appointment basis. Such offices or reception areas are termed "audience space."	Library Lawyers' Lounge East Conference Room West Conference Room
Civic	Rooms in which formal meetings are held by governing bodies. Examples are legislative chambers, courtrooms, and hearing rooms. Drawing on a concept developed elsewhere by Goodsell (1988, 13), such rooms are called "civic space."	Court Chamber
Circulation	Lobbies, vestibules, corridors, open stairs, the rotunda, and public restaurants and restrooms in the statehouse are termed "circulation space."	Great Hall Spiral Staircases John Marshall Statue Visitors' Film Exhibits Cafeteria Gift Shop
Perimeter	Exterior steps, walkways, and grounds encircling the building are considered "perimeter space."	Front Plaza

SOURCE: Adapted directly from Goodsell's (1998, 9) analysis of classes of civic space.

the press. Further, the library is one of the most beautifully decorated spaces in all of Washington, D.C. Professional attorneys who are members of the Supreme Court Bar are granted access to the library and may bring a single guest. (There is also a basketball court on the fifth floor of the building, which is accessible to Supreme Court workers. It was converted from storage space in the 1940s and is nicknamed "the highest court in the land," as it is one floor above the courtroom.)

The most iconic space of the U.S. Supreme Court Building is the courtroom. Located in the heart of the building, it is an intimate space measuring 82 by 91 feet (U.S. Supreme Court 2021c). At any given time, only 250 people can attend a session of the court. The proceedings are open to the public on a first come, first serve basis, but no personal belongings are allowed in the room other than a pad of paper and a writing utensil. The majority of visitors to the court do not experience the court in session but rather view the exhibits and educational video available in the circulation space on the first floor. The Great Hall is also open to the public, but there is not much to observe in this space. The primary function of the hall is to serve as a grand entrance to the courtroom. The two other attractions in the building are the John Marshall Statue and the two spiral staircases.

Central to media coverage of the Supreme Court is the image of protestors on the Front Plaza before the steps of the Supreme Court Building awaiting the release of a seminal opinion. The Front Plaza welcomes visitors to the court and bids them entry between two symbolic statues and a set of gargantuan bronze doors. Though recent administrative changes have closed the front entrance to visitors, this space still nicely fits the criteria for perimeter space.

THE U.S. SUPREME COURT AS CIVIC SPACE

Having considered the Supreme Court Building in terms of *classes* of civic space, the analysis now turns to a more in-depth examination of the *quality* of these spaces and the social meaning inherent in their design. The analysis moves through spaces in a reasonable order of public procession from exterior court space to interior court space, starting with the initial space encountered by visitors to the Supreme Court, which is the perimeter space on the west side of the building, and then continuing deeper into the building through classes of exclusion.

Figure 4.1. The West Pediment of the U.S. Supreme Court Building, 2005. Photograph by Matt Wade. Image courtesy of Wikimedia Commons.

Perimeter Space

The exterior public approach to the U.S. Supreme Court Building begins with the Front Plaza. This 252-foot-wide oval plaza leads visitors to the steps of the building and provides a forum for public protest of court decisions. Several powerful symbols of judicial iconography are embedded in the statuary and ornamentation of the space. As Barbara Perry (2001, 319) notes, even the allegorical figures decorating the lampposts symbolize the strength of the court and the deliberate nature of its proceedings. The architecture of this space emphasizes three particular features: the West Pediment, the two statues, and the bronze doors.

Designed by Robert I. Aitken, the West Pediment incorporates nine allegorical figures (see figure 4.1). At the center of the pediment sits *Liberty* on a throne. In her lap rest the Scales of Justice. She is guarded by *Order* and *Authority*. These figures are flanked by depictions of *Council*. The final two figures at the edges of the pediment are *Research Past* and *Research Present* (U.S. Supreme Court 2009).

Figure 4.2. *Contemplation of Justice*. Statue by James Earle Fraser on the left front steps of the U.S. Supreme Court Building. Photograph 2016. Image courtesy of Wikimedia Commons.

Two statues on the Front Plaza guard the entrance to the U.S. Supreme Court Building. They are intended to be a "prelude to the spirit of the building" (U.S. Supreme Court 2010d). The architect Cass Gilbert persuaded the United States Supreme Court Building Commission to hire James Earle Fraser to sculpt both statues. Fraser designed one to represent the "contemplation of justice" and the other to represent the "authority of law" (ibid.).

To the left of the building's entrance sits *Contemplation of Justice* (see figure 4.2). Fraser designed this female figure to express "the beauty

Figure 4.3. *Authority of Law*. Statue by James Earle Fraser on the right front steps of the U.S. Supreme Court Building. Photograph 2007 by dbking. Image courtesy of Wikimedia Commons.

and intelligence of justice" (ibid.). One arm rests on a book of laws, while she holds a small figure in her other hand. The female figurine in her right hand is blindfolded and represents the objectivity of justice (ibid.). The depiction of justice in female form originates in ancient mythology. The Greeks worshiped Themis, the Goddess of Justice and Law. The Romans worshiped Justicia, the Goddess of Justice. The detail of a blindfold dates to the sixteenth century and signifies impartiality (U.S. Supreme Court 2003b).

To the right of the building's entrance sits *Authority of Law* (see figure 4.3). Fraser intended this male figure to symbolize execution of the law. In other places, he is described as the "Guardian or Executor of Law." The statue depicts a Greco-Roman soldier armed with a helmet and a sheathed sword. Depicted by Fraser as "powerful, erect, and

Figure 4.4. "The Bronze Doors." U.S. Supreme Court. Office of the Curator, Supreme Court of the United States, Infosheet. Accessed November 18, 2020, https://www.supremecourt.gov/about/infosheets/bronzedoors.aspx?rwndrnd =0.2755968610290438.

vigilant," the soldier holds a tablet of laws inscribed with "LEX" ("law" in Latin; U.S. Supreme Court 2010d). The placement of the sword in this composition is significant. Located behind the tablet, the sword signifies the power necessary to enforce the rule of law. Interestingly, the new Supreme Court Building opened in 1935—the same year that the court declared the National Industrial Recovery Act unconstitutional. This action on the part of the court (as well as consistent opinions issued against the constitutionality of other New Deal programs) gained little favor with the other branches of government or the public at large. Lacking general support, the court soon retreated from its position to protect its composition and independence from President Franklin D. Roosevelt's infamous "court-packing plan." No stately statue could resist the strong current of Depression-era public sentiment.

The main entrance of the Supreme Court Building is hallmarked by two monumental doors, measuring 17 feet high and weighing approximately 13 tons (U.S. Supreme Court 2018). Gilbert designed these doors made of bronze to signify the timelessness of the law (see figure 4.4). The doors draw inspiration from Classically inspired gates sprinkled throughout Western architecture. (Take, for example, the doors to the Battistero di San Giovanni [Baptistery of St. John] in Florence, Italy, or the doors to the Pantheon in Rome, Italy.) Whereas the Baptistery doors in Florence use bas-reliefs to capture the life of St. John the Baptist, the Christian virtues, and the chronology of the Old Testament, Gilbert used bas-reliefs on each door to chronologically trace and "illustrate significant events in the evolution of justice in the Western tradition" (U.S. Supreme Court 2018). From lower left to upper left and then from lower right to upper right, the doors depict important events such as the development of the Justinian Code and the signing of the Magna Carta (ibid.). See table 4.3 for the full chronology. During business hours, the doors are kept open. Thus, the doors are only available for public viewing during nonbusiness hours (ibid.).[3]

In response to two security studies, the court decided in May of 2010 to close general public access to the building through the grand entrance designed by Gilbert. According to a press release issued by the court regarding the change in operating procedure, "The [new] entrance provides a secure, reinforced area to screen for weapons, explosives, and chemical and biological hazards" (U.S. Supreme Court 2010e). Visitors now enter the building on the ground level through access points on either side of the plaza. Only employees, special guests, and authorized press officials may use the front entrance (ibid.).

TABLE 4.3. The bronze door panels of the U.S. Supreme Court Building

Left Door	Right Door
4. Justinian Code This panel depicts the publishing of the Corpus Juris by order of the Roman (Byzantine) Emperor Justinian in the sixth century AD. This is considered to be the first codification of Roman law.	**8. Marshall and Story** The Donnellys describe this event as Chief Justice John Marshall and Associate Justice Joseph Story discussing the 1803 Marbury v. Madison opinion in front of the U.S. Capitol. It should be noted that Justice Story did not join the Supreme Court until 1811, eight years after this historic decision was handed down.
3. Julian and Scholar Julian, one of the most prominent law teachers in Ancient Rome, instructs a pupil. According to the Donnellys, this represents "the development of law by scholar and advocate."	**7. Coke and James I** England's Lord Chief Justice Coke bars King James I from the "King's Court," making the court, by law, independent of the executive branch of government.
2. Praetor's Edict A Roman praetor (magistrate) publishes his edict proclaiming the validity of judge-made or "common" law. A soldier, perhaps representing the power of government to enforce the common law, stands by.	**6. Westminster Statute** King Edward I watches as his chancellor (secretary) publishes the Statute of Westminster in 1275. The Donnellys' description labels it "the greatest single legal reform in our history."
1. Shield of Achilles Two men debate a point of law, with the winner to receive the two gold coins on the pedestal. This scene is described in the Iliad as part of the decoration on the Shield of Achilles forged by Vulcan. It is re-created here by the Donnellys, who described it as "the most famous representation of primitive law."	**5. Magna Carta** King John of England is coerced by the Barons to place his seal upon the Magna Carta in 1215.

SOURCE: Adapted from U.S. Supreme Court (2018).

Figure 4.5. The Great Hall looking toward the courtroom. "Supreme Court Building." Architect of the Capitol. Accessed November 18, 2020, https://www.aoc.gov/media/4611.

Circulation Space

Gilbert's design called for visitors to enter the building through the bronze doors into the Great Hall before proceeding to the courtroom (see figure 4.5). While access through the front entrance is denied to the general public, the Great Hall still serves as the major circulation space of the building. In addition to this space, visitors are welcome to tour portions of the first and ground floors to see the John Marshall statue

TABLE 4.4. Metopes and their meaning

Thunderbolts	Minerva	Armor Suit	Lion Heads and Swords
Power	Goddess of Wisdom	Trophy of Victory	Guardianship
Shield, Sword, and Helmet	**Scales and Lamp**	**Book and Torches**	**Moses**
Trophies of Victory	Justice and Wisdom	Education and Knowledge	Lawgiver and Seer
Juno	**Zeus**	**Mercury**	**Solon**
Genius of Womanhood and Guardian of Female Sex	Father of Gods and Men; God of Heavens and Fertility	Herald and Messenger of the Gods	Athenian Lawgiver and One of Seven Sages of Greece

SOURCE: Adapted from U.S. Supreme Court (2019b).

(discussed below), the two spiral staircases, and the exhibits on display (U.S. Supreme Court 2021e). There are no guided walking tours, but thirty-minute courtroom lectures are scheduled during normal business hours at regular intervals around the public sessions of the court (ibid.).

In the frieze surrounding the Great Hall, Gilbert incorporated fifteen metopes (see table 4.4). The allegorical images draw from Greek, Roman, and Judeo-Christian mythology to emphasize the themes of law and lawgiver, wisdom and knowledge, power and victory, guardianship, and divine authority and foresight. There is a repeating sequential pattern in which each metope appears eight times. The only exception is the thunderbolt, which appears twelve times (U.S. Supreme Court 2019b; see figure 4.5).

The ground floor provides visitors with a theater for continuous viewing of a twenty-four-minute educational film on the Supreme Court (U.S. Supreme Court 2021e). Due to the irregularity of sessions of the court as well as the limited seating available to the public in the courtroom, this film most likely provides visitors with the only opportunity they will have to see and hear the justices of the Supreme Court. As we noted previously, figuring prominently on the ground floor in the center of the Exhibit Hall is the John Marshall statue. It is the only full-sized statue in the Supreme Court Building, and it is framed with famous quotes from the opinions written by Chief Justice Marshall during his tenure on the court (1801–35).

Figure 4.6. "The Courtroom of the Supreme Court of the United States." Court Interior, Image 2 of 5. "Photographs," Supreme Court of the United States. Accessed November 18, 2020, https://www.supremecourt.gov/about/photos.aspx.

The Symbolism of the Space

The focus of the courtroom is the elevated bench at which the nine justices sit to preside over each session. In the center of the bench, under the clock, sits the chief justice, and other justices are seated in order of seniority to his right and left sides. Each justice is provided with a traditional pewter drinking cup and spittoon (used today for waste disposal; Maroon and Maroon 1996, 135). The parties to each case present oral arguments before the court at the advocate's lectern.

The courtroom is replete with imagery and meaning. On the frieze to the left of the central figures stands *Wisdom* holding a lantern, and to the right of the central figures stands *Statecraft* holding a shield adorned with the Scales of Justice. The remaining figures on the left-hand side of the frieze are led by a judge with a book of law. This group of figures depicts the role of the judiciary in "the defense of human rights and protection of innocence" (U.S. Supreme Court 2010a). The remaining figures on the right-hand side of the frieze depict the role of the judiciary as a "safeguard of the liberties and rights of the people in their pursuit of happiness" (ibid.).

The corollary to the East Wall Frieze is the West Wall Frieze. In this composition, the sculptor Adolph Weinman creates a dualism between good and evil. The *Powers of Good* are assembled to the left of *Wisdom*, and the *Powers of Evil* are assembled to the right of *Truth* (U.S. Supreme Court 2010a).

These figures are supported on either side by *Wisdom* and *Truth* (U.S. Supreme Court 2010a). The allegorical representation of truth in Weinman's work is somewhat intriguing. This figure holds a mirror and a rose and looks directly at the viewer. There are many possible interpretations for this design element. The gaze of the figure (away from both good and evil) might suggest the impartiality of the truth. Further, the mirror is directed toward the viewer. As a representation of truth, this could mean that the truth should be the standard by which the beholder is judged or that the truth is in the eyes of the beholder. The rose could symbolize the beauty of truth in the laws of nature. Alternatively, the rose could depict the Judeo-Christian Rose of Sharon— a representation of the divine nature of truth.

The North and South Wall Friezes depict lawgivers through history. The procession of lawgivers moves from the south left-hand corner to the north left-hand corner. Incorporated in the design are eight allegorical figures—four in the South Frieze and four in the North Frieze. The figures in the South Frieze are *Fame, Authority, Light of Wisdom,* and *History.* The figures in the North Frieze are *Philosophy, Equity, Right of Man,* and *Liberty and Peace* (U.S. Supreme Court 2003a).

The Function of the Space

For the most part, the Supreme Court hears oral arguments from October through April on Mondays, Tuesdays, and Wednesday mornings in two-week intervals (U.S. Supreme Court 2021d). Occasionally the court will schedule afternoon sessions, but that is the exception rather than the rule. In a typical session, the two sides of a case are each permitted thirty minutes for oral argument. During this time, advocates are often interrupted and forced to respond to substantive questioning by the justices concerning the merits of their arguments (ibid.). Due to limited seating, visitors are offered two options for viewing the court in session. They may attend a session of the court in its entirety, or they may move through a separate line to observe the court for a three-minute interval (ibid.). The justices also use the civic space of the courtroom to release orders and opinions from May through June (ibid.).

As an operational space, the courtroom serves to promulgate certain traditions through both ritual and spectacle. First, the Supreme Court reinforces a tradition of formality. The black robes worn by justices of the Supreme Court date back to the early 1800s (U.S. Supreme Court 2021b). Until the twentieth century, those making an appearance before the court were expected to wear formal attire. The Marshal of the Supreme Court maintains this tradition, wearing a morning coat for all public sessions. The only attorneys who now wear formal dress are those representing the United States government (ibid.). Nonetheless, the court maintains a dress code for counsel appearing before the justices for oral argument. The resource provided to attorneys suggests that "appropriate attire for counsel is conservative business dress in traditional dark colors (e.g., navy blue or charcoal gray)" (U.S. Supreme Court 2019a, 3).

Second, the Supreme Court reinforces a tradition of deference to seniority. Not only do the justices sit in order of seniority flanking either side of the chief justice, who sits at the center of the bench, they also uphold seniority in their private conference proceedings. Justices generally speak and vote in order of seniority—practices that grant more influence and leverage to the most senior members of the court.

Third, the Supreme Court reinforces through its ritual a tradition of unity. Since the late nineteenth century, justices have prefaced their public and private sessions with a handshake. Though done out of sight, this ritual underscores the belief of Chief Justice Fuller (who instituted the practice over a hundred years ago) that "differences of opinion on the Court did not preclude overall harmony of purpose" (ibid.). The official seal of the Supreme Court further emphasizes this symbolism. Though nearly identical to the Great Seal of the United States, the Seal of the Supreme Court depicts one star below the eagle to separate the text encircling the image. This single star represents "the Constitution's creation of 'one Supreme Court'" (U.S. Supreme Court, 2021a).

Audience Space

Goodsell classifies certain spaces as *audience space*. Unlike civic space, where the general public views the operations of government, audience space includes rooms where government elites meet with visitors by

Figure 4.7. "The Main Reading Room in the Supreme Court Library." Court Interior, Image 4 of 5. "Photographs," Supreme Court of the United States. Accessed November 18, 2020, https://www.supremecourt.gov/about/photos.aspx.

invitation or appointment, such as office space or reception areas (Goodsell 1998, 9). The Supreme Court Building does limit public access to certain rooms. These include the Supreme Court Library, the East and West Conference Rooms, and the Lawyers' Lounge.

On the third floor of the Supreme Court Building is the library (see figure 4.7). This space boasts a collection of more than 500,000 volumes as well as electronic databases and microform collections. Ornate hand-carved oak panels decorate the library's Main Reading Room (U.S. Supreme Court 2021b). Supreme Court Rule 2.1 stipulates that the Supreme Court Library is a space reserved for a select audience: "The Court's library is available for use by appropriate personnel of this Court, members of the Bar of this Court, Members of Congress and their legal staffs, and attorneys for the United States and for federal departments and agencies" (U.S. Supreme Court 2010c, 1). Elsewhere, the justification for this rule suggests that "the Supreme

Court Library's main mission is to assist the Justices in fulfilling their constitutional responsibilities with the best reference and research support in the most efficient, ethical and economic manner" (U.S. Supreme Court 2021c). Consequently, Rule 3.1 stipulates that only justices and their staff may remove books from the building (U.S. Supreme Court 2010c, 1).

The library as audience space is one of the most beautiful spaces in all of Washington, D.C. Above each of the columns stands an owl, a recognized symbol of wisdom. Elsewhere, carvings represent various academic disciplines (science, law, and the arts), fifteenth- and sixteenth-century printers' shields, and profiles of Classical lawgivers in the Western tradition (Maroon and Maroon 1996, 95).

Gilbert created two distinct and elegant spaces to the north of the courtroom on the building's first floor. While Gilbert did not necessarily know how they would be used, he imagined a future need for space for "international conferences or arbitrations" (Maroon and Maroon 1996, 77). Instead, these spaces have been privatized for the use of the justices; these conference rooms are inaccessible to the general public and instead provide a private space to host events of the court or for media appearances by the justices (Maroon and Maroon 1996).

Events hosted in these rooms include speaking engagements before larger audiences, press conferences, biennial meetings of the Judicial Conference of the United States, and a variety of social functions, including receptions, dinners, and reunions for law clerks serving the court (Maroon and Maroon 1996, 78). Chief Justice Roberts administered the Judicial Oath of Office to Elena Kagan on August 7, 2010, in the West Conference Room before a small gathering of Justice Kagan's family and friends (U.S. Supreme Court 2010b). The Supreme Court grants occasional access to affiliated groups, such as the Supreme Court Historical Society, for meetings or receptions. In addition, the conference rooms sometimes function as operational space for staff meetings.

The Lawyers' Lounge provides a separate audience space adjacent to the Great Hall for attorneys to prepare for oral argument before the Supreme Court. Those attorneys arguing before the Supreme Court who are planning to sit at the counsel tables in the courtroom report to the Lawyers' Lounge before the session begins. The Clerk of the Court uses this space to brief attorneys on courtroom protocol, to answer questions, and to issue identification cards. Counsel is prohibited from taking electronic devices into the courtroom, and the use of these devices is also prohibited in the Lawyers' Lounge (though these items may be stored in the lounge during a session; U.S. Supreme Court 2019a, 3). Such a space is needed for the attorney acting in the distinct role of private citizen as officer of the court. Lawyers appearing before the court are engaged in the most important and intense argumentation in the judicial process. Unlike lobbyists before Congress or lay citizens, they have a special status before the law and in relationship to the court. This status confers both the privilege and necessity of such space.

This is also the space where those appearing before the court are socialized to the experience. Maroon and Maroon (1996) detail the Clerk's briefing experienced by attorneys before their day in court. "They are told where to sit, when to approach the podium, what the white and red lights on the podium mean, and when to begin speaking (only when invited by the chief justice). They are instructed how to address the Court: 'Mr. Chief Justice,' 'Justice So-and-so,' in a pinch, 'Your Honor,' but *never* 'Judge.' Attorneys are advised to walk around the Courtroom prior to the session to get a feel for the ambience; some have found the unexpected proximity of the counsel's podium to the bench unsettling" (ibid., 161).

Operational Space

A separate class of space includes those areas serving to support the operations of the governmental agency. Goodsell (1998, 9) includes among these spaces staff offices, storage areas, and equipment rooms. In the Supreme Court Building, these spaces are hidden from public view. Unlike the House and Senate office buildings that house operational spaces but also host constituent visits, the Supreme Court's operational space is housed in private areas of the building and rarely accessed by the public. The support areas included in this category of space would be the Office of the Clerk of the Court, the Counselor to the Chief Justice, the Police Headquarters, the Public Information Office, the Press Room, the Curator's Office, the Personnel Office, the Marshal's Office, and the Solicitor General's Office. One might also include the fifth-floor basketball court in this category.

Sanctum Space

Gilbert designed the building to accommodate the general public and also provide the justices of the court with sanctum space. "Justices were to be spared the potential annoyance of being accosted in the building by citizens angry over an opinion with which they disagreed" (Maroon and Maroon 1996, 57). In addition, Gilbert recognized the need to provide the court with private areas for confidential deliberation. The sanctum space of the Supreme Court Building includes the justices' private chambers, the Conference Room, the Justices' Dining Room, and the Justices' Library Reading Room. These spaces as well as the courtroom can be accessed without public interaction. As Maroon and Maroon (ibid.) note, "It is a far cry from the days when the brethren lived and worked in boarding houses, met in taverns, and donned their judicial robes in full view of the public."

Each justice enjoys a three-room suite for his or her private chamber. The suites are assigned based on seniority. "When a vacancy occurs on the bench, the most senior justice has first claim on the empty suite, and can start a potential chain reaction down through the entire bench" (Maroon and Maroon 1996, 111). The Conference Room is located in the Chief Justice's suite. Gilbert designed the first floor to accommodate the justices' chambers so that "they would all be but a few steps away from the Courtroom, the Conference Room, the robing room, and each other" (ibid., 112). Justices decorate their suites according to personal tastes, sometimes utilizing artwork from various Washington museums (ibid., 113).

During a session, the Supreme Court typically meets on Wednesdays and Fridays in the Conference Room to discuss petitions for certiorari and cases heard for oral argument. When the justices meet in conference, no other personnel are allowed in the space. So strict is this norm that "the most junior justice is always assigned to the seat nearest to the door; it is his or her job to act as doorkeeper and to hand messages or requests for material to the messengers stationed just outside the room" (Maroon and Maroon 1996, 161). Strict codes of conduct govern these meetings. Upholding the tradition of seniority, the chief justice calls the session to order from his seat at the head of the conference table. Upholding the tradition of unity, the justices shake hands "as a sign of the collegial nature of the institution" (United States Courts 2011). What we know about the proceedings of these conferences is gleaned from oral histories of retired justices and interviews with sitting justices. This sanctum space insulates the deliberations of the nine members of the Supreme Court from public scrutiny and serves as a physical manifestation of the independence of the judicial branch.

Gilbert also designed less-formal sanctum space. The Justices' Dining Room originally provided the court with an informal space for justices to eat food prepared at home. Today, the room serves as a formal dining area for special occasions "such as dinners in honor of the arrival of a new justice or the retirement of a departing one" (Maroon and Maroon 1996, 79). The Supreme Court Building includes two additional private dining rooms—the John Marshall Dining Room and the Ladies' Dining Room.[4]

THE CONSEQUENCE OF SECURITIZATION

The twenty-first century was ushered in with a heightened awareness of political terrorism in the United States. The September 11 attacks followed a decade of periodic domestic and overseas terror acts, but it was only after the 9/11 attacks that heightened security measures became the norm. The introduction of heightened security screening in transportation and public spaces was accompanied by the hardening of both existing and new public structures. The consequence was a lasting change in the culture and character of the national city.

Physically these changes reached the Supreme Court both inside and out. Increased security measures have changed the experience of entering the Supreme Court Building and also of navigating the inside of the structure. The public's approach to the building is still from the west, coming from First Street and across the plaza. But entry has changed from the intent of the architect. The public does not climb the grand steps between the statues of the *Contemplation of Justice* and the *Authority of Law* (or *Guardian*). The public does not enter the Great Hall with its forty-four-foot-high ceiling through the pair of six-and-a-half-ton bronze doors. The public instead enters through plaza-level doors on either the north or south side of the stairs, and passes through an electronic metal detector. The northside entrance is for the general public and is wheelchair accessible. The southside entrance has more limited hours and is for the use of arguing attorneys, members of the Supreme Court Bar, and the press.

The general public then turns east into the Lower Great Hall, with ceilings about a third of the height of the Great Hall. In addition to the John Marshall statue, here are exhibits on the history of the court, including landmark cases, prominent justices, and the story of the building itself. To get up to the Great Hall with its soaring ceiling, the public climbs an enclosed arched-ceiling stone staircase to then enter the

Great Hall from the side. The public then confronts the grandeur of the greatest public space, with the oak doors of the courtroom at the east end.

The ground floor is the main location of the offices and services that the elite public (lawyers, the press) will interact with, including the press office, HR, the curator, and the clerk of the court. In this manner, the new security design meets the need for access and circulation for elites having business with the court and is consistent with design guidelines for federal courthouses (see Judicial Conference of the United States 2007). Securitization and closing access to the bronze doors does not change the experience of the elite public. Other interior security measures also create a sense of separation that departs from the intent of the architect. Locked movable partitions separate the public from the corridors leading into the building's wings, disrupting the natural flow and circulation of the building. Such circulation controls are a common feature of new and also retrofitted federal courthouses.

The effect of enhanced security considerations and the need to balance security with other concerns is not lost on the courts or the designers of judicial space. The federal government's guidelines for future courthouses note that "security concerns, including demonstrations, weapons, witness and jury intimidation, bombs, and so on, are inherent to courthouses. Optimal courthouse security is a fine balance between architectural solutions, allocation of security personnel, and installation of security systems and equipment" (Judicial Conference of the United States 2007, 16–1). The security adaptations to Gilbert's design are minimally intrusive. However, they come at the cost of an experience for the visitor as they engage with the building.

CONCLUSIONS

The social meaning of the U.S. Supreme Court Building is the product of both the physical structure of the space and the unique behavior of the justices who occupy it. The building designed by Gilbert and his team of artisans carries rich legal symbolism borrowing heavily from Western cultural traditions. Public access and scrutiny are highly regulated. The place for public dialogue is limited to the perimeter, yet ceremony and ritual performed on behalf of the citizenry take place within the controlled confines of the building's interior civic space—the courtroom.

Goodsell (2003, 372) challenges us to consider the "democratic content of place-bound public spaces" such as the Supreme Court Building. A consideration of his work compels us to pose the following questions:

- Is open access portrayed by clear entrances, ample fenestration, and generous interior dimensions?
- Is participation encouraged by downplaying the conveyed superior status of official power in terms of height, barriers, and separation?
- Are excessively theatrical presentations of leaders forgone in favor of emphasis on more egalitarian staging?
- Is staging accomplished by the governed as well as the governing?
- Are furniture arrangements in spaces intended for deliberation actually conducive to that form of interaction?

The bronze doors at the entrance of the Supreme Court Building are kept open to portray accessibility, yet this is little more than a gesture, since the public is not allowed to enter them. Public participation is extremely limited, and power is indicated through physical barriers and separation (within public spaces and between public and private spaces). Participation by members of legal counsel is limited to oral argument at the discretion of the justices. The heavy symbolism of the Supreme Court Building's spaces emphasizes theatricality over practicality and authoritarianism over egalitarianism. The governed contribute little to staging beyond the confines of perimeter space on the Front Plaza. Finally, the furnishings of the courtroom are designed to facilitate observation by a small and subdued public audience. The courtroom is a space of dialogue but not of significant or prolonged deliberation. Justices use sanctum space for deliberation. In answering all of Goodsell's questions, it is clear that the U.S. Supreme Court is democratic in its mission—to protect the rule of law as well as to provide equal protection under the law—but not democratic in its space.

Competing with the first and second branches of government, which symbolize popular sovereignty and unitary will, the court portrays itself as the "final arbiter of the law and guardian of constitutional liberties" (U.S. Supreme Court 2021d). Through longevity of tradition, formality of ritual, extreme theatricality, and limited accessibility, the court stands as a physical reminder of the limits and dangers of democratic government and calls for sacred respect of justice in the name of civil society.

As Edelman (1985, 4) suggests, "a key characteristic of myth [is] that it is generally unquestioned, widely taught and believed, and that the myth itself has consequences, though not the ones it literally proclaims." Brigham examines the physical manifestations of judicial institutions, suggesting that these attributes structure public associations with the institution. Taking the Supreme Court as a case in point, he notes:

> In law, the bench, the robes, and the marbled walls signal that something is going on, and that the activity is important. We know that these "things" are not just physical, but we treat the physical presence as the institution. And although it is no secret that the Court had makeshift quarters until only fifty years ago, we lose track of that fact. After Chief Justice William Howard Taft acquired a new building for the Supreme Court in the 1930s, his successor referred to the black robed justices in their new home as "Beetles in the Temple of Karnak." The new building was a little more than many of the justices believed appropriate for the Court. The institution evident in the pictures we have of it has changed dramatically since ratification of the Constitution established the legal foundations for the American Republic (Brigham 1987, 15).

Even if the justices of the New Deal era felt uncomfortable with the grandeur of the Supreme Court Building designed by Gilbert, the establishment of a permanent and monumental space for the judicial branch of the federal government marked a significant moment in the court's institutional history. According to Perry (2001, 339), the majestic building "solidified the other symbols and images of the rule of law and judicial independence that the U.S. Supreme Court had fostered for nearly a century and a half of constitutional interpretation" (see also Perry 1999).

The Supreme Court Building also stands as a testament to the role of the architect in shaping public space. Gilbert was a product of the Beaux-Arts tradition. He and the sculptors with whom he worked internalized the Beaux-Arts philosophy of *architecture parlante* (speaking architecture)—the idea that architectural design and artistic detail should be used to reveal the function and identity of the space. The architecture of the U.S. Supreme Court Building manifests this philosophical orientation through rich legal symbolism (U.S. Supreme Court 2015). Through form and function, the Supreme Court reinforces Gilbert's emphasis on the wisdom, truth, and majesty of the law and the authority and power of the government to execute justice. The spatial procession one experiences moving through the building highlights liberty's dependence on order and authority, the intelligent design of justice, the sacred power of the law, the heritage of our legal system, the seminal moral truths of humanity, and the unique role of the judicial branch in safeguarding the rights of the minority from the tyranny of the majority.

5   A Cultural Interpretation of the U.S. Supreme Court Building

The stone temple motif is one of the standards of American public architecture. A variety of Greek Revival, Roman Revival, and Neoclassical courthouses, public buildings, and capitols have been erected since the late eighteenth century, starting with Jefferson's Virginia State Capitol and followed by others. The style was so closely associated with public buildings before the Civil War that it was termed the "National style." The architecture of the U.S. Supreme Court Building is unmistakably Neoclassical, and its exterior façade clearly borrows from the building type of a Greco-Roman temple. The architect Cass Gilbert purposefully incorporated a number of symbolic elements from ancient civic structures, including columns, pediments, bronze doors, and flanking sculptural guardians. What is less clear, however, is the symbolism of the interior space in Gilbert's design. Understanding the U.S. Supreme Court Building as a temple in form and a courthouse in function, we examine in this chapter the unique symbolism offered by this national civic structure by paying particular attention to the symbolic dimensions of its interior spaces.

This analysis asks us to notice the ever-present "cult of the court" in American culture and society. As Perry (2002, 32) succinctly states:

Although recent academic literature portrays judges as political actors—differentiated from those in the other two branches only

111

by their unique institutional milieu—the "cult of the robe" continues
to play a role in the imagery and symbolism of the court. Scholars
will continue, as they should, to explore the reality behind the
court's famed red curtains; but to the extent that the general public
still judges the court by its external imagery, we must recognize the
importance of judicial symbolism. Moreover, social scientists have
noted that political symbols convey "emotional, moral, or psychological impact" that may not be "independently true" but may "tap
ideas people want to believe in as true."[1]

In this part of our work, we recount the decision to build a home
for the Supreme Court and engage both the vision Cass Gilbert developed for this important structure and central features and materials
he incorporated into the design. From there, the analysis turns to the
expressive, behavioral, and societal meaning of the Supreme Court
Building as a temple for priests of justice. An examination of three
significant historical temples then provides a backdrop for understanding
the temple motif chosen by Gilbert and its ultimate form as expressed
through architecture and perceived by visitors to the Supreme Court
Building. Then we consider the symbolism of the court as temple as
reinforced in the popular culture.

An important assumption of this work is that the social meaning
of civic space is related to the political culture in which the space is
situated. Here, the focus is on cultural interpretation of the civic space
dedicated to the U.S. Supreme Court Building. Grana and Ollenburger
(1999) reflect this understanding of the primacy of culture to political life in their introductory discussion of the social context of law. They
state: "Culture permeates all aspects of our social life; it is passed down
from generation to generation. As individuals, we use the framework
of our culture to assist us in solving problems and fulfilling basic human
needs. Culture is made up of three interrelated components: the cognitive component, which defines how we think and communicate; the
normative component, which defines our beliefs and values; and the
material component, which includes all the material possessions used
in a society" (ibid., 2). These three components intersect and provide
the cultural milieu in which law is created. Further, this relationship
between law and culture is interdependent. Culture shapes law, and law
shapes culture (ibid.).

The three "realities" influencing this social context in which law
is created, according to Grana and Ollenburger, include "people and

groups, ideas, and social conditions" (ibid., 3). It makes sense to the cognitive component of culture as related to people and groups, the normative component as related to ideas, and the material component as related to social conditions. Taken together and acting interdependently, these realities shape the contours of law for a society. In sum, and important to our analysis, "laws are socially created phenomena; there is no way to study law without recognizing the influence of human lives on their genesis and evolution (ibid., 10).

Political socialization leads citizens to love some institutions and actors and hate others. The political scientists John Hibbing and Elizabeth Theiss-Morse (1995) demonstrate that while the average American citizen loves his or her member of Congress, the public hates the membership of Congress as a whole. In part, this socialization to authority is related to education, and in part it is due to sanctions individual citizens experience during formative years (Grana and Ollenburger 1999, 137). Through the socialization process, members of society develop a definition of self and a sense of place, a definition of community, and a sense of place within the broader community (ibid.). Both formal and informal controls contribute to this process. The law as a formal social control dictates interpersonal behavior and prescribes sanctions for those who violate its edicts. A norm of conduct is an informal social control further shaping interpersonal behavior (ibid.). The relevance of this brief discussion of culture and political socialization to the social meaning of the Supreme Court should be clear. The court is the final interpreter of the formal social controls governing American society. In addition, it promulgates strict yet informal social controls through its judicial processes, course of business, and daily rituals. To understand the meaning of the Supreme Court as an important civic space, one must first appreciate the theoretical parameters of culture and political socialization and the role of formal and informal social control in public life.

There is substantial debate about the extent of judicial power over policymaking in the United States. Members of the court have significant discretion by virtue of the parameters of the office and the development of American jurisprudence. They enjoy lifetime appointments for good behavior, and they claim the power of judicial review—the ability to interpret the constitutionality of a law or government action.

Due in part to Americans' strong natural law tradition based on inalienable rights of the individual, in part to the arduous task of legislative efforts at political change, and in part to recent successful civil

TABLE 5.1. Three lenses for examining the social meaning of civic space

	Expressive	Behavioral	Societal
Types of social meaning sought	Ideals and values embedded in features of design	Design elements that shape user conduct	Symbolic impact of design on the public
Issues faced in interpretation	Unstated, subjective, and culturally bound nature of meaning	Degree of causality, individualized and interactive effects	Ambiguity and subjectivity of symbolic meaning

SOURCE: Goodsell (2001, 9).

rights movements, increasing numbers of citizens are using the legal system for political redress (Grana and Ollenburger 1995, 107). As a vehicle for social change, the court holds several distinct advantages. First, the law is perceived to be a source of legitimate authority. Second, the law is perceived to be binding. Whether through natural or supernatural ordination, the law requires obedience. Finally, the law carries with it the possibility of sanction (Vago 1997, 296–306).

Though legal realists emphasize the role of self-interest in judicial decision-making, there is much to be said for the perceived power of the court as a collective, independent, and somewhat deified governing body. Weber ([1905] 1992) would suggest that this power stems from the "rational-legal authority" of these officers as justices of the Supreme Court. They are not powerful by hereditary tradition; they are not powerful because of charismatic leadership; they are powerful because of a legal system of rules and regulations found to be rational and thus legitimate.

A CULTURAL INTERPRETATION

In his analysis of American state legislatures, Goodsell (2001) identifies three lenses for understanding the social meaning of civic space. Table 5.1 illustrates these lenses.[2]

Structures embody "broad conceptions of what was considered right and proper within a system of state governmental authority during their era of construction" (ibid., 8). From this architectural imprint, citizens can glean insight into the dominant cultural "ideals, values, and concepts" of government at the time of construction (ibid.).

Gilbert's design may tell us something about the values of the societal culture in which the Supreme Court was built. But his scheme also shapes the contemporary behavior of the political actors who work in the environment. We examine through this lens not what buildings say about their originators or eras of construction, but how they may shape the attitudes and conduct of contemporary users and others affected by them. This frame is used to look for ways in which the built environment affects, not reflects, the social world. Putting the distinction another way, architecture is seen not as an imprint of earlier ideas, but as a pathway that steers or conditions current behavior (Goodsell 2001, 10–11).

Goodsell further draws our attention to the refurbishing of the House of Commons in London after the attacks of World War II. Winston Churchill argued for a reconstruction of the original design due to certain critical features of the chamber that affected behavior. As Goodsell recounts, the benches designed for government and opposition minimized the potential for ideological faction; the lack of desks kept member lid-banging to a minimum; and the intimate size of the chamber gave the illusion of members at work. Contrast this setting with the U.S. House of Representatives, which has ample room for every member. On average workdays, the chamber is relatively empty and is covered by C-SPAN for all to see (ibid.).

We noted Churchill's architectural vision of the House of Commons as a behavioral setting in chapter 2 and reiterate here that "there is no doubt whatever about the influence of architecture and structure upon human character and action. We make our buildings and afterwards they make us. They regulate the course of our lives" (Brand 1994, 3). Goodsell (2001) draws our attention to the similar quote of Charles de Secondat Montesquieu from which Churchill perhaps drew his inspiration of institutional determinism. Montesquieu (1968, 25) suggests in a text on Roman history, "At the birth of societies, the rulers of republics establish institutions; and afterwards the institutions mold the rulers." Whether in legal architecture or physical architecture, form and behavior necessarily interplay.

From this brief summary, the use of the behavioral lens in this context assumes that the architectural design and setting of the Supreme Court holds implications for political behavior. While individuals are autonomous agents and can resist this architectural influence, on the whole there is an impact of design on group behavior. In this way, the behavioral lens offers us a unique perspective from which to evaluate the architectural space of the Supreme Court.

The final lens through which to examine Gilbert's design is the societal lens. Through this lens we examine "how buildings present themselves to the external society" (Goodsell 2001, 12). There exist distinct building types. Take, for example, a church. Stereotypically characterized by a steeple, the church as a building type symbolizes not only a social or religious subculture of people, but also a certain orientation to the physical world—the proper relationship of citizen to community. Similarly, certain stereotypical features characterize the American statehouse. The dome of many state capitols, for example, has become the symbol of legislative government. As a symbolic representation of the cap or crown of government, it suggests the sovereign authority of the people's house in a separated system of government. Very often this dome is centered on a bifurcated structure balancing the two chambers of the legislative branch. It is the symbolic institutionalization of the Neoclassical style.

The expressive lens begs us to take heed of the ideas, values, and concepts at play in the original design of the structure. The societal lens in turn begs us to examine the impact of the design on the public. These are not the same. As Goodsell (2001, 185) argues, "The societal lens draws attention to the effects of the statehouse on the public at large. Citizens do not notice the capitol's detailed embedded expressions or subtle behavioral effects, but they do experience the structure as a whole, in important ways."

It is possible that the values incorporated in the design of the Supreme Court Building fail to have the desired impact on citizens. Nonetheless, the symbolism perceived by the public is just as important a question as the expression embedded in the design.

The next section recounts the decision to build a home for the Supreme Court, the vision developed by Cass Gilbert for this important structure, and central features and materials incorporated by Gilbert into the design. From there, the analysis turns to the expressive, behavioral, and societal meaning of the Supreme Court Building as a temple for priests of justice.

THE SUPREME COURT FINDS A PERMANENT HOME

Central to the history of the U.S. Supreme Court is its nomadic existence for the first 145 years of its operation. After World War I, new Chief

Justice William Howard Taft determined to secure a permanent rest-ing place for the court and lobbied Congress for a separate building "appropriate to a branch of government coequal with the Congress and the presidency" (Urofsky 2005, 200–201). In 1925, Congress designated space adjacent to the Library of Congress for a new judicial building. Ultimately, Cass Gilbert received the commission to design and super-vise construction of the project.

Cass Gilbert drew inspiration from the City Beautiful movement to build both commercial and civic spaces. This orientation to architec-ture combined "artistic excellence with social improvement," drawing from Classicism to counter the effects of materialism and enliven Ameri-can culture with an ennobling urban environment (Stern 2001, 15). He is most remembered for the Woolworth Building in New York City, the world's tallest skyscraper in 1913. In addition, he helped found the Architectural League of New York and served as the president of the American Institute of Architects from 1908 to 1909. Yet it is his con-tribution on the U.S. Commission of Fine Arts (CFA) and his archi-tectural oversight of the Supreme Court Building that gave him great influence over the landscape of civic space in Washington, D.C. Through his appointment to the CFA in 1910, he influenced the implementation of the McMillan Plan of 1902—a report released by the commission "for the development and improvement of the entire park system of the District of Columbia" (Moore 1902, 7). This charge included instructions to consider the location of public buildings and grounds.

According to Flanders (2001, 9), Gilbert was particularly interested in courthouse architecture. Along with the Supreme Court Building, he built the Essex County Courthouse and the Thurgood Marshall United States Courthouse. He also designed the West Virginia State Capitol building, which included a courtroom for the state Supreme Court of Appeals and is subsequently echoed in the later design of the high court's courtroom in Washington. In conceptualizing the new space for the Supreme Court, Gilbert took particular note of the unique responsibilities and environment required for judicial work. "His office surveyed all forty-eight state supreme courts and the needs of the new building's users—justices, staff, librarians, clerical force, lawyers, and press—to ensure ample working room for all" (Blodgett 1985, 632).

In bringing his work to life, Gilbert enjoyed incredible artistic dis-cretion. Chief Justice Taft gave Gilbert free reign over the conceptual design and the general budget (Byard 2001, 273). Gilbert used this auto-nomy to contract with fellow Beaux-Arts adherents to design and sculpt the pediments, statuary, metopes, and friezes associated with the project.

This autonomy permitted Gilbert to make sense of his building to the world. Realizing an architect's dream, Gilbert used this commission to make a "palpably coherent" design "say something illuminating about the human condition" (ibid.).

THE VISION FOR THE SUPREME COURT BUILDING

The initial commission for the Supreme Court Building belonged to Henry Bacon, the architect responsible for the Lincoln Memorial—an awe-inspiring Doric temple. Though Bacon developed a scheme for the project, his death in 1924 created an opportunity for Cass Gilbert to lobby for the contract. William Howard Taft, serving as the chief justice in the 1920s, gave the commission to Gilbert based in large part on their longtime friendship and similar political views. In his diary, Gilbert reflected on the commission: "Thus opens a new chapter in my career and at 70 years of age I am now to undertake to carry through the most important and notable work of my life. . . . God grant me the strength, courage, and intelligence to do it well" (Gilbert 1929). From Bacon, Gilbert inherited the design inspiration of a temple motif. Byard (2001, 276) suggests that the commission's initial approval of Bacon's temple sketch and Gilbert's admiration for Henri Labrouste's vision of an "ideal Beaux-Arts courthouse" cemented this design concept for Gilbert. It is not surprising that temple design was the motif of choice for Bacon and later Gilbert. "The first real works of architecture we know of are temples" (Glancey 2000, 9).

    With a vision in mind, Gilbert turned to the original Greco-Roman models as well as the early American and Parisian renditions of Neoclassical public architecture. He recently had toured the Mediterranean and visited the Athenian Acropolis for the first time. In personal correspondence, he reflected that "to have seen it is to have received a benediction from the gods it was built to glorify" (Gilbert 1927). Against the backdrop of world war and the impending economic depression, the Classical world "still enforced orderly virtues worth sustaining in American life" (Blodgett 1985, 627). While the Parthenon provided an iconic representation, the Maison Carrée in Nîmes, France (figure 5.1), provided a greater sense of processional directionality and, perhaps most important to students of the Beaux-Arts architectural tradition, "an unequaled measure of right, as represented by the exquisite perfection

Figure 5.1. Maison Carrée, Nîmes, France. Photograph 2011 by Danichou. Image courtesy of Wikimedia Commons.

of all its proportions" (Byard 2001, 276). Gilbert had built in this fashion before. We noted the influence of his West Virginia State Capitol on the Supreme Court Building's courtroom. But there is also a strong echo in the exterior design of the Charleston capitol, dedicated in 1932, just three years prior to the opening of the U.S. Supreme Court Building. The major difference between the exteriors of the two structures is the dome on the capitol and Gilbert's greater infusion of Colonial Revival and Italian Renaissance elements into the West Virginia design. Others had attempted singular temple forms before Gilbert. Jefferson's use of this motif for both the Virginia State Capitol and the University of Virginia Library are among the earliest.

It should be noted that Gilbert understood the success of these "temples" to be somewhat dependent upon their siting—that prominence and also the relationship to surrounding structures mattered in communicating the importance of both the building and its purpose.

The Parthenon, for example, sat atop the highest hill in Athens. It punctuated the Acropolis and was visible to every Athenian in the valley below. Similarly, the Maison Carrée was elevated on a podium in the forum of Nîmes, where it commands an elevated presence. The library of the University of Virginia served as the focal point at the end of a central axis constituting the academic village designed by Jefferson. According to Jonathan Glancey (2000), Jefferson used this university plan to articulate modern renditions of Classical architecture for the new nation. Central to the University of Virginia campus, "the Library . . . stands proudly at the end of a long, raised rectangular lawn . . . designed to resemble the Parthenon" (Glancey 2000, 125).

To accomplish the same glorified effect, Gilbert argued for a change in venue. He pictured the "temple of justice" at the end of an east ceremonial axis from the Capitol Building. This placement would reinforce the philosophical separation of powers undergirding the constitutional arrangement of American government and bestow upon the judicial branch the power and authority it perceptually deserved. The commission had set aside dedicated space for the Supreme Court Building next to the Jefferson Library of Congress across the street from the Capitol Building and in close proximity to Union Station. This location threatened to dwarf the meaning of the Supreme Court Building and overshadow its architectural significance. The ornate Library of Congress would appear as a coequal to the Supreme Court Building, and both would be subsumed by the focus of Capitol Hill—the Capitol itself (Byard 2001, 277–78).

Aside from the issues associated with architectural competition for prominence, this location frustrated Gilbert's design in terms of the actual size of the building's footprint. According to Byard, "the Supreme Court building did not have to be very big to function. Its program was tiny, to house nine individuals engaged in the most cerebral of tasks, big in stature but still small in actuality" (Byard 2001, 278). To compete with its surroundings, however, the building would have to be enlarged.

As a student of the Beaux-Arts tradition, Gilbert easily adapted the Classical design to the challenges of siting, producing a larger, more powerful statement of the "rightful" authority of the Supreme Court. This tradition of Classicism had a normative thrust—one to be appreciated as an important influence on Gilbert's design ethos. "The effort was corrective: Beaux-Arts Classicism would will the world not to be the way it was, but the way its sponsors thought it ought to be" (Byard 2001, 274). Its particular focus was on "authority, continuity, right, the way things ought to be" (ibid., 275). Gilbert embraced this tradition, and it defined his architectural career.

References to Greco-Roman Classicism further drew upon the roots of Western tradition and reinforced the values of popular sovereignty and representative democracy. In the New World, this style was particularly well suited to public architecture because of its symbolic expression of "longevity and order, qualities that some found reassuring" (Sweeney 1993, 92). Additionally, the revival of Classicism heralded the wisdom and virtue of the ancient Greeks and the rights and responsibilities of Roman citizens. As a dominant force in American architecture until the second quarter of the twentieth century, Neoclassicism stood for "Classical learning, and such decorations were taken as an indication of good taste" (Glancey 2000, 129).

THE LAYOUT OF THE SUPREME COURT BUILDING

With the temple motif securely established in Gilbert's mind, he turned to the basic layout of the building. Of central importance was the location of the courtroom. As Byard notes, Gilbert struggled with two distinct choices. He could locate the courtroom in the center of the building. This siting would mimic the use of domes in legislative architecture to articulate the center of authority and the role of consensus to shared governance. Within the context of the court, this placement would highlight the central activity of the courtroom for legal proceedings and the "role of the court as an agent of reconciliation" (Byard 2001, 278). Alternatively, Gilbert could locate the courtroom at the far end of a central axis within the building. Like a processional temple, the room would be placed "at the end of a directional axis, as the end of a directional axis, as the end of the line, the ultimate authority, the final appeal" (ibid.). The processional nature of this design option would more strongly express the temple motif and harken to iconic architectural references such as the Parthenon or the Maison Carrée (ibid.; figure 5.2).

Without a dome, the building stood out as distinct from the U.S. Capitol and the Library of Congress, which bordered the proposed location of the building, nicely illustrated in a souvenir postcard from the early 1930s (figure 5.3). Gilbert's ultimate design resembled the Maison Carrée with two wings. Even without a long ceremonial axis to the front steps of the Supreme Court Building, Gilbert used the ascension from street level to the temple entrance as well as the procession to the courtroom

UNITED STATES SUPREME COURT, WASHINGTON, D.C.   5334-29

Figure 5.2. Model of the United States Supreme Court Building, Washington, D.C. Postcard, issued between 1935 and 1955. From the authors' private collection. Image by C. T. American Art Colored, Curt Teich Co.

to accomplish his vision for the space (Byard 2001, 280). The front plaza leads visitors up to the staircase. After ascending the stairs, they enter through two great bronze doors opening to the entrance of the building. From here, they walk through the great Memorial Hall, a long processional space leading to the courtroom itself. Byard (2001, 283) offers an astute reflection on this punctuated axis:

> The courtroom is a square. It has no direction. It is a stable, non-processional destination at the end of the long procession. Like the sphere of enlightenment offered at the top of Jefferson's University of Virginia, Gilbert's perfect square, almost cube, comes at the end of his line like a decision. In final presentation drawings and in the design that was followed in construction, the central temple is strongly in charge, very different from the Library of Congress, powerfully and purely white, with the great steps up from the sidewalk setting up the progress toward "Equal Justice Under Law," presented by the building either as a fact to be found in the square of

Figure 5.3. U.S. Capitol, Supreme Court, Library of Congress and House Office Buildings. Postcard, issued between 1935 and 1955. From the authors' private collection. Image by Todd Aerial Mapping, in association with Metrocraft, Everett, Massachusetts.

the courtroom, or as an enduring goal at the end of the procession made tirelessly and over and over again along its halls.

The directionality of the space is clear, and the processional walk is narrow. Most of the building is inaccessible to the public at large. According to Blodgett (1985, 632), Gilbert's plans "provided justices with maximum privacy and isolation from the public, thus enforcing the ritual mystery of their movements and the oracular nature of their judgments."

THE MATERIALS AND MEANING OF THE BUILDING

Just as important as Gilbert's vision for the layout of the building was his design aesthetic for the building's construction materials. The entire structure is white marble. At once appearing both noble and pure, this material accentuated the importance and character of the judicial enterprise. In the early twentieth century, construction of the building did not require marble as it perhaps did for the ancient Greeks. Rather, Gilbert chose this material to express awe-inspiring reverence for the rule of law (Byard 2001, 283). "Gilbert had a purpose and a conviction about what he was doing. He was trying to use his Beaux-Arts architecture to drive home points about authority and right for the sake of the Court" (ibid., 287).

The marble for the building mostly came from Vermont, Georgia, and Alabama. The exterior of the building is adorned with Vermont white marble. For the interior spaces, he used marble from the other two states. For the court and its courtroom, however, Gilbert required stone with a level of warmth and richness only possible with the finest Spanish ivory marble and Italian marble (Blodgett 1985, 633).

COMPLETION AND RECEPTION

Gilbert did not live to see his Supreme Court Building occupied. He died on May 17, 1934, and the Supreme Court Building opened its doors in 1935. Only two of the sitting justices of the court moved their offices from the Capitol Building to the new facility. Several found the new quarters to be far too grandiose for their liking. Associate Justice Harlan Fiske Stone called it "almost bombastically pretentious . . . wholly inappropriate for a quiet group of old boys such as the Supreme Court" ("Homes of the Court" n.d.). Another justice quipped that the members of the court would be "nine black beetles in the Temple of Karnak" (ibid.). In an interview with C-SPAN on Justice Louis Brandeis's reaction to the new Supreme Court Building, Frank Gilbert, Brandeis's grandson, reflected on his grandfather's sentiment.

> Grandfather was opposed to the Supreme Court Building. He thought the plans were too grand; he liked the intimate chambers . . . in the Capitol Building. He thought that the . . . new proposed building would not contribute to the justices' humility, which they needed. And he voted against the Supreme Court Building. Grandfather refused to use the chambers . . . in the new Supreme Court Building. In fact, he never set foot inside the chambers and continued to work at home in his apartment. Actually I'm told that the staff of

the Supreme Court . . . used the suite in the 1930s to point out what Justices' offices would look like . . . with his empty office. . . .

I think Grandfather didn't need all that space. The bedroom and the efficiency apartment in which he and the law clerk worked were quite modest. But back at home he had the law books spread out on the floor of his bedroom office, which was not a large room. And that served him . . . in a very fine fashion, so he saw no need for this Marble Palace. He didn't want to be any part of it, although he had very good relations with his fellow Justices. (Gilbert 2012, n.p.

The distancing of the justices from the building would be short-lived. Within five years, over half of the court would turn over, and within ten years, only Justice Harlan Stone would remain among those justices who sat in the Old Senate Chamber. The brethren were soon all together occupying the east half of the main floor of the building.

The justices were not alone in their criticism of the new structure. Cass Gilbert and his design represented a dying breed of architects. Against the formalism and Classical grandeur of the Beaux-Arts tradition, proponents of Modernism and especially the International style suggested a new architecture focused on realism, efficiency, transparency, and functionality. According to Byard (2001, 283), "The modernists thought that the world had had enough of pomp and papering over. The modernists thought one had to start fresh by seeing what was actually going on and finding a way to make sense and beauty out of that." The Supreme Court Building was a failure insofar as it was not real, efficient, transparent, or functional. "For all its strenuous effort, it was out of touch with the times. It was, arguably at least, in the then-devastating word of a modernist argument, irrelevant" (ibid., 285). In addition, through Gilbert's effort to broadcast the authority of the judiciary as a coequal branch of government, the building alluded to oppressive authoritarianism in its grand imperial design. In fact, Gilbert relied on his relationship with Mussolini to secure Italian marble for the columns of the court chamber (Blodgett 1985, 633).

Gilbert had built a reputation as one of the leading Beaux-Arts architects of his day, and the Supreme Court commission came at the end of his long career and also his waning day. The new tradition of Modernism stood at odds with everything Gilbert's work represented. The new U.S. Supreme Court Building, the hallmark of Gilbert's career, was mostly ignored as outdated and irrelevant (Flanders 2001, 11). Not until the occasional references by Postmodernists would the Classical forms so dearly loved by Gilbert be revived and returned to the national stage (Glancey 2000, 212).

METAPHOR: THE SUPREME COURT AS A TEMPLE

It is important to consider not only the expressive meaning of the architect in designing the built environment but also the behavioral and societal meaning carried by the space (Goodsell 2001). For this reason, the Supreme Court Building should be understood as a temple motif designed by Gilbert, shaping the behavior of its occupants—veritable priests—and being interpreted by its occupants through the perceptual screens of dominant historical and cultural reference points.

From Gilbert's personal correspondence and diary entries, we know he intended the space to reflect a Greco-Roman temple. With the exterior essence of the Maison Carrée and the interior processional layout of the Parthenon, the structure was designed by Gilbert to stand in stark contrast to its neighbors.

It is important to note that Gilbert was not alone in his deification of the rule of law and reverence for the judicial task of constitutional interpretation. During the ratification debates of the 1787 Constitutional Convention, Alexander Hamilton suggested the enlightened role of the judiciary as the guardian of the rights of the people. The judiciary is necessary "to guard the Constitution and rights of the individuals, from the effects of those ill-humours which the arts of designing men, or the influence of particular conjunctures, sometimes disseminate among the people themselves, and which, though they speedily give place to better information, and more deliberate reflection, have a tendency, in the meantime, to occasion dangerous innovations in the government and serious oppressions of the minor part in the community" (Hamilton 2003, 2).

Chief Justice John Marshall reflected on the priestly function of members of the court. In service to the law, "judicial power is never exercised for the purpose of giving effect to the will of the Judge; always for the purpose of giving effect to the will of the Legislature; or, in other words, to the will of the law" (*Osborn v. Bank of the United States*, 22 U.S. 866 [1824]). Mason (1991, 12) elaborates on Marshall's doctrine, suggesting that "constitutional interpretation consists in finding meanings which are clear only to judges. To judges, the meaning of the Constitution is obvious. To others, whether legislators or executives, its meaning is hidden and obscure."

Reviewing the 1957 decisions of the Supreme Court, President Eisenhower noted the "transcendental wisdom" of the court, characterizing it as a sort of "brooding omnipresence in the sky" (ibid.). According to Mason, "the only final and authoritative mouthpiece of the Constitution is the Supreme Court, and its every version . . . has the special virtue of never mangling or changing the original instrument" (ibid.).

THE COURT AS TEMPLE TO THE CONSTITUTION: AMERICA'S ARK OF THE COVENANT

Extending the sacred imagery even further, the Constitution has frequently been likened to a national "Ark of the Covenant" and the court as a temple to guard it. As early as the late eighteenth century, political elites such as Benjamin Rush, signer of the Declaration of Independence and delegate to the Continental Congress, described the Constitution as a miraculous, divinely inspired document (Meyer 2001, 88).[3]

Representative Caleb Cushing referred to the Constitution as "our Ark of Covenant" (ibid.). In the late 1870s, American Bar Association president Edward J. Phelps condemned the profaned politicization of the Constitution. In the words of Mason (1991, 25), he "deplored the spectacle of unhallowed hands on the Ark of the Covenant."[4] In 1880, President Garfield lauded the sanctity of the law, stating: "More sacred than the twelve tables of Rome, this rock of the law rises in monumental grandeur alike above the people and the President, above the courts, above Congress, commanding everywhere reverence and obedience to its supreme authority" (Garfield 1880).

Senator Warren G. Harding (soon to be president) gave a speech in 1920 on "Americanism" in which he used similar language: "The Federal Constitution is the very base of all Americanism, the ark of the covenant of American liberty, the very temple of equal rights. The Constitution does abide and ever will, so long as the Republic survives" (Harding 1920). Just two years later, Taft made similar reference to the Constitution as an Ark of the Covenant (Meyer 2001, 88). According to Rodgers (2011, 84), Taft further viewed "the judiciary as a priestly class guarding (the Constitution's) sacred principles." Given this sentiment, it is understandable that the chief justice fought so persistently and vehemently to secure the site and the funding for the new Supreme Court

Building. In 1928, Louis Marshall suggested on national radio that the Constitution serves as America's "holy of holies, an instrument of sacred import" (quoted in Kammen 2006, 225). John Gerring (1998, 91) argues that the authority conferred upon the Constitution and the sacrosanct reverence granted it held significance for a young democratic nation "with few symbols or myths legitimating the value of tradition."

Not every reference of this sort was reverential. Thomas Jefferson noted in 1816 with distaste: "Some men look at constitutions with sanctimonious reverence, and deem them like the ark of the covenant, too sacred to be touched" (quoted in Kammen 2006, 47). Contemporaries of Cass Gilbert who opposed such constitutional reverence claimed: "To most Americans, a Constitution is merely a fetich [sic]. They don't know what is in it, and to them it is as the Ark of the Covenant was to the Jews, the Bible to the uneducated Catholic, or the Sacred stone to the Mohammedans" (quoted in Kammen 2006, 225).

ANALYSIS OF TEMPLE MOTIFS

Before turning to possible sources of inspiration for Gilbert as well as to temple motifs of which Americans are possibly most culturally aware, it is useful to review the major elements of Gilbert's exterior and interior design for the Supreme Court. The procession through the public space begins with a great ascension from the Front Plaza up the stairs to the bronze doors, entering the building on its west side. Gilbert commissioned Adolph Weinman to sculpt two statues for the Front Plaza. A seated female figure holding a small female figure of Justice blindfolded flanks the north side of the plaza, and a seated male figure holding a book of law in front of a sheathed sword flanks the south side of the plaza. These two sculptures are called *Contemplation of Justice* and *Authority of Law*.[5] We grapple with the multiple meanings associated with these representations, including both contemporary associations with impartiality and Renaissance associations with the inability to see the pain of punishment and the potential for error in judgment, as well as the negative connotations of blindness abounding in Babylonia and Egypt, in Greece and Rome, as well as in Judeo-Christian traditions (Kammen 2006, 63–64).

The face of the building's west front boasts an ornate pediment punctuated with the inscription "Equal Justice under Law." The allegorical message of this pediment, according to its designer Robert Aitken, is liberty holding justice, protected by order and authority and informed by counsel (U.S. Supreme Court 2009). The first interior space is the Great Hall. With little ornamentation, this long, narrow room guides visitors into the next space, the courtroom. It is important to note, however, that Gilbert did decorate the friezes surrounding the ceiling of the Great Hall with metopes. The fifteen separate images depicted major mythical beings (Greek and Roman gods and lawgivers and Israeli kings and lawgivers) of the Western tradition as well as images of Victory, Guardianship, Knowledge, Contemplation, Wisdom, Justice, and Freedom (U.S. Supreme Court 2019b).

The courtroom, with extremely limited access to the public, is a relatively small, square room focused on the long judicial bench for the nine justices of the Supreme Court, which is backed by four great columns and a heavy red curtain from which the justices emerge to preside over a session. Four friezes surround the courtroom. Above the bench, Adolph Weinman centered two seated male figures: *Majesty of Law* and *Power of Government*. Between them is a pylon with Roman numerals I through X. This single feature of the courtroom has stirred controversy, with the informational materials from the Curator's Office associating this image with the Bill of Rights and some religious organizations associating this image with the Ten Commandments (U.S. Supreme Court 2010a; see Millard [1991] for further detail on the debate concerning the pylon's meaning). Similar tablets appear on the ten sets of bronze gates on either side of the courtroom, along with other representations of eagles, torches, lions' heads, acorns, and oak leaves (Resnik and Curtis 2011, 151). On the opposing wall, Weinman depicted the struggle between good and evil. Two female figures, *Justice* and *Divine Inspiration*, hold the central position in the composition. The powers of good and evil flank these figures and provide allegorical representations of several virtues and vices.

For the North and South Wall friezes, Weinman chose to trace the evolution of the law from Menes of Egypt (ca. 3200 B.C.) to Napoleon (1769–1821) and, interestingly, John Marshall (1755–1835). Interspersed among these great lawgivers are allegorical representations of fame, authority, light of wisdom, history, philosophy, equity, right of man, and liberty and peace. Taken together, these figures provide a chronology of great lawgivers (Resnik and Curtis 2013, 208–10).

The final space, one that is off-limits but suggested to the public, is the gathering place of the judges behind the veil. This space includes the Robing Room where justices gather, dress in their robes for a session, and exchange a handshake of goodwill and unity of purpose before entering the courtroom. In addition to this space is a further sacred room that is off-limits to all but the justices but figures prominently in the public mind: the Conference Room where the justices collectively deliberate case selection, discuss oral argument, and reach agreement before drafting opinion(s) of the court. Having sketched the contours of this familiar civic space, we turn now to some of the historically dominant temple motifs of our heritage. Three cases provide a general understanding of some of the primary vehicles of symbolism in temple design: the Temple at Karnak, the Temple of Solomon, and the Parthenon.

THE TEMPLE AT KARNAK

The Egyptians worked on the temple complex at Karnak for over two thousand years under numerous consecutive pharaohs. As in many ancient temples, the Temple of Amun-Re is oriented along an east-west axis. The original design called for an avenue of ram-headed sphinxes serving as guardians of the temple. The procession began with an initial pylon leading to the first court—an open-air courtyard that included a colonnade of columns. From here, the procession led through a second pylon into the Hypostyle Hall, a hall full of sandstone columns. The next space included tall stone obelisks made of granite. The final space in the center of the temple was a sanctuary dedicated to an enshrined statue of Amun-Re. Also important to the temple was the sacred lake, holding water used for rituals of worship. Much of the space was accessible only to priests (Sullivan 2008, 2). (See figure 5.4 for a floor plan of the Temple at Karnak.)

Two features are of particular note as symbolically significant. First, the most striking feature of the Temple at Karnak to Amun-Re is the massive columns in several halls proceeding to the shrine. In the Hypostyle Hall, the largest of its kind, there are 134 separate pillars, signifying "the dense, papyrus-filled marsh, where, according to myth, Isis reared young Horus after Seth slew his father, Osiris" (Yurco 1990). Doors in the temple were also symbolically significant. They often were constructed of rich wood covered in fine metals, including gold, and fastened with bronze and iron (ibid., 108). Finally, sphinxes figured prominently in Egyptian temple and tomb design. Originally, these sculptures were signs of royal power, but they took on different meaning in the New Kingdom. Often located at the gate to the structure, the sphinx served

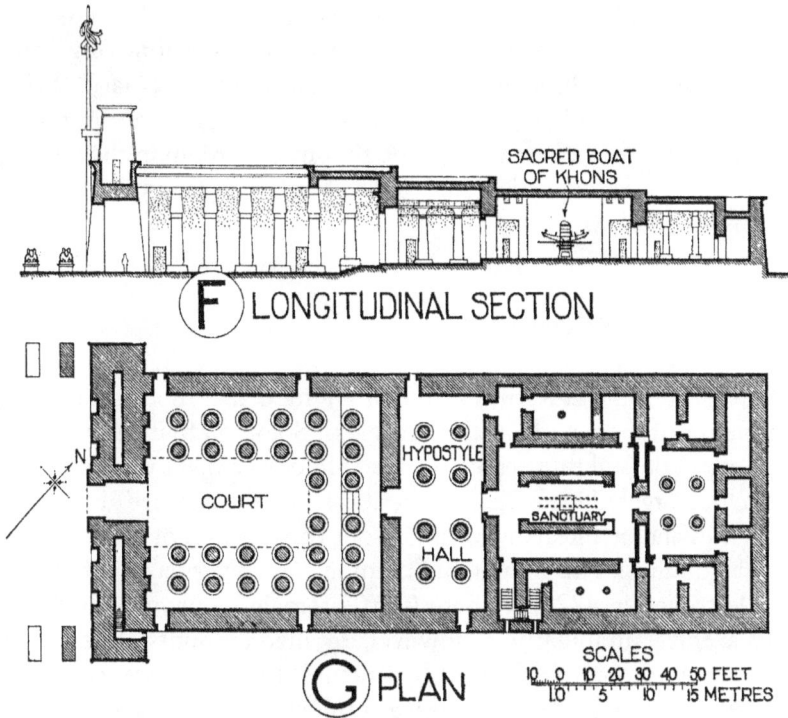

Figure 5.4. Plan of the South Temple at Karnak. From Baedeker 1885, 169.

as a watcher or guardian. "In the New Kingdom, the sphinx was then placed in relationship with the sun god, Amun-Re, and received a ram's head instead of a human head" (Owusu 2000, 155). Hundreds of ram-headed sphinxes were built to represent Amun-Re at Karnak.

The strong processional orientation of the Temple at Karnak is not only an important defining characteristic of the structure; it is also clearly constructed to worship the solstice, and it shapes behavior to accomplish this through an axis that is "absolutely open, straight, and true," according to Lockyer (1894, 100). As one proceeded through the pylons, the openings were narrowed and increasingly covered so that a "dim religious light" was created in the innermost sanctum space (ibid., 106). The precise construction of this temple to channel light strategically permitted astronomical observation by the priests who kept the temple. "The priests having this power at their disposal . . . ruled by knowledge," according to Lockyer (ibid., 109).

From this structure, we see "an increasing gradation in sacredness beginning with the outer court and proceeding to a zone of greater holiness and then climaxing in an inner womb-like sanctuary" (Beale 2004, 54). Finnestad (1997, 210) argues that the Egyptians purposefully designed the holiest space to be the smallest room in the temple, with other spaces expanding outward to symbolize the expanding and expansive cosmos.

THE TEMPLE OF SOLOMON

While the Temple at Karnak stands as an important model of ancient temple motifs, it is perhaps the Temple of Solomon that captures the most attention and thus serves as a ready reference point for Americans due to our largely Judeo-Christian heritage (and the heritage of the political elites and architects who carried out construction of the Supreme Court Building). The Temple of Solomon was constructed in 832 B.C. and destroyed in 422 B.C. There is little remaining physical evidence of its architectural features; however, detailed accounts of its design features are recorded in the Old Testament. Just as siting was central to Egyptian temple planning, so it was important to the Israelites. The temple was to be constructed on a mountain—Mount Zion. This holy place was thought to be the original site of the Garden of Eden.

Figure 5.5 provides an illustration of the layout of the temple. The procession began with the great court where the people worshiped God around the temple. The next space was the inner court, or the court of the priests, with the altar of burnt offering, the brazen sea, and the ten lavers. The two pillars of Jachin and Boaz stood at the entrance of the temple porch. Behind a curtain was the holy place, or the greater house, where the priests performed rites of worship. The veil, a heavy curtain of purple, crimson, and fine linen, separated the priests from the most sacred space of the temple. It hung in front of a golden door. Behind the veil and door was the inner house, or the holy of holies. This space was considered the dwelling place of God (Easton [1897] 2007, 621).

The two bronze pillars that met people at the entrance of the temple on the porch, Jachin and Boaz, served as a gateway to the structure. Some suggest that these pillars indicated the presence of God in the temple as well as the magnificence, strength, and stability of God to those who passed through them (Ryken, Wilhoit, and Longman 1998, 645). Understood as a temple gate, these figures reminded the Israelites of

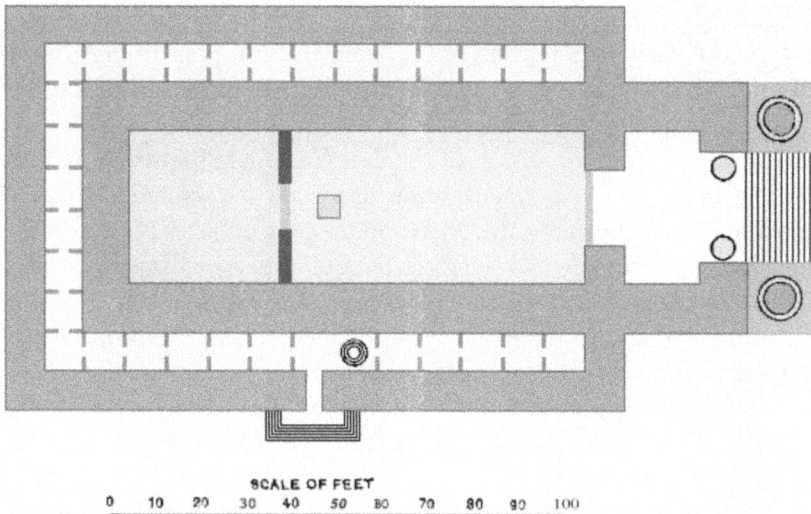

Figure 5.5. Plan of the Temple of Solomon. Procession from white space (the Outercourt), through the barrier represented by a medium gray line (the Curtain), to the interior spaces in light gray (the Holy and the Holy of Holies, separated by the dark-shaded Veil). From Blavatsky 1888, 13.

their wandering in the wilderness and the time of the judges (before the construction of Solomon's Temple), when the gate served as the place for legal proceedings and public demonstrations. In fact, Boaz negotiated to marry Ruth in the town gate. As Ryken, Wilhoit, and Longman (1998, 321) observe, official deliberations took place by community elite while "sitting in the gate." Thus, one's position near the gate served as a status symbol to the community at large.

Beale (2004, 32) examines the general symbolism of the Temple of Solomon and argues that the temple was divided into three primary sections. Each of these sections held cosmic symbolism. In his analysis:

(1) The outer court represented the habitable world where human-ity dwelt; (2) the holy place was emblematic of the visible heavens and its light sources; (3) the holy of holies symbolized the invisible dimension of the cosmos where God and his heavenly hosts dwelt. (Ibid., 32–33)

The procession established by the temple design was one of increasing holiness demonstrated through increasingly rich ornamentation and dress

(Haran 1978). This orientation (temple as microcosm of universe) was not unique to Israel's temple, notes Beale, but was present in Ancient Near Eastern archaeology as well.[6] Within the innermost sanctum space of the temple was the Ark of the Covenant. The creation of the ark coincides with the provision of the Ten Commandments on Mount Sinai. The Ten Commandments reside in the ark as a reminder of God's moral will. Accompanying this artifact in the holy of holies (God's dwelling place) are reminders of the great Exodus—tokens of Israel's deliverance or saving grace. Taken together, these items symbolized the covenant between God and Israel (Beale 2004, 118–19). Of further importance is the association of the law with wisdom (Numbers 24:25–32).

It has further been suggested that the temple of Israel symbolically reflected the first temple or dwelling place of God in the Garden of Eden. In this created space, God communed with Adam, in the same way that God communed with the priests of Israel in the temple on behalf of the people. Adam's charge in the Garden of Eden was to "cultivate and keep" or "serve and guard" the garden (or temple). Similarly, the priests of Israel were charged with guarding the Word of God and servicing the temple (Beale 2004, 66–67).

Another important component to the Old Testament instructions for Israel's initial tabernacle and later temple concerned the attire of the high priest. The high priest not only wore a robe but also a breastplate adorned with twelve jewels representing the twelve tribes of Israel—or the representation of the people in God's presence by the priest.

The role of the priest was symbolically aligned with the role given to Adam by God. As the first priest in the Garden of Eden (the first temple), God charged Adam with "maintaining its order and keeping out uncleanness" (Beale 2004, 85). God's dwelling place was to be distinguished by order in contrast to disorder outside the garden. The role of Adam as teacher of Eve further illustrates the role of priest as knower and teacher of the law of God (ibid.). Interestingly, John H. Walton (2001, 174) argues that Adam's role should be understood not merely as a gardener but as a steward of the orderliness of the sacred garden sanctuary. This included, according to Walton, "cultivating" and "guarding." As an image of humanity, both male and female, and as stewards, both cultivating and guarding, this depiction bears a striking resemblance to the two statuary sphinxes situated in front of the Supreme Court Building. Seen through the societal lens, *Contemplation of Justice* and *Authority of Law*, whether intended by Adolph Weinman as images of

Adam and Eve or not, hold possible meaning for visitors concerning the "sacred" work of the court.

Consequently, the temple through its unified symbolism depicts "justice, peace and blessing," according to Ryken, Wilhoit, and Longman (1998, 851). "The temple is related to the dispensation of law and justice; in it the law was both taught and practiced. The prophets were quick to remind people of the offensiveness of temple worship if not accompanied by justice" (ibid.). The priests who maintained and guarded the temple were expected not only to know and teach the law but also to demonstrate obedience through their behavior. As Ryken, Wilhoit, and Longhman explain, "the physical ascent of the temple mount into God's presence must be matched by an ethical ascent" (ibid.).

Further elaborating on this theme, Cheyne and Black (1902, 3845) suggest that several factors combined to confer power on the Israeli priesthood, including "the unity of the altar, its inaccessibility to laymen and to the inferior ministers of the sanctuary, and the specific atoning function of the blood of priestly sacrifices." It is through the intercession of the priesthood that national holiness was maintained. The temple represented the holiness of God; the priests protected the order and sanctity of this place; and the site served to provide continual atonement for "breaches of holiness" (ibid., 3844).

From here, it should be apparent that there are several symbolic parallels between the role of the priest and the temple for the Israelites and the role of the justices and the court for our system of government. Table 5.2 details some of these parallels.

From this broad and general comparison of the characteristics and responsibilities of the tribe of priests and the priestly tribe, some distinct parallels emerge. Though the formal qualifications for Supreme Court justices are quite limited in the U.S. Constitution, the informal qualifications increasingly limit service to an exclusive group of elite, highly educated, legally experienced, professional jurists.

These members of the court are expected to be of the highest moral character and the soundest mind, and be the most prolific of communicators. They are knowers and teachers of the law. To preserve independence and protect justice, they are independent of the people. They are not elected, and they can only be removed from office for lack of "good behavior." This buffer against public or institutional retaliation is further enforced through limited accessibility—even in public sessions of the court.[7] With all of this secrecy comes an aura of sanctity, and the

TABLE 5.2. Comparing priestly tribes:
Members of the tribe of Levi and members of the U.S. Supreme Court

	Members of the Tribe of Levi	Members of the Supreme Court
Criteria for Membership	High priests were sons of Aaron of the tribe of Levi. They were members by bloodline.	While there are no formal requirements, judicial appointees have elite education, have legal experience, and are often career jurists.
Expectations of Character	High priests were expected to be holy and strong. They served as guardians of the temple and as a role model to the people.	Justices are expected to be wise, analytical, prolific, and of high moral character.
Attire	Robe of blue; ephod of gold, blue, purple, and scarlet; breastplate with jewels representing twelve tribes of Israel. These garments symbolized the glory of God, the holiness of worship, and the role of the priest as aintercessor for the whole people.	Black robes; William Rehnquist added gold bars to his sleeves to designate his status as chief justice.
Responsibilities	Intercessor between God and people; received sacrifices and offerings; performed rituals; guarded the temple and its contents; taught the law	Intercessor between legislature and executive and people; to know the law, to interpret the meaning of the Constitution, and to resolve conflict
Resources	The Torah	Law clerks and law library
Accountability	Appointed for life terms by birth	Appointed for life terms subject to good behavior
Accessibility to Public	Limited to receiving sacrifices and offerings	Limited to oral argument, pronouncement of decisions, and special invitation
Access to Sanctum Space	Only ones permitted in the holy place	Only ones permitted in the conference room
Public Opinion	High; viewed as the representation of God on earth	High; consistently held in higher regard than members of the other two branches of government

SOURCES: Column 1: Adapted from Vanderkam (1991). Column 2: Adapted from materials from the Office of the Curator of the U.S. Supreme Court and Perry (2002).

court enjoys the highest level of public approval (though accompanied by the lowest level of public knowledge) of all the institutions of American government. While these features are actor-specific rather than architecture-specific, the actors in this setting serve to shape the expression of the space to the public, the behavior of the judicial body and the public, and thus the social meaning of the space for its occupants. The justices are sometimes referred to as "priests" because their status, surroundings, and behavior are in fact reminiscent of Biblical priests.

From examination of the Temple at Karnak and the Temple of Solomon, one can draw clear referential meaning at the Supreme Court Building. Gilbert, however, specifically chose to express the temple motif most directly through the architectural style of the Greeks and Romans. The Parthenon of the Acropolis clearly shaped his thinking.

THE PARTHENON—TEMPLE TO ATHENA

Perhaps most Americans associate the Supreme Court Building with the Parthenon, a temple built by the Athenians to celebrate and enshrine the city-state's patron goddess, Athena. This iconic Greek temple sits at the center of the Acropolis—a set of structures built on a hilltop above the surrounding Athenian community. After the Athenians warred with the Persians for fifty years and finally conquered them in 449 B.C., Athens assumed responsibility for nearly two hundred cities. The Athenians used these territories to finance their ambitious construction projects. The temple is considered to be a thankful offering by the Athenians for the military victory over the Persians (Neils 1999, 11).

The Parthenon was a crowning glory for the Athenian landscape. The construction of the Parthenon incorporated major features of Classical Greek architecture (figure 5.6). Massive columns surrounded the entire structure. Pediments graced either end of the temple with friezes illustrating the story of the birth of Athena and her struggle with Poseidon to be the patron deity of Athens.

Within the inner chamber, friezes encircled the shrine to Athena. Some archaeologists suggest that these friezes depicted the quadrennial Great Panathenaia—a festival for the people. "By incorporating this scene of civic celebration . . . the Parthenon served not merely as an imperial propaganda statement but also an expression of Athens' burgeoning democracy" (Hadingham 2008, n.p.). The east frieze includes a group of twelve seated figures who represent the earliest depiction of the twelve

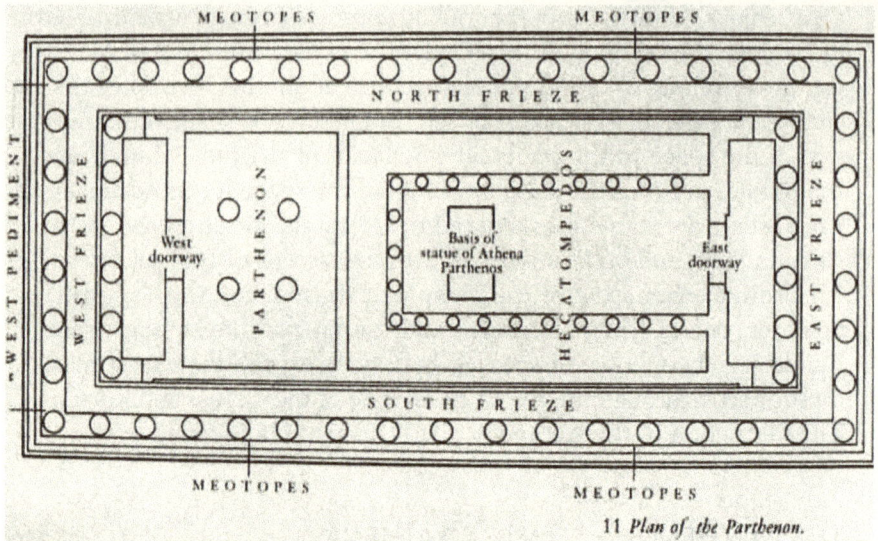

Figure 5.6. Plan of the Parthenon, 432 B.C. "Greek Art," PBWorks. Accessed November 28, 2020, http://sasgreekart.pbworks.com/f/parthenon_flooplan.jpg.

gods of Greece and Rome (Neils 1999, 6). At the Parthenon's entrance, with the statue of Athena facing the spectator, this collection of deities sit in two groups of six and include both male and female mythological figures (ibid., 6–8). It is interesting to note that goddesses were often winged in Classical Greek art, as is the winged female figure on the west wall frieze of the Supreme Court courtroom (ibid., 8). It also appears that youthful figures were incorporated into the frieze as a symbol of hope (ibid., 11); young figures are incorporated into the friezes of the courtroom as well as the outdoor lamp posts as well.

Metopes surrounded the entire building. Most of the subject matter involves mythical battles. For example, on the east front, the metopes illustrate the battle between the gods and giants. The compositions differ in terms of subjects and groupings (Yeroulanou 1998, 413–14). Similarly, the metopes of the Supreme Court Great Hall alternate between gods and symbols of strength, victory, knowledge, wisdom, and justice.

The most important feature of the Parthenon was the figure of Athena. Surrounded by metopes depicting mythological battles of justice and injustice or order and chaos, the statue of Athena Parthenos (made of ivory and 2,400 hundred pounds of solid gold) stood approximately forty feet tall. In her hand was a statue of Nike, the goddess of victory (adapted from Hurwit 2007). This sculptural detail bears a striking resemblance to the *Contemplation of Justice* on the Front Plaza of the Supreme Court, who holds a miniature, blindfolded statue of Lady Justice.

One of the important differences between the temple motif of Israel and the temple motif of the Egyptians and Greeks was the absence of an idol or image of the god in the innermost sanctum space. Nevertheless, a dominant consistent symbolic theme across all three temple motifs is that of the temple as a place of rest—rest after creation, rest after bringing order to chaos, rest from war, and rest on holy or festival days (see both Beale 2004 and Ryken, Wilhoit, and Longman 1998).

From this examination of three iconic temples of ancient civilization, we can draw some striking observations about the references used by Gilbert (or used by the occupants of the space when perceiving the building) related to the Supreme Court as a temple of justice. From the overall Greco-Roman style demonstrated through the Maison Carrée, to the flanking sphinxes on either side of the Front Plaza, to the ascent up the famous steps, to the large bronze (gold) doors tracing the evolution of justice, this exterior space is rich with temple symbolism. From the bronze doors to the ivory-colored marble Great Hall surrounded by metopes depicting ancient deities and virtues; to the smaller sacred space of the courtroom with friezes depicting the timeless themes of good versus evil, the rule of law, and the great lawgivers; to the veil behind which the most sacred work of justice takes place, the interior space of the Supreme Court Building is saturated with temple symbolism. And the actors who play a part in the action of the building add to this meaning through their dress, the pomp and circumstance of their public sessions, the privacy with which they conduct most of their business, and the public's impression of their interpersonal behavior (through personal interviews with justices, autobiographical accounts of justices, and media coverage of the court).

THE NEOCLASSICAL COURT IN POPULAR CULTURE

Courtrooms make attractive venues for fiction, providing key elements to fuel both drama and comedy, conflict and adversity. Courtrooms and litigation are vehicles for the portrayal of important issues and the opportunity for social commentary. The courts are historically a source for public drama that predates mass media and attracts the public to attend and witness the search for truth and the pursuit of justice, which provide theater at no charge.

The public's relationship with courts as theater and the ability to perceive the courts in action changed in the twentieth century, almost coincidental to the construction of the Supreme Court Building. The rise of the talking motion picture in the 1930s and later of television brought both the physical symbolism of the courts and the art of legal argumentation to the lay public. A vehicle is made for the mass consumption of the courtroom as theater space. Stage presentation forces a single perspective on the participant. In film, the viewer is able to consume multiple perspectives on courthouse and courtroom as set and setting.

The temple form is omnipresent. Television dramas routinely use the "establishing shot" of a courthouse's pediment and columns or steps to convey the transition to an interior trial scene. Discourse among players often takes place on the steps as well. Arguably the best-known use of this technique is found in the opening credits of the long-running television program *Law & Order*. The early seasons of the series used interiors of the Italianate/Neoclassical Old New York County Courthouse until interior courtroom sets were constructed. And, every week, in the credits of this show, in the montage of slides presenting law enforcement and the social order of legal process, the transition slide halfway through the credits shows the broad pediment and columns of the New York State Supreme Court Building on Foley Square. Other slides show aspects of courtroom procedure: examination, consultation, a falling gavel, and the symbolic scales of justice.

These elements matter in understanding both legal fiction and the communication of judicial symbols through popular culture. Stefan Machura presents a scheme for analyzing law films that illuminates several elements of courts and courtrooms to consider in the analysis of courtroom films: Is the court criminal, civil, or military? Was it a court of original jurisdiction, an appellate court, national high court, or a special court? Is there a jury and judge? Only a sole judge? A judicial panel? What is the architecture of the court (Modern, Classical, ornamental, other symbolism; Machura 2007, 333)? All of these elements come together to create a combination of venue and vehicle for compelling storytelling. The literature on legal film and legal fiction explores these themes and elements beyond our concern with courthouse and courtroom. Among these, Bergman and Asimow's book *Reel Justice*; Laster,

Breckweg, and King's *Drama of the Courtroom*; and Erickson's *Encyclopedia of Television Law Shows* are especially expansive in cataloging and analyzing the genre.

The application of Machura's scheme shows that jury trials are "very frequent" in movies, as are courts martial. Both comedy and drama make use of the trial court venue, as do the countless television lawyer shows aired over the decades, starting with *Perry Mason*. Appellate and high court films and shows are rare, and when they do occur, it is often as a vehicle for either historically based stories such as the films *Recount*, *The People vs. Larry Flynt*, *Amistad*, or *Gideon's Trumpet*, or as televised vehicles to add heightened attention to commentary on important social issues. Dramatic vehicles centered around the Supreme Court often focused on noncourtroom interpersonal interactions and social commentary, such as the 1981 film *First Monday in October* or the 2002 television series *First Monday* on CBS and *The Court* on ABC (both of which lasted less than a full season). The politics of confirmation occupied several episodes of the series *The West Wing*. Regular, successful series such as *Boston Legal* and *Picket Fences* used the Supreme Court chamber and oral arguments as story vehicles.

Machura notes the faithfulness of film to these courthouse venues, albeit with a bias informed by the symbolism seen in the courthouses we study. There is a tendency to show in these films Neoclassical architectural elements of the sort seen in the evolution of the U.S. Supreme Court's homes, as "filmmakers devote much effort to finding the appropriate court architecture for their story. A nineteenth-century court building with pillars, allegorical figures, paintings of former judges, and the interior of a jury court provides a very different atmosphere compared to a typical 1970s German functional building, where the judge and the parties are sitting at the same table surrounded by blank walls" (Machura 2007, 333). The symbolism and architectural features of courtrooms and courthouses further enhance the drama. The nature of these courtrooms, with their dark wood, ambient light, and variable and different perspectives that can easily be forced by camera angles, enhances the noir quality of legal drama (Grossman 2015/2019; Rosenberg 1994).

The courtroom sets used in three of the most highly regarded courtroom films reflect the role of architecture—*To Kill a Mockingbird*, *Inherit the Wind*, and *My Cousin Vinny*. The 1962 film adaptation of Harper Lee's *To Kill A Mockingbird* is widely considered to be the greatest legal movie ever, winning three Academy Awards (including one for Gregory

Peck as Atticus Finch) for the dramatization of racism and injustice in Depression-era Alabama. Another of the Oscars was for set decoration. The unusual hexagonal courtroom closely resembles the unusual oval courtroom in the historic Walker County Courthouse in Jasper, Alabama, which served as Lee's inspiration. The design emphasized postbellum Neoclassical elements often found in courtrooms of the Deep South. The prominent segregationist balcony gallery features columns, and the elevation of the jury and judge conveyed the power actors in the courtroom. *Inherit the Wind*, the 1960 dramatization of the Scopes Monkey Trial, was nominated for five Academy Awards. The tight courtroom set was conventionally square, with an elevated bench, witness stand, and jury box. Indirect lighting through windows added to the dramatic elements. The 1992 dramatic comedy *My Cousin Vinny*, which is lauded as one of the most technically, legally accurate courtroom films ever, presents all of the symbolism associated with courtroom fiction. The noncourtroom scenes were shot at a historic Neoclassical courthouse in Monticello, Georgia, which features all of the temple motif elements we describe here, including grand columns and a pediment, a cupola and rotunda, and the symbols of the judiciary. The courtroom is a constructed set, but it is a faithful representation of a Neoclassical southern courtroom, again with elevated bench, jury box, and witness stand, and also a prominent legacy balcony at the back of the courtroom. A high ceiling and great windows convey the majesty of the room. The elements of the courtrooms we describe here appear in these fictional courtroom sets.

The portrayals of Supreme Court chambers are also generally faithful to the elements described in our analysis of the historic court. The film *Amistad* dramatizes events from 1839 to 1841 that led to the U.S. Supreme Court case *United States v. Schooner Amistad* (40 U.S. [15 Pet.] 518 [1841]). An eleven-minute sequence of Anthony Hopkins portraying former president John Quincy Adams combines dramatic camera work with the presentation of a relatively faithful reproduction of the Old Supreme Court chambers in the basement of the Capitol. The vaulted ceiling, pillars, curtains, and rail reflect the intimate confines of the chamber. The rear wall is curved, with limited audience space. The justices sit low. The intimacy of the old cloistered chamber is communicated in the shooting of the courtroom scenes. And, in an homage to the high court, former associate justice Henry Blackmun portrays Justice Joseph Story, who delivered the opinion of the court in the case. The 1950 film *The Magnificent Yankee* dramatized the life of Oliver Wendell Holmes Jr. The film used symbolic Washington backdrops, such as the

White House, the Capitol, and the Reflecting Pool. And, in portraying the Supreme Court, a set that generally resembles the Old Senate Chamber was used. The columns, curtains, and orientation of the bench are faithful to the refurbished legislative chamber as a courtroom.

Portrayals of the modern high court are normally faithful to the key elements of Cass Gilbert's courtroom. The forty-four-foot ceiling, ambient light, heavy red curtains, surrounding columns, and prominent bench for the justices are faithfully portrayed. The close proximity of the lectern to the bench is useful for the dramatic effect sought by filmmakers. The 1980 television movie *Gideon's Trumpet*, in which Henry Fonda plays appellant Clarence Earl Gideon's effort to obtain the right to counsel in *Gideon v. Wainwright* (372 U.S. 335 [1963]), features extensive backroom scenes of justices in chambers and in conference. The viewer gets a dramatic look at a rendition of the courtroom when José Ferrer as attorney Abe Fortas makes the oral argument in support of Gideon's appeal. The 1981 film *First Monday in October*, which portrayed the appointment of a conservative first woman (Jill Clayburgh) to the Supreme Court, similarly presents a combination of backroom scenes— justices' chambers, conference and robing room, and the "movie day" practice of reviewing pornographic films recounted in the book *The Brethren*—and also use of a courtroom that is faithful to Gilbert's basic design. Other films and television shows (*Swing Vote, The People v. Larry Flynt, Recount, Boston Legal, Picket Fences*) used renditions of the courtroom that highlight these elements. In terms of the conduct and behavior of participants, the sometimes freewheeling nature of the justices during oral arguments is balanced against the ritual, dignity, and mystery that surround the "cloistered" court.

Many courtrooms portrayed in film and television exhibit a Modern architectural style. And the scope of architectural styles in courthouse and courtroom design has evolved since the opening of Gilbert's building (taken up in chapter 6). However, in the portrayal of the high court, and among the most notable courtroom films that historically impress the public, the Classical elements associated with the high court are both popular and reinforced.

CONCLUSION

When the Supreme Court was given a final resting place in the early twentieth century, the commissioned Beaux-Arts architect, Cass Gilbert, chose to build for the justices a Neoclassical temple. The building complex is dense with symbolic social meaning, including expressive, behavioral, and societal. The Neoclassical design drew heavy reference from Greco-Roman temples such as the Parthenon and the Maison Carrée. Yet this motif reflects in some clear ways earlier examples of religious structures.

This chapter included three notable cases of temple architecture that set the stage for consideration of the Supreme Court Building as a temple form. From the Temple at Karnak, the Temple of Solomon, and the Parthenon, we gather important themes of procession, guardianship, deification, and civic education. This frame makes sense as an architectural expression by Gilbert and a behavioral mechanism of social control because of the responsibilities of the court and the role of the judiciary in American politics.

Assuming that culture imbued with material, cognitive, and normative meaning shapes law in society (Grana and Ollenburger 1999, 3), this building holds interpretive value for students of judicial process and politics. American rhetoric until the time of the court's construction illustrates a socio-cultural lens thick with Judeo-Christian references that cast the Constitution as sacred and the role of the court as guardian of its precepts.

As Perry (2002, 32) notes, despite controversial judicial nomination processes, questionable forays of the court into unprecedented political territory, and polarizing majority opinions, "the justices have managed to preserve an image of themselves as a 'priestly tribe.'"[8]

Understanding the Constitution as an Ark of the Covenant communicates meaning about our valuation of the tenets of social contract theory, our respect for fundamental law, and our notions about the importance of the rule of law in democratic society. Understanding the role of members of the bench as "priests of justice" communicates meaning about the independent and isolated nature of their work; the role of the judiciary as a form of intercessor on behalf of the people in the name of justice; and the character expected of justices in terms of intelligence, wisdom, and ethical conduct. Finally, understanding the Supreme Court Building as a temple explains the reverence with which the court is treated (in theory), the significantly limited access given to the public, and the ceremonial nature of its public (and private) activities.

From this perspective, contemporary architectural reflections of Gilbert's design make sense. The contemporary effort to build federal courthouses across the country illustrates this renewed interest in Gilbert's aesthetic. As Flanders (2001, 9) notes:

> Gilbert's architecture became central to a process by which late-twentieth-century architects relearned how to design courthouses that are both appropriate to their functions and settings and pleasing and useful to their multiple publics. The federal courts developed programs to celebrate Gilbert because his buildings function preeminently well among the vast variety of designs and settings that house the work of the courts. Gilbert buildings enlarge the lives of those they touch, a discovery that resulted in the rapid and spontaneous spread of Gilbert's program beyond the courts, throughout New York and on to many other places. Everyone who enters a Gilbert building designed for public use realizes that they have arrived at a significant place.

Some contemporary architectural critics have developed a renewed appreciation for Cass Gilbert. His various public spaces have inspired recent tributes to Classical architecture. Flanders (2001, 10) expresses the value of Gilbert's approach to design, particularly of public buildings, suggesting that he "serves as an essential link in teaching the federal government how to create civic architecture all over again, and how to think about civic architecture through the troubled aesthetic of our time." Similarly, Byard (2001, 287) notes the way in which Gilbert used refined architecture to pronounce "the courthouse's standard of integrity," describing his buildings' "rigorous classicism," "beautiful materials," "strict consistency of . . . detail." In some way, Gilbert's quest to get things right finds its complement in the court's effort to "nakedly and humanly" engage in the enduring quest for the sacred truth, the right, the honorable (ibid.).

Contemporary scholarship, such as the sweeping treatment of judicial iconography offered by Resnik and Curtis (2011), challenges one to consider the expressive, behavioral, and societal meaning of modern adjudication as increasingly inaccessible to the public at large—as an activity performed out of sight. They suggest: "Adjudication is itself a democratic process, which reconfigures power as it obliges disputants and judges to treat each other as equals, to provide information to each other, and to offer public justifications for decisions based on the interaction of fact and norm. Thus Jeremy Bentham's insistence on 'publicity,'

Jürgen Habermas's interest in the 'public sphere,' and Michel Foucault's understanding of the power of surveillance inform our thesis of a distinct place for courts in producing, redistributing, and curbing power" (ibid., xv).

While the Supreme Court might gain legitimacy in the public eye through its symbolic trappings, the choice to shape justice in this way might have philosophical and practical implications for the democratic quality of American judicial proceedings.

6 Establishing the Federal Presence

As the Supreme Court moved from home to home, the architecture of the court's home changed, but the court itself nonetheless carried forward notable elements from home to home. The homes of the inferior federal courts have similarly changed over time, often borrowing from the past. In this chapter we consider the shift in judicial architecture used for the federal presence in the states. We begin with an examination of the pattern of federal courthouse construction over time. There is periodicity in the construction of new courthouses and also notable context found in when and where new federal courthouses are built. And whether intentionally or unintentionally, the uneven dedication of federal resources to local communities for federal buildings to serve as post office and courthouse led to the dominance of certain architectural styles. Visualizing the pattern at the macro level through mapping of construction and design and also at the micro level through close examination of representative cases highlights the use of style to carry social meaning in the cultural landscape. From the Neoclassical temple refashioned from the mold of a town meetinghouse to the Brutalist administrative complexes that emerged in the last part of the twentieth century, court spaces frame the everyday experience of law in society.

We ask the reader to contemplate in this chapter the strength of different forms as reflections of democratic values. And then we highlight the possible tension created when the local federal presence invokes one stylistic motif and the national invokes another. How do we make meaning from the ecotones of the federal presence in built form?

THE FEDERAL COURTHOUSES AS CIVIC ICONOGRAPHY

An important theme of this volume is that the courts are among the oldest, most revered, and perhaps most powerful democratic institutions of American politics. It might seem counterintuitive to say that an appointive body is the most democratic. Of course, legislatures represent popular sovereignty and consent to be governed. Presidents have often asserted their unique role as a nationally elected officer, staking a claim to being a "tribune of the masses." But the courts represent the secularization and rule of law, the limits of executive power, the primacy of collective judgment, the rights of the citizenry, the accessibility of the state, and the protection of the minority. Courts use democratic processes and rely on democratic theory to serve all of these functions. Tracing the contours of federal court architecture therefore highlights the consonance of the function and form of justice.

In chapter 2, we presented the etymology of the American courthouse and how it presents as an iconic form of civic space. As the American democracy has grown and expanded, so too federal courthouses have been established in communities to house a system of justice and to project the authority and power of the national government to provide the rule of law. The proliferation of federal courthouses throughout the country in the twentieth century brought the federal presence to localities. And, in so doing, these structures convey meaning beyond their technical charge to shelter the courts. In this chapter, we extend our work on the homes of the high court to uncover the social meaning of other federal court spaces for everyday democracy. We do this mindful of the role of the Supreme Court's current home as a physical disruptor both of the architecture of Washington and of federal judicial architecture in general.

The theoretical lenses we have used throughout this work represent just a sample of the myriad methods available to scholars of American political development and judicial institutions. We seek to build a bridge from the political scientists who study institutional development to the architects and urban designers who make the dynamic spaces to house those same institutions and consequently shape human behavior. Introducing these techniques to a problem of politics informs our understanding of the puzzle. It also leads us to believe that the study of political culture and behavior has a great deal to offer to academics and practitioners of architecture and urban design. The current focus on smarter and more sustainable design, higher-quality public space, and deeper community engagement involves public building and thus public construction (see, for example, Francis et al. 2012). How have we built public space to facilitate democratic governance? And how should we build public space moving forward?

A focus on the courts brings into full view the seminal values undergirding the American political community. Courts are fundamentally about equity and freedom (Richardson 1951), and judicial buildings attempt to embody these values while holding relevance as works of design at the monumental scale. Does the architecture of the federal court system reflect empowerment of the American citizenry in the administration of justice? Has the institutionalization of the court throughout the twentieth century shifted the social meaning of places of justice in local communities? As we look back at the "century of building" of federal courthouses, what architectural styles have been used over time to shape the buildings? How do those choices in turn shape us and our understanding of justice?

THE PATTERN OF FEDERAL COURTHOUSE CONSTRUCTION

Article III of the Constitution empowered Congress to create lesser courts beyond the constitutionally mandated Supreme Court. Congress subsequently acted, with the Judiciary Act of 1789, to create a federal "district" in each state, with an accompanying court that most often dealt with matters of admiralty law. Over time, these courts had their jurisdiction subsequently expanded by Congress, and as states were added or states grew in population, additional districts were established. Congress specified cities where the courts could meet, crafting a geographic foundation for the presence of justice that continues to this day. Establishing a federal court system created a need for homes for those courts. However, the pattern of creation of courthouses is not constant and flat. Instead, it varies across time and by geography, necessarily accompanying the expansion of the nation and the need to establish visible symbols of authority and justice.

Figure 6.1 illustrates the general pattern of federal courthouse construction from the end of the Civil War to the second decade of the

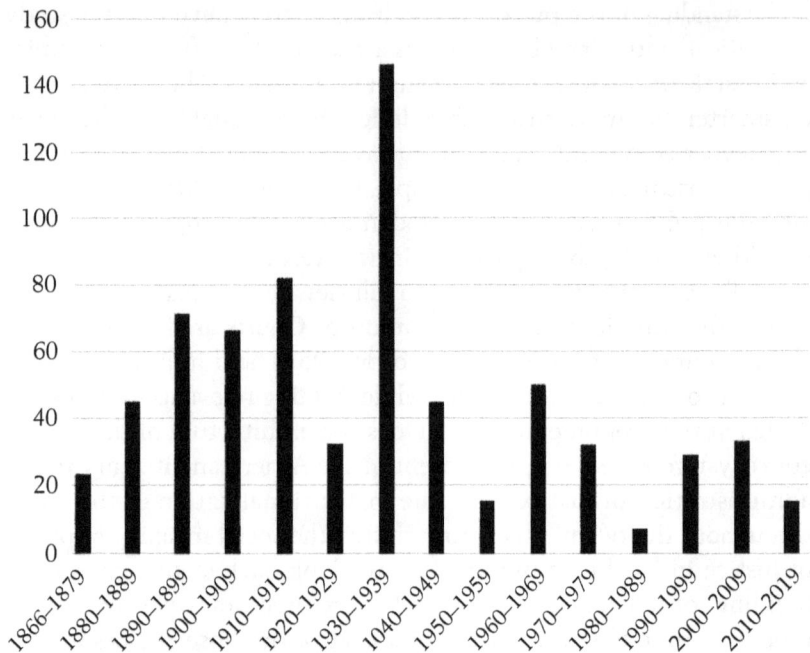

Figure 6.1. Postbellum U.S. federal courthouse construction over time. Created and compiled by the authors.

twenty-first century. The end of the American Civil War was accompanied by the unleashing of settlement forces and efforts at nation building on several dimensions. These efforts had begun during the war with the passage of the Homestead Acts and the initiation of the construction of the transcontinental railroad, which further sped territorial expansion into the Great Plains and the Rockies (see, for example, Ambrose 2000; Foner 2019). The end of the conflict in the east brought the subsequent Reconstruction effort in the South to accompany westward territorial expansion. As a consequence, the national government engaged in a massive construction program throughout the latter half of the nineteenth century and early part of the twentieth century. Lois Craig suggests in *The Federal Presence* (1978, 163) that "towns everywhere clamored for federally funded buildings as an indication of stature. And Congressmen obligingly served them up. For example, Memphis received a courthouse even though no federal courts were held there."

In part, the surge in construction stemmed from demographic and transportation changes. Waves of European immigration brought urban population growth. The expansion of the railroad, coupled with the invention of the automobile, paved the way for the development of new cities in rural communities across the country. "In 1899, the Office [of the Supervising Architect] had responsibility for construction or management of 399 buildings; by 1912, the number was 1,126" (Craig 1978, 213). The pace of new construction was so rapid that the secretary of the treasury in 1916 observed that the federal construction effort was "being increased at the rate of a new building every fourth day in the year" (ibid.). Congress began passing comprehensive omnibus bills to fund public buildings in the first decade of the twentieth century. Within a decade, media criticism of pork barrel politics and governmental waste led Congress to establish a new Public Buildings Commission in 1913. Under its watchful eye, Congress failed to pass another omnibus bill until 1926 (ibid., 239–40).

Following this general moratorium on new project construction, the Roosevelt administration addressed the catastrophic turn of the nation's economy during the Great Depression with expansive investment in public works.[1] Part of this development of infrastructure included new federal courthouses built during the 1930s. By comparison, the construction of new court facilities across the country over the last several decades is quite limited in scope, which is in part a testament to the scope and durability of the infrastructure built for the courts by the New Deal.

In Figure 6.2, the data on federal courthouse construction is further broken down by decade and three categories of states: states that joined the Confederacy; states that remained in the Union; and states that were admitted after 1863, starting with Nevada. We treat West Virginia as a state that stayed in the Union.[2]

Disaggregating the data by region reveals a more complete picture of federal courthouse construction over time and helps illuminate the effort to establish a national federal presence in communities throughout the country. For states admitted after the Civil War, most construction took place between 1900 and 1940. Construction in the former Confederate states begins in earnest in 1880 and peaks in the 1930s. This pattern clearly reflects the effort by the federal government to physically shape the federal presence in counties across the region as a means of ensuring access to due process for newly enfranchised African Americans living in the Jim Crow South. For remaining states, a general

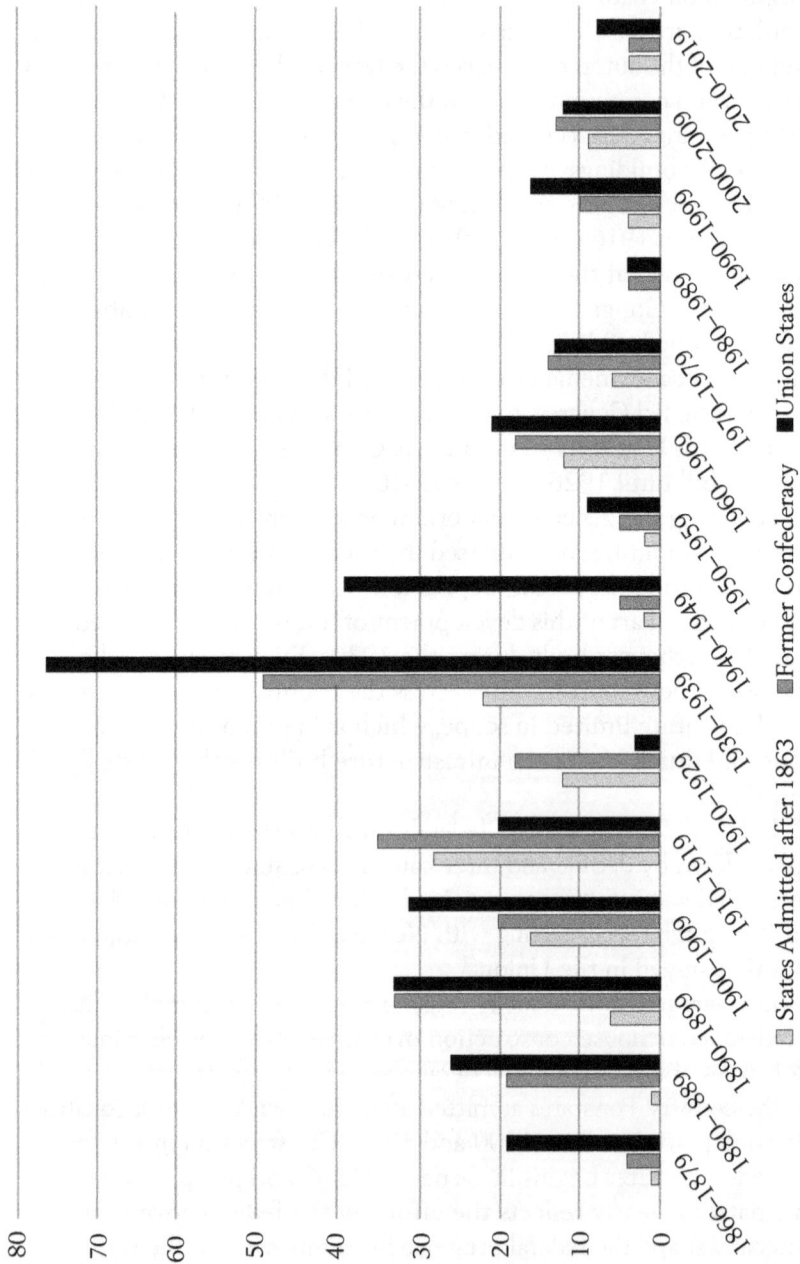

Figure 6.2. U.S. federal courthouse construction by region. Created and compiled by the authors.

Legend: States Admitted after 1863 | Former Confederacy | Union States

surge in construction occurs prior to the 1920s. After a moratorium on new construction in the 1920s, the building effort spikes in the 1930s and then gradually but fairly steadily declines throughout the remainder of the twentieth century and into the twenty-first century.

PHYSICALLY DEFINING THE FEDERAL COURTHOUSE

Tracing the construction effort of federal courthouses since the Civil War illustrates waves that coincide with major periods of federal expansion, including territorial expansion, greater protection of individual civil rights against acts of discrimination, and growth of the social welfare state. Courthouse construction is part of a wider effort to establish a federal presence. It also reflects the economic policy of governing administrations, with growth led by Democratic presidents to address economic downturns and to implement domestic policy reform.

For purposes of this analysis, we examine the decade of the most construction for all regions except new territories. Figure 6.3 illustrates the construction of federal courthouses between 1930 and 1940. It is worth noting that construction doesn't just happen; it is a lengthy process. And one of the great wonders of the New Deal is the scope of and speed with which "shovel ready" projects were implemented to transform American infrastructure and also push money into the economy (Smith 2006). A great surprise is the extent to which construction took place in the 1930s, but not just as a product of the New Deal. Of the 151 federal courthouses built in that decade, over 70 were built before the end of 1933, with 1933 being the peak year. The allocation of the money to construct these buildings, the letting of the contracts, and even the breaking of the ground for construction in many cases preceded FDR's swearing in and the passage of the New Deal through Congress; the ramp-up of federal courthouse construction appears to have started under the "Great Engineer," Herbert Hoover. So, to the extent that the courthouse constructions were rampant in the 1930s, they are as much a part of a general response of the national government throughout the 1930s rather than only a consequence of the realigning and defining New Deal election.

The decade of the 1930s captures both the construction and inhabitation of the U.S. Supreme Court Building in Washington, D.C, as well as federal courthouses throughout the nation. While Cass Gilbert's design for the Supreme Court Building stands as an archetype of Neoclassicism,

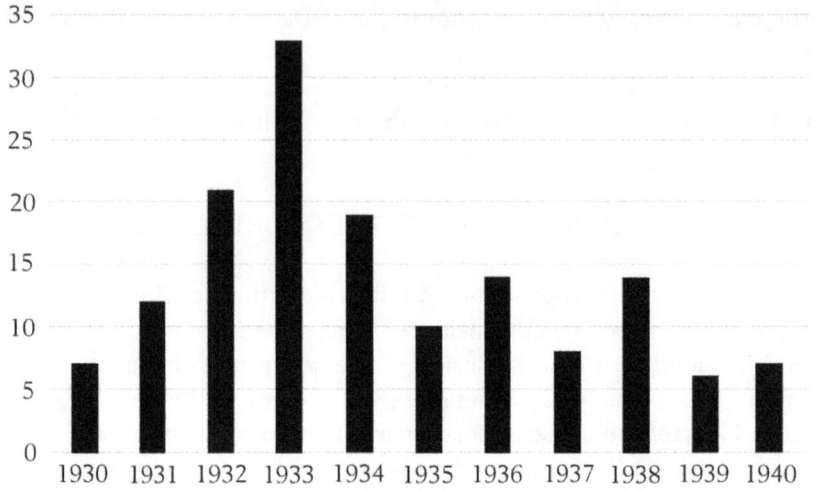

Figure 6.3. Construction of federal courthouses from 1930 to 1940. Created and compiled by the authors.

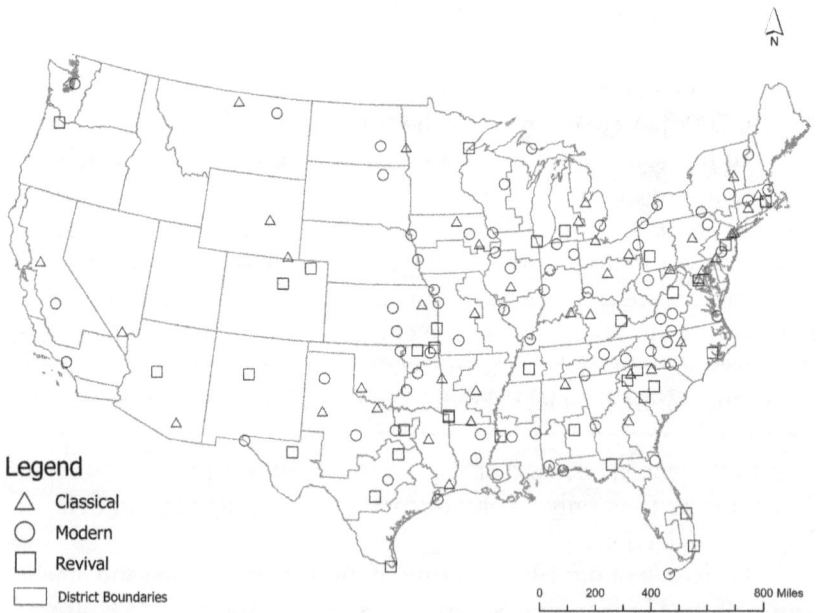

Figure 6.4. Map of architectural styles used from 1930 to 1940 in the contiguous United States. Created and compiled by the authors.

TABLE 6.1. Tracing the federal architectural heritage

Classical	Revivalist	Modern
Colonial	Beaux-Arts	International
Neoclassical	Renaissance	Art Deco
Georgian	Second Empire	Stripped Classicism
Federal	Egyptian	PWA Moderne
	Spanish Mission	

SOURCE: Compiled by the authors.

firms commissioned to carry out the federal building program used a nearly full range of architectural styles. Numerous architectural styles emerged in the last two centuries, and many made their way into public construction. We find it useful to distill architectural style in American public building into three major periods: Classical, Revivalist, and Modern. Though individual styles carry clear and meaningful distinctive features, considering them within the context of larger stylistic periods reveals themes of social meaning otherwise obfuscated. The following three figures map the construction of federal courthouses during this decade by architectural style (figure 6.4), trace the evolution of these periods, and differentiate the styles attributed to each (tables 6.1 and 6.3).

Early American judicial architecture took on Classical form. Generally, courthouses in the Classical form (Greek Revival and Classical Revival) were constructed between 1780 and 1850, preceding the Civil War. The temple motif predominated. With the recurring features of Greco-Roman columns, friezes, and façades, courthouses in the Classical style bespoke republican virtues of popular representation, state order, individual liberty, and the sacred rule of law.

The architectural styles descendant from Neoclassicism include Federal, Georgian, Empire, and Greek Revival. Courthouses in this style dot the American landscape, appearing as temples of justice in communities throughout the country. When Cass Gilbert designed the U.S. Supreme Court Building in Washington, D.C., the Neoclassical pattern had grown worn and unpopular, and the larger architectural community had moved toward Modernist and international forms that broke with the old patterns. (Table 6.2 presents a summary of stylistic features, symbolic values, and characteristic examples seen in federal courthouse construction.) Visitors to the nation's capital would be justified in dating the building to the early nineteenth century.

TABLE 6.2. Motifs of justice expressed in architectural styles

Neoclassical

Federal (1780–1830); Georgian (1720–1840); Empire (1800–1830); Greek Revival (1820–50)

General Features: Palladian, isolated and clearly articulated, autonomous, complete, planar rather than sculptural, flatter projections and recessions, friezes and tablets, ancient façades and building layouts

Values: Greco-Roman virtues, accessibility, rationalism, republicanism, radicalism/revolution in the name of individual liberty

Example: U.S. Customhouse, Savannah, Georgia (1852)

Revival

Gothic Revival (1840–1930); Romanesque Empire; Renaissance; Beaux-Arts (1880–1920)

General Features: Ornamentality, purity, decorative patterns, finials, cathedral-like, use of buttresses and vaults, emphasis on height; later a return to ornamental Neoclassicism.

Values: Conservative, pious, religious conformism, purity, truth, Christian, sacred, sacrifice, superiority

Example: U.S. Post Office and Federal Courthouse, Charleston, South Carolina (1896)

Modern

Functionalism (1900–1930); Modernism (1920–60); Art Deco (1920–40); PWA Moderne (1950–70); Brutalism (1950–present)

General Features: Simplicity, minimalism, bare, modular, emphasis on function, repetitive, international structural, geometric, monolithic, massive, concrete, imposing

Values: Egalitarian, truthful, unrefined, revealing, transparent, universality, power, strength, authority, control, cultural cohesion, repetition, equality, directness

Example: William Kenzo Nakamura U.S. Courthouse, Seattle, Washington (1940)

Postmodern I

Deconstructivism (1980–)

General Features: Surface manipulation, fragmentation, distortion, dislocation, discontinuity, instability, dysfunctional, asymmetric, unpredictable, unstandardized

Values: Contradiction, irrationality, imagination, play, untraditional, unconventional, uniqueness, inequality, dishonesty, disharmony, fluidity

Example: Long Island Federal Courthouse, New York (2000)

Postmodern II:

Sustainable (2000–)

General Features: Green, sustainable, integrated, energy efficient, renewable, balanced, natural, high quality

Values: Vision, stewardship, self-control, efficiency, nature, protection, placeness, responsibility, balance, planning

Example: Wayne L. Morse United States Courthouse, Eugene, Oregon (2012)

SOURCE: Compiled by the authors.

Breaking from Neoclassicism, Revivalist styles emerged in American civic architecture in the mid-nineteenth century. Early examples date to the 1840s, with construction in this style generally continuing until the 1920s. As a broad stylistic category, Revivalist architecture is characterized by greater ornamentation and use of decorative pattern, with an emphasis on vertical elements such as buttresses and vaults. These cathedral-like structures reference the grand cathedrals at town centers in medieval Europe. Consequently, they carry social meaning embodied in religious architecture of the Judeo-Christian tradition. It is a conservative style, emphasizing conformity, ritual, truth, sacrifice, and superiority, and as we noted earlier in this work, we can see these values also at work in the meaning of law in American society. Another form of temple, the Revivalist courthouse emphasizes equality in the eyes of the law, the ritual of judicial process, the sacred role of the robed judge in the holy place, the price of freedom, and the gift of mercy. The law is hard and fast, and its source is fundamental and enduring.

Most American federal architecture, however, dates to the twentieth century—a period in which Modernism reigned as the international style of choice for monumental architecture. In the early part of the century, Functionalism dominated. From it stemmed the complementary styles of Art Deco and High Modernism. In the United States, federal architecture took on characteristics unique to the public works building program in the form of Public Works Administration (PWA) Moderne. And Brutalism emerged around midcentury at the apex of the period.

In contrast to the ornamentation of Revivalist architecture, all Modern structures emphasize simple lines, bare façades, imposing and regular geometric shapes, and massive sizing. (See table 6.2 for a comparison of justice motifs expressed in architectural style.) Rather than the expensive imported marble or granite of the Neoclassical courthouse, the Modern courthouse is concrete. It exudes equality, transparency, directness, universality, power, and permanence. This courthouse is not a temple. It is an administrative complex. Equality under the law is represented in the predictability of bureaucratic processes. The court has become institutionalized. The law transcends culture. It is a law grounded in universal human rights. An international standard is represented in an international style.

Few courthouses in the United States are built in the Deconstructivist style. It is an important period in the evolution of public architecture, and examples of it appear in communities across the country.

Deconstructivists broke from the Modern tradition in the 1980s. The characteristic features of this style include elements that are playful, unconventional, discontinuous, and fragmented. Symmetry of form is thrown off in favor of the unpredictable. In court architecture, the Deconstructivist style is particularly powerful as social critique. It relishes contradiction, disharmony, and inequality. It embraces fluidity rather than stasis. What does this portend for the nature of law and society? Deconstructivism reveals the contradictions of a hyperlocalized court system—with federal and judicial systems and constitutions at odds and in flux. It points out the role of judicial imagination and the sometimes unpredictable nature of judicial interpretation. It emphasizes the role of argument and tension in conflict resolution, the tenable nature of witness testimony, and the unequal process and outcome of law enforcement.

GILBERT'S COURTHOUSE AS A PERIOD INFLECTION

Classical elements persist in courthouse architecture, but throughout the interwar period and especially in the 1930s, the Classical and Neoclassical "stone temple" designs and early, ornate Beaux-Arts designs give way to Modern derivatives of the Beaux-Arts, mainly in the form of Stripped Classicism and Moderne architecture.

One lasting stylistic effect of the 1930s construction can be attributed to the New Deal: the emergence of the architectural style PWA Moderne, and the widespread use of this Art Deco–derivative style on federal courthouses in the latter part of the 1930s. The Public Works Administration (PWA) was the principal federal public works construction agency of the national government, created in 1933 as the Federal Emergency Administration of Public Works program under the National Industrial Recovery Act (NIRA). Among the PWA's projects were dams, airports, housing projects, and also federal buildings. (The PWA is sometimes confused with the Works Progress Administration [WPA], which largely implemented shovel-ready small-scale public works and improvements and directly employed unskilled labor. The PWA, by contrast, hired private professional firms to do quality construction [see Ickes 1935; Smith 2006].)

PWA Moderne descends from the same Beaux-Arts tradition that had inspired and been perpetuated by Cass Gilbert. Buildings in this motif clearly reflect the Art Deco emphasis from the latter period of the Beaux-Arts movement and are sometimes referred to as examples of Stripped Classicism. PWA Moderne structures in particular radiate power and have a more monumental feel than the often more modest Stripped Classicism and Streamlined Deco construction of the same era. In addition to being used in public construction, including courthouses, it was also used in private construction for banks and other office towers. It can readily be argued that as much as Gilbert's design was criticized for the strong Beaux-Arts influence on its design, it was also entirely in the mainstream of a transition in American power architecture that was shedding the more flourished and ornate elements of the Beaux-Arts tradition, and was instead a work that bridged to Stripped Classicism and a subset of Moderne that was prominent in the period.

The most recent stylistic development in court building is Sustainable design. Emerging at the turn of the twenty-first century, this style is driven by values more than by general form. Sustainable civic buildings are well integrated, and they are energy efficient. Designs emphasize balance and the use of natural resources. If we unpack the social meaning of Sustainable design for understanding justice, we see a picture of the law that is restrained and responsible. The scales of justice are balanced and calibrated to the fundamental laws of nature, in an ecological sense rather than an Enlightenment sense. We are stewards of this Earth, and we are but one species in one cultural habitat. These designs incorporate regional materials, emphasizing the placeness of justice. The law is a construct, dependent on cultural understandings that are specific to time and place. In this respect, we see a nod back to the very earliest courthouse constructions in North America—the vernacular building, which relied on existing styles but also the practicality of local climate and local materials for its final form.

THE COURT AS A DEMOCRATIC INSTITUTION TODAY

Returning to the argument that the court is the original democratic institution, what does the evolution of our nation's federal judiciary in built form tell us about the democratic character of the court today? Considering the expansion of the federal presence and its manifestation over time in the architectural design of courthouses, it behooves us to consider the evolution of values invoked through design concerning the nature of law and the dispensing of justice. Table 6.3 illustrates the evolutionary track of the values and characteristics of each major period

TABLE 6.3. The evolution of social meaning of the law across architectural styles

Classical	Revivalist	Modern	Deconstructivist	Sustainable
Republican	Conservative	Equal	Imaginative	Integrated
Secular	Conformist	Transparent	Unpredictable	Efficient
Enlightened	Ritualized	Direct	Dissonant	Balanced
Ordered	Honest	Universal	Conflictual	Natural
Traditional	Sacrificial	Powerful	Unequal	Restrained
Sacred	Superior	Permanent	Asymmetrical	Responsible
	Equal	Bureaucratic		Stewarded
	Sacred	Predictable		Localized
	Fundamental	Institutional		Contextual
	Enduring			

SOURCE: Compiled by the authors.

in a way that visually illustrates the meaningful shift from sacred and enduring temple to bureaucratic and institutionalized judicial complex.

Further, the coordinated building program of the federal government embarked on courthouse construction projects to achieve certain explicitly stated goals. As stated in the 1991 U.S. Courts Design Guide section "Aesthetic Considerations": "Federal Court architecture should symbolize the Judiciary as a co-equal branch of Government. Courthouse design should reflect the seriousness of the judicial mandate and the dignity of the judicial system. The scale of a courthouse should be monumental, and the materials used on its exterior durable. The spirit of the architecture should be impressive and inspiring" (1991, 58).

As Resnik and Curtis (2011, 59) note, the guide expanded its charge in the 1997 edition of the document and retained this charge in the 2008 version. The section entitled "General Design Guidelines" states:

> The architecture of federal courthouses must promote respect for the tradition and purpose of the American judicial process. To this end, a courthouse facility must express solemnity, stability, integrity, rigor, and fairness. The facility must also provide a civic presence and contribute to the architecture of the local community.
>
> To achieve these goals, massing must be strong and direct with a sense of repose, and the scale of design should reflect a national judicial enterprise. All architectural elements must be proportional and arranged hierarchically to signify orderliness. The materials

TABLE 6.4. The American court as a democratic institution in function and form

	County Courthouse	Federal Courthouse
Functions	Record keeping (birth, marriage, death), taxation, licensure, jury deliberation, law enforcement	Post office, courthouse, federal judicial complex
Values	Collective memory, local autonomy, civic duty, accessibility	Respect, solemnity, integrity, rigor, fairness, civic presence, artistic, mediation, hierarchy, orderliness, naturalness, permanence
Social Meaning		
Expressive	Community identity, local power and authority	National power and authority
Behavioral	Regular access for legitimizing social relations, accessing vital records, paying taxes, serving as jurors, receiving due process, paying fines	Little access or use in everyday life; securitization
Societal	Local law and order	Federal presence, dominance of the unfamiliar and inaccessible

SOURCE: Compiled by the authors.

employed must be consistently applied, natural and regional in origin, durable, and invoke a sense of permanence. Colors should be subdued and complement the natural materials used in the design.

Here we see the full picture of the establishment and evolution of federal presence in communities throughout the nation. These buildings were designed to be monumental, durable, impressive, and inspiring. Commissioned architects should therefore build to evoke respect, project power and order, and emphasize permanence. The resulting courthouses constitute major landmarks of the cityscape. They stake claim to prominent public space, often situated proximate to county courthouses.

How does this juxtaposition of spaces of justice give social meaning to courts as democratic institutions? As citizens approach physical systems of justice, what do they encounter and experience? Table 6.4 compares the function and form of local courthouses and federal courthouses.

A citizen might pass by a federal court on a daily basis and not once enter its doors. By contrast, a citizen would be hard-pressed to avoid visiting the county courthouse or a circuit court, for these judicial facilities serve as archives of community memory, preserving certificates of birth, marriage, and death. They process the payment of fines and taxes; they house law enforcement; and they facilitate jury duty. They function as familiar civic stages for the performance of citizenship. In terms of values, these county and federal courthouses carry different meanings by design as well as by use. Federal courthouses have been built as artistic monumental spaces to project federal authority and respect for the rule of law. County courthouses, through exterior and interior design, speak of local identity and autonomy. The increasing securitization of federal buildings further alienates the average citizen from the space. Federal courts speak to the presence of law without revealing much of the practice of law.

One way current and former federal courthouses are finding broader meaning for the public is by serving public cultural memory and literacy. Current and former federal courthouses do serve educational and exhibition roles that bring knowledge, art, and culture to the public. Courthouses often exhibit permanent and rotating historic and art exhibits. Examples of gallery space can be found in both historic and new courthouse construction, including exhibits of commercial art. However, exhibit space cannot display pricing on art even if it is available for sale.

Historic functions are often tied directly to the building and its role in landmark litigations. Two examples are found in Kansas and Missouri. The old federal courthouse in Topeka was the site of the 1951 district court in the *Brown v. Board of Education of Topeka* case (347 U.S. 483 [1954]). Still functioning as a post office, the building hosts exhibits of the history and development of Topeka and Kansas, with particular attention to the school desegregation case. In Saint Louis, Missouri, the Old Courthouse on the Mississippi River currently stands with the Gateway Arch in the background. Built over a half century, from 1816 to 1864, the building hosted the Missouri Supreme Court trial for the infamous *Dred Scott* case. It is now operated by the National Park Service as part of a national monument.

Other examples exist of courthouses either hosting or being repurposed for educational and historical missions. In Las Vegas, the

Neoclassical federal courthouse and post office built in 1933 was turned over to the city in 2002. A decade-long rehabilitation resulted in a home for the National Museum of Organized Crime and Law Enforcement. The modern Dirksen Courthouse in Chicago still serves as a courthouse but also hosts the Northern District of Illinois Court History Museum, including exhibits on famous prosecutions such as Al Capone and four former governors of the state. In Oklahoma City, the Federal District Court for the Western District opened a Federal Court Museum and Learning Center one block from the Murrah Federal Building Memorial commemorating the 1995 domestic terror act.

Still other courthouses found new life as local monuments. For example, the Richardson Romanesque courthouse built in 1890 in tiny Jefferson, Texas, was sold to the local historic society in 1965 and turned into a local museum; the old federal courthouse in Newcastle, Delaware, is similarly purposed. In Wheeling, West Virginia, the antebellum Custom House was sold in 1963 to the state. The structure has historical significance. Subsequent to Virginia's secession from the union, the Wheeling Convention met in the building in May 1861 to separate from the Commonwealth, and then hosted another meeting a month later to establish the "Restored" government of Virginia; still later, the drafting of the state's constitution occurred there. The structure is now a museum known as the Independence Hall of West Virginia and is a National Historic Landmark.

CONCLUSION

What is to be made of a courthouse? How do values, history, and function come together in the process and product that will become a hall of justice? The U.S. Supreme Court Building heralds justice in the language of Classicism, but this is only one design language used to convey the purpose and function of a government building. Cass Gilbert had other stylistic options at the time of its construction, but he chose to invoke ancient symbols of law used throughout the history of Western civilization. The resulting temple to justice became a visual shorthand for public perception of the federal judiciary.

However, the third branch of the U.S. government is more than the Supreme Court. Its district and appellate court facilities are present in communities across the country. This chapter pushes beyond the U.S. Supreme Court Building as an exploration into the physical

manifestations of the federal judicial system in monumental civic structures across the country. What we uncover is a massive building program that accelerated in the early twentieth century, with particular
emphasis on the 1930s. Focusing on this decade provided a vehicle for
systematically considering the social meaning of major architectural styles
used to build federal courthouses.

Fundamentally, we are concerned with the symbolic significance of
courthouses as democratic institutions committed to the administration of justice. The proliferation of federal courthouses provides rich
cases to consider the ways in which the language of justice manifests
in local communities. As federal buildings share prominent space in the
city with county and state courthouses, the social meaning of justice
in built design becomes layered and potentially complex. Do these
structures reflect empowerment of the citizenry? If citizens have greater
familiarity with local courts than with federal ones, then the exteriors
of federal courthouses take on even more symbolic meaning. From our
view, the language of Neoclassicism and Revivalism carry familiar messages about the nature of justice and the rule of law. The language of
Modernism is complicated. On the one hand, it speaks of equality, transparency, and universality. On the other hand, it speaks of bureaucrati-
zation and centralized authority. Deconstructivism carries an even more
problematic meaning in that it calls into question the predictability of
the law and the symmetry of power relations. Further, it finds inspiration in dissonance, inconsistency, and conflict. Perhaps this is the true
nature of the law in society, but we would do well to recognize the
symbolic message of our civic buildings built in this style.

Conclusion

We seek an appreciation of the social meaning of the American courts in built design, using the U.S. Supreme Court as our vehicle. This is the story of a unique court that both informs and is informed by the story of American courthouses in general. The local experience with courts and courthouses shapes the nation's court and the national governing experience. Through the evolution of vernacular architecture as well as the language used to describe it, the courthouse (and thus the Supreme Court Building) became an extension of the public meetinghouse. As we described in chapter 2, the local courthouse was the physical manifestation of an emerging democratic zeitgeist. As a central feature of a parish or county, it oriented the public by way of landmark and function. The Supreme Court and its building serve in this way for the nation.

The emergence of local courthouses in early American history echoed the Classical democratic model of the Athenian agora or the Roman forum. Jackson (1987, 120) notes (with emphasis added):

> As we might expect, the ideal public square in the political landscape has a strong architectural quality. It occupies the most prestigious location in the principal town and is surrounded by politically significant buildings: law court, archives, treasury, legislative hall, and often military headquarters and jail as well. . . . Typical of the political

emphasis on boundaries, the area is well defined by markers and has its own laws and its own officers. Finally, it is here in the agora or forum that history is made visible and where speech becomes a political instrument, eloquence a form of political action.

The local courthouse was the secular censor and the secular center, the place where communities met and where people governed the boundaries between institutions and defined individual rights. The influence of early religious traditions in the American colonies guided architecture for worship, which in turn guided architecture for secular public structures. These influences carry through to the high court's home. We also learn that the individual is important in the origin of American architecture through the characteristics of the individual house of a freeholder that carry into the design of the community house and courthouse. Fittingly enough, these echo the importance and primacy of the court in defense of the rights and freedoms of the individual in the American experience. And, as a result, the high court, too, finds a postbellum role as secular censor and secular center.

The high court—America's first court—was among the very last to get a home of its own. As such, it spent decades following an old model of court adaptiveness that was not so far removed from the circuit-riding experience. The court was not originally seen as a permanent sitting institution most of the time. Only institutional growth of the government in general as well as the courts made a true permanent home a necessity. The messy challenge of nation building in the eighteenth and nineteenth centuries contributed to the court's tenant existence. The initial U.S. capitals were chosen out of a combination of politics and necessity. The new American republic was intent on creating a governing place. But unlike for Congress and the executive, the capital city did not provide the high court an original home, though L'Enfant clearly intended one in his design. Instead, the court found itself in residence in a general government building, sharing inferior space with other institutional actors.

The journey from marketplace to city hall to Capitol basement to tavern to refurbished legislative chamber would shape the court. Physically, institutionally, and operationally, the court found elements of identity, intellectualism, and intimacy that might not otherwise have emerged in a grand palace for justice. It grew. And as the court grew in size, caseload, power, and permanency, it both added to and projected out its definition of space and developed more and more perimeter control, even within the Capitol Building.

THE BUILDING AS CONFLICT RESOLUTION

The construction of the Supreme Court Building alters the cityscape of Washington, D.C. But it does so out of necessity, and in so doing, resolves a variety of conflicts for the client (the Supreme Court) and in its alteration of the cityscape. The Supreme Court was intended to have an independent and coequal space of its own, as befits a branch of government. In the early capitals of New York and Philadelphia, the high court enjoyed temporary though visible and independent quarters just like Congress and the president. And around the country, the presence of the federal courts through their courthouses became the most explicit reminder of federal power, much as the presence of post offices was the most explicit reminder of federal services.

This was not to be the case when the government moved to Washington, where the court lacked its own walls and its own symbol of authority. (This function is filled for the executive by the front pediments and columns of the White House, and for Congress by the Capitol dome.) Before the 1930s, we had no external expression of the high court through its architecture. As the court found a home of its own, it took on greater imagery that honored the tradition of the rule of law and the notion of justice. Rich legal symbolism is infused into all aspects of the structure, as the chosen stylistic motif proves to be a suitable vehicle for capturing distinct legal and democratic traditions that are in and of themselves otherwise tied to distinct architectural traditions. The placement of the Supreme Court Building relative to the Library of Congress and the Capitol Building almost dictates that Gilbert make the court's home larger, grander, and more remote if only to maintain the institution's relative prominence.

Practical need drives the construction of a building. The high court's caseload and function had grown. It had taken up more and more Capitol space, even as the justices and their clerks largely worked from home and used a messenger system to circulate briefs. The future of the courts, like the rest of the national government, was growth. This required a building to grow into as well. So, for Gilbert, the first conflict to resolve was a need for professional space that incorporated both practicality and

Figure C.1. Aerial view (looking west) of Capitol Hill and the National Mall in Washington, D.C. Photograph 2007 by Carol M. Highsmith. Library of Congress, Prints and Photographs Division, LC-DIG-highsm-01901.

prominence, and that would allow the justices a professional space that was for each of them a sanctuary while allowing professional interaction.

Practical need also drives the choice of location, which created the second conflict requiring resolution. Though D.C. was a new capital, the U.S. Supreme Court Building was a late addition. It materialized after the urban commitments had been made. The building had to articulate justice in a way that would contribute to the existing civic fabric of the National Mall and other surrounding structures (figure C.1). We note in our analysis that the building, with its Neoclassical elements and strong temple motif, looks as old as the buildings started over two hundred years ago. The conservatism for which Gilbert is criticized can also be seen as a wise architectural choice, that is, to not make the building's statement through its departure from the surrounding styles, but instead through its ability to reconcile the elements around it. By starting with the Maison Carrée as inspiration for the central part of the construction, and then crafting the office space surrounding the atriums and presenting them in a modest Stripped Deco design, he presents a building that complements the Capitol to the west and the Library of

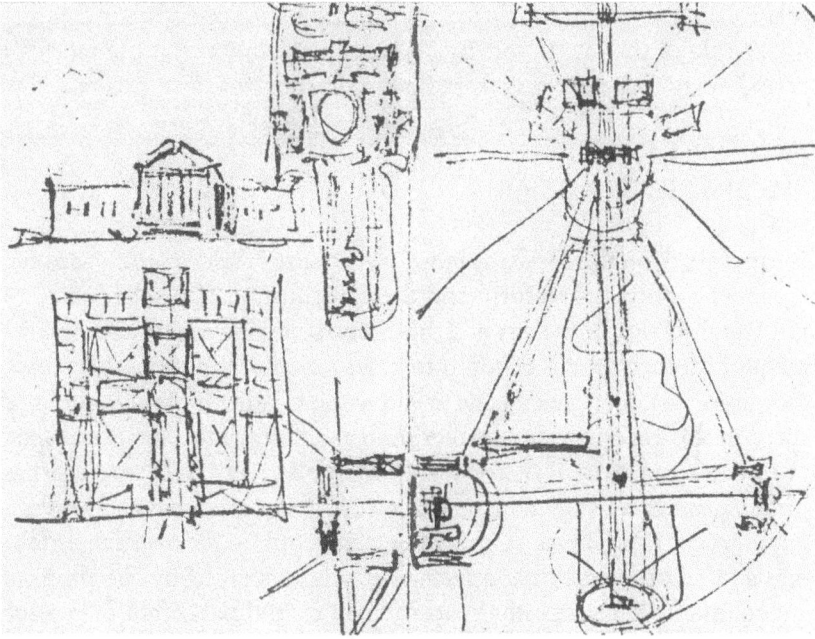

Figure C.2. Cass Gilbert's informal sketch of the Supreme Court Building and location. Cass Gilbert Papers, Library of Congress.

Congress to the south, and also emulates the horizontal elements of the Cannon House Office Building. A sense of the resolution as articulated by his own hand appears as figure C.2. This sketch, found in Gilbert's papers at the Library of Congress, shows the prominent face, aerial view, and relational placement of the building in a manner that makes these conflict resolutions quite plain.

The building stands out, with its height, powerful stairs, pediment, and columns. The court appears to rise slightly above the Capitol Building. This is an illusion, but the broad horizontal design of the Capitol and the vast eastern plaza and underground visitor's center deemphasize the rising steps beneath the dome. The Supreme Court Building, in contrast, is approached across a plaza with periodic elevation and a more prominent portico that emphasizes the front steps—the grand entry to the high court. Cass Gilbert's Neoclassical design was neither original nor on trend, but it wove into the cityscape seamlessly. As Greenberg (1987, 213) notes, "The exterior articulation of a courthouse and the relationship of the building to its surroundings expresses our concept of the role of the law in society." It is in this manner that the fabric of courthouses is given rich symbolic importance.

THE SPACES OF JUSTICE

Current work on the social meaning of civic space divides neatly between those who study urban form and the contribution of public spaces to the overall vitality of the city and those who study the design and arrangement of interior spaces devoted to governmental functions. When we look inside the court's home, we see how the treatment of judicial public space in this way provides a richer understanding of the social meaning of the court in American civic life. Goodsell (1987, 192) argues that "interior spaces may be more significant in affecting citizens and expressing political ideas, because it is in enclosed public rooms such as lobbies and auditoriums that citizens are fully embraced by the physical environment." These are the spaces where civic rituals often take place and where democratic deliberations actually happen. Because interior spaces are self-contained, Goodsell suggests that they normally provide "the most concentrated architectural statements of official values and ideas" (ibid.).

In chapters 4 and 5, we explored the types of civic spaces housed in the U.S. Supreme Court Building, including the important public protest spaces of the courthouse and its perimeter, which does project beyond its walls. Then we dissected the social meaning of the building as a temple of justice. Jackson (1987, 120) notes that "every traditional public space, whether religious or political or ethnic in character, displays a variety of symbols, inscriptions, images, monuments, not as works of art but to remind people of their civic privileges and duties—and tacitly to exclude the outsider. . . . The public space was not for relaxation or environmental awareness; it was for *civic* awareness." The symbols, inscriptions, and sculptures refer to history's lawgivers to illustrate the timeless nature of the law. The staging establishes for the observer the dignity of the rule of law and sanctifies the dispensation of justice provided in this place. The heavy curtain, the black robes, and the prohibition on photography as well as audio or video recording of court proceedings shrouds the activity of the court in mystique. It conveys a sacred space for the expansion of the Constitution to include all citizens, though it does so through the ritualistic practice of exclusion. Few see the justice for all.

These chapters use the U.S. Supreme Court to illustrate the social meaning of judicial space, but the analysis has implications for understanding the meaning of courthouses throughout the nation. Courtrooms showcase the crucial role of symbolism in architecture, with deliberately planned staging, seating, security, and ornamentation. These interior civic arenas reinforce the ritualized judicial process through highly formal court procedure. We have argued that courts are the original democratic institutions. We meet at the courthouse for conflict resolution, expecting to be treated with dignity and respect.

The architectural roots of the American courts in the original meetinghouses of the young colonies bespoke democracy. The courtrooms at the heart of these civic buildings interpret American values through a system of signs meant to communicate an idealized version of the relationship of the actors involved in the court's proceedings (Greenberg 1987, 210). Compared to other countries, the materialized relationship expresses the rights of the accused, according to Greenberg (ibid.). We have no dock to hold the person on trial. The accused sits with counsel, on par with the state as an actor in the proceedings. Greenberg (1987, 209–10) summarizes:

> The layout of a typical criminal courtroom in the United States differs markedly from courtrooms in other countries and reflects our unique system of justice. The American judge is an impartial arbiter and is therefore positioned on a raised podium in the center of the front of the room. Defense and prosecution are equal adversaries and, as such, are each provided with seats at assigned tables in the well of the courtroom facing the judge. The public are silent observers, sitting at the rear of the courtroom facing the judge. Their role is just as crucial as that of the other parties for, as silent arbiters, they influence the law through the political processes of election and legislation. The jury box is placed at the side of the room, deliberately divorced from the axial relationship of judge, counsel and public. This placement reflects the impartiality of the jurors, who must decide guilt or innocence. The witness box is located adjacent to the judge's bench facing the two parties. This provides the latter with their constitutional right to confront the opposing counsel's witness

DESIGNING JUSTICE

In chapter 6, we illustrate the theaters of justice checkering the American landscape, which represent diverse architectural styles. They speak to us in different symbolic languages. Drawing from Hubbard (1987), we can identify at least four means by which courthouses communicate to the public at large. At a basic level, these buildings can "denote the identity of the institution housed inside" (ibid., 129). On a different level, buildings can speak to the function of the institution. In the case of courts, the public space could use images of justice and law. The courthouse can present an ideology. "It can propose to us what this institution means (or wants to mean) to society" (ibid.). Finally, it can claim an aspiration that is separate from the current regime. Through its design, "the building talks not only about the role an institution plays in society, but also about how society itself ought ideally to be organized, the ideas which ought ideally to govern society's operation" (ibid., 130).

Every civic building represents a design solution to the problem of housing democratic processes. In this way, each building constitutes an idealized image of the political realm (Vale 1992, 277). The sponsoring government agency and the commissioned architects and designers determine what this image will look like. Consequently, it is our job to "analyze both ideals and their architectural depiction carefully" (ibid.).

Architects hold great power in designing justice in the city. They have a vast repertoire of forms and symbols from which to draw. In tracing Cass Gilbert's intention for the U.S. Supreme Court Building in chapters 4 and 5, we see the fruits of his imagination—his purposeful choice to speak in the language of Neoclassicism with reference to American Judeo-Christian heritage.

DEMOCRATIC POLITICS AND THE THEATER OF JUSTICE

Democracy is more than systems and structures. It is more than positive and negative rights. Democratic politics is deliberative and performative. Parkinson (2012, 23–24) suggests that "democracy is not merely the interplay of arguments and reasons in some abstract public sphere but is performed by people, with aims, on stages. This performative, dramaturgical understanding of democracy has roots in Classical understandings of politics." We concur, and it is in this spirit that we conclude that the American courthouse serves as *theater* for the democratic activities of witnessing, demonstrating, petitioning, arguing, persuading, and deciding (ibid.; see Young 2000, 16), and that the U.S. Supreme Court is the ultimate theater for conflict resolution in the American polis.

How does the high court manifest as democratic performance? Its proceedings include the four major roles of democratic performance: "narrating interests, opinion and experience; making public claims; deciding about those claims; and accounting for decisions and actions" (Parkinson 2012, 48). It provides a national, dignified single location for the public to petition the government. In this way, it facilitates focused scrutiny of the American political order (ibid., 66). Democratic theorists and scholars of rhetoric emphasize the role of the audience in the performances of democracy (ibid., 43; see Sauter 2000).

But there are limits to the audience's access to the Supreme Court. There are few recordings of the proceedings of the court and only one or two photographs of the justices sitting in session. There are no public records of the deliberations of the justices in the sacred Conference Room. What we know of these democratic performances is from audio recordings of oral arguments and scrutiny of court opinions and dissents once they have been released to the public at large. Secrecy shrouds deliberations of the high court, and there is little to no relationship of the court with public opinion. Ultimately, this dynamic might be the source of public trust in the institution relative to the other branches of the U.S. government. Consider the two primary questions Gallup asks of the American public to measure political trust of the judicial branch. When asked in the 1970s about trust and confidence in each of the three branches of government, approximately 65 percent of Americans expressed a great deal or fair amount of trust in the judicial branch. This number peaked in the late 1990s at approximately 80 percent. It has wavered between these two figures in the intervening decades. By contrast, the legislative branch has dropped from approximately 60 percent in the 1970s to 30 percent in more recent years (see Jones 2017).

We might ask why the Supreme Court makes public appearances at all. What would be lost if oral arguments took place in the elite spaces of the building? Is face-to-face presence actually important? We make the case throughout this book that the deliberative and performative nature of democratic politics requires a physical public space. Parkinson's (2012, 23) account of democracy argues that it takes seriously the "process of opinion formation and narration in the public square, and the ways in which public claims are transmitted to formal institutions for action." We agree. Oral arguments give litigants their "day in court."

The process of listening and clarifying the positions of each side in a case signals to every witness in the courtroom—the litigants, the members of the audience, and even the justices themselves—just where the fault lines lie.

THE TRANSFORMATIONAL IMPACT OF THE BUILDING

In *Architecture, Power, and National Identity*, Lawrence Vale (1992) considers the use of national capitals to establish and affirm the political legitimacy of the existing regime through urban design. Capitals can be categorized as evolved capitals, evolved capitals renewed, or new capitals. In the U.S. context, Washington, D.C., was designed from whole cloth. The strong axiality of the National Mall embodies Jefferson's hope and L'Enfant's vision for the capital city. Civic building for Jefferson provided the opportunity to make a promise in stone—a monumental commitment to uphold certain fundamental values. How does this commitment influence design? Glazer and Lilla (1987, 157) suggest that "all buildings should be seen as opportunities to build the city—as fragments of a covenant with the future." Public building serves a greater purpose than private building. It is the obligation of the architect and commissioning government to "include considerations of place, of the dignity of persons, and of the connection with a larger, more enduring order" (ibid., 158).

A consequence of Gilbert's design is to create something that was previously lacking in modern politics, namely, a visual source of identity for American justice. The Supreme Court Building achieved that by acting as a visual aid for the media and the public to identify the high court and justice. The building's iconic design is reflected in many district courthouses and local courthouses throughout the United States. Forced perspective photographs and drawings of the building emphasize the pediment and columns to create a soaring sense of the temple design. The effect is to evoke the powers, philosophy, and wisdom that are meant to accompany the concept of justice under the law. Such images often appear in print and broadcast stories and reinforce the relationship between the temple motif and law in the republic.

The influence on Gilbert of Classical architecture and also twentieth-century Italian architects from the fascist period provides a second important element, namely, the broad plaza to the west of the building between the front steps and First Street. The delimited space and close proximity of the front steps of the court create an important civic ritual space, with a backdrop that is more proximate than the White House and not as overwhelming in magnitude as the Capitol or the Mall. The oval plaza, nearly a football field in length, quickly turned into a prominent location for public demonstration, though Congress banned such protests on the oval proper in 1949. (This decision was found to not encroach on First Amendment rights in litigation sixty-five years later in a case before the D.C. Court of Appeals [see *Hodge v. Talkin*, 799 F. 3d 1145 (2015)]. The high court affirmed the finding without comment in a rare ruling that directly addressed an issue *of* the court.) Between the plaza and First Street is a sidewalk space nearly as large, which is regularly used for gathering, demonstration, and protest over issues before the court. It is a well-designed theater for civic action and protest.

Finally, while giving the justices an easily identified "home," the Supreme Court Building's design and the court's luddite approach to technology and privacy have allowed the "nine" to maintain their mystique. Before 1935, the court's mystique resided in the relative anonymity of being lost in the vastness of the Capitol, with no external perimeter and with the justices mainly working from home. The new building perpetuated the mystery in a different manner, by bringing the mystique of the temple to the high court. No cameras are allowed in the courtroom. Until recently, sound recordings of hearings were not released either. And the practice of justices giving interviews and doing conferences where there is regular media present is also relatively recent. So, unlike the president and the Congress, who regularly and almost gleefully perform for the cameras, the justices stay behind their walls in their stone temple, issuing opinions and writing the occasional article or book, mystics of the Constitution.

SOCIAL MEANING WHEN CONSIDERING THE COURT IN PLACE

Buildings hold social meaning. They frame our understanding of governmental processes, stage our civic engagement, and physically manifest that which is felt and thought: "Real places have a power over the mind because they are the locus of our actions; the events of our lives are connected with the settings in which they take place. Places take

Figure C.3. "Nettie Hunt explaining to her daughter Nikie the meaning of the high court's ruling in the *Brown v. Board of Education* case on the steps of the U.S. Supreme Court." Bettmann Archive via Getty Images.

on meanings through our participation in them. . . . Places matter to us because we come to care about them; we have a telling experience there" (Glazer and Lilla 1987, 157).

Why do we care about the Supreme Court as a real place? What are the telling experiences we have had there as a nation of liberty and justice for all? Perhaps no other image captures the American imagination more readily than the Corbis photograph taken on May 18, 1954, the day after the Supreme Court ruled on *Brown v. Board of Education of Topeka* (figure C.3). The photo is captioned "High Court Bans Segregation in Public Schools." It features a mother and daughter seated on the steps, framed by the temple façade of the U.S. Supreme Court Building. The image amplifies the original commitment made by the building to justice because it extends that commitment to Nettie and Nikie Hunt, individual citizens fighting for equal rights under the law regardless of race or ethnicity. The steps of the Supreme Court are the locus for their petition, and they become the locus of every final judicial petition in the decades that follow.

At the national level, the U.S. Supreme Court Building provides the architectural setting for *the ideal public square*. "It occupies the most prestigious location in the principal town and is surrounded by politically significant buildings" (Jackson 1987, 120). It neighbors the legislative assembly and associated staff office buildings, the old and new national libraries, the monumental avenue of national memorials, the train station, and the historic commercial district of Eastern Market. It has clear boundaries, upholds a written constitution, and has dedicated personnel. About the court, we can say, "It is here in the agora or forum that history is made visible and where speech becomes a political instrument, eloquence a form of political action" (ibid.). A critical reader might challenge the idea that the judiciary ideally is apolitical—impartial and nonpartisan. Here we use the term "political" to mean *of the polis*, in this case the nation. The U.S. Supreme Court decides matters of law, the impact of which concerns individual citizens and the political community as a whole. The home of the high court is the place we look to, to watch the story of the U.S. Constitution unfold.

A LAST THOUGHT: AFTER THE TEMPLES

The American republic has drawn on Classicism and Neoclassicism for much of its public architecture since the eighteenth century. But there has also been an evolution in the architecture of the public space. Indeed, public architecture has often reflected conventional yet contemporary tastes. In the wake of the Civil War, Second Empire style was popular in federal construction, so much so that it was termed "General Grant" architecture. The fall of France to Prussia led to the fall of its popularity. Competing influences took hold in architecture and made their way to public construction. And so, too, Modern, International, and Postmodern architecture have all been embraced in public construction throughout the post–World War II period.

Yet the temple endures in the presentation of American justice. But will this change? Will design and construction change with enduring evolutions of the needs of courts, of structural materials, of public tastes in architecture? Vale (1992, 278) asks the question, "Who decides which ideals are to be pursued" when determining the appropriate spatial form to convey a political ideal, while considering the current cultural pluralism? Charles Goodsell observes that "the links between architecture and politics are subtle and indirect, of course." Only in a totalitarian regime do we find dictated architectural styles. This does not mean that architects are freed from political influence. They participate in a society, one in which the politicians and consumers and architects experience the same range of political, cultural, and social tastes (see Goodsell 1987, 193).

A book is many things—the book the author thinks they wrote; the book the reader thinks they read; and the book as it was actually written. None are quite the same. Invoking Walt Whitman, Vale (199, 279) reminds us that "not the book but the reader need be the complete thing," so as to remind us that any work—a book, a painting, a song, a construction—requires the eye, the heart, and the body of the ordinary citizen to be fully appreciated. What has the architect of monumental civic buildings designed? The publics who encounter and use a public building therefore bring to us the final answer to the question. The artistic intent, the actual use, and the broader interpretation (what Goodsell [2000] terms the expressive, the behavioral, and the societal) all give social meaning to the final design. For this reason, the architect as artist must consider all of the competing publics and their needs to build a public building, or square, or capital city: "In the design of a capitol complex, there would seem to be two very different objectives at work. On the one hand, the complex is intended to advance the consolidation of political rule; on the other, it is expected to advance the cause of national unity. In many places, this implies a contradiction: the leaders want the capitol complex to symbolize the person or group holding power and, simultaneously, to represent the nation-state as a whole. It must symbolize both faction and state, both part and whole" (Vale 1992, 283).

So how does one achieve balance? One approach is abstraction, the stepping away from symbolism, design, and elements that are deemed too divisive, too political, too partial to one element of society at the expense of the feelings and values of others in the public. We can be certain that political decision makers with input on public spaces will shape these toward their tastes in some manner, if only because these legislative chambers, courtrooms, and hearing rooms are the stages of their political theaters (Goodsell 1987, 193).

It is important to remember that, once built, public buildings tend to stay, but as Vale (1992, 276) observes, their meanings "never remain static." Their impact on the user through their design and meaning can render them "good" buildings or "bad" buildings. This is at least in part a function of their qualities that cannot be named but are known and that manifest in good buildings through the application of good patterns. As Christopher Alexander (1979) observes, good patterns embody and make physical good values, which reside in the human heart and mind.

But events can change their meaning for a public. A crime scene takes on the quality of the crime. A place of triumph or accomplishment or the finding of true love takes on the qualities of those events. Sentiment does attach to place. Politics and public events will similarly define and redefine spaces through time. Cass Gilbert invoked the temple imagery of Neoclassicism to reference the great temples of the ancient world and the democratic and republican virtues of the Greek polis and Roman forum. Yet he could not know that within a decade of the building's construction, European dictators would use the same architectural language to frame a uniquely fascist style to provide the staging for monumental rallies and processions.

We asked whether the temple motif will persist as an American presentation of justice. The reality is that spaces of American courts have changed. New courthouses serve very different functions in dispensing justice. They are complexes, with the courts supported by a large administrative bureaucracy, and they are also dealing with heightened threats to the physical security of the courts themselves from both criminal and terrorist sources. And here we meet the challenge Vale (1992, 285) lays down for dealing with the placement of a capitol in capital design in general, the "contradictions of security: the capitol must be defendable yet appear to be open to the public." So, too, for the court; it must defend democracy and also defend itself. Can it be democratic and public yet also hardened and defensive?

How does this change our perceptions of courthouses and their designs? Perhaps it requires that we step away from the implicit assumption made of courthouses for nearly two hundred years, that these were easily accessible public venues wrapped in architectural symbols that embodied a majoritarian consensus about republican democracy. The architectural inflections toward abstraction and Modernism since the latter twentieth century strip away the familiar symbolism of the old majoritarian consensus. Nathan Glazer and Mark Lilla (1987, 215) observe in *The Public Face of Architecture: Civic Culture and Public Spaces* that "perhaps the most damning characteristic of many new courthouses is the lack of a coherent and symbolically significant relationship with the surrounding buildings and environment. The messages which these buildings communicate to the taxpaying public and attorneys, witnesses, jurors, and litigants in the courthouse are that their needs, both functional and psychological, do not warrant attention or expression."

Scale matters. Temples are daunting in their way, with the stairs and columns and legacy of the mythology of the Classical era as well as the infused symbols transmitted from Athenian democracy. But the temples pale compared to the soaring edifices of corporations that are embodied by skyscrapers. The movement of the courts toward the sky, toward greater perimeter control, toward crafting a complex that can house a judicial leviathan, creates a different world of awe that is disconnected from the romance of Classicism.

These changes might render Gilbert's courthouse to be the last institution of American democracy to be physically defined by the old republicanism of Classical architecture. For this reason, we devote so much attention to the ways it carries meaning. We interrogate the heritage of the American *courthouse*, the symbolic and referential meaning it carries, and the ways in which it provides a critical democratic public space prioritizing the rights of the individual. In so doing, we pave a way for intentional and rigorous examination of future sites of American justice as intentional community buildings with significant social meaning. We lay out a roadmap for comparative work on the portrayal of justice in facilities around the world. And we make an argument for the application of diverse theoretical frameworks, including those provided by architecture, to the range of physical structures that house democratic politics. Legislative assemblies, city council chambers, meeting halls, civic auditoriums, and public plazas all serve a vital function in supporting political behavior. Our politics could not happen without them. The U.S. Supreme Court Building stands as a remarkable example of a temple to "equal justice under law," but it is just one example among many in the American republic. May we protect those edifices that reflect who we want to be as a people and seriously question those that fail to do so.

There is one last question to answer: Did Cass Gilbert design a good building? His style for the Supreme Court Building did not reflect the emergent Modernism of the times; it did use the evolving styles that were expanding on Neoclassicism to provide an appropriate cultural metaphor. It has an elegant professional space in the "back of house" where the work is done, and it also enjoys grandeur, intimacy, and good circulation in all of its realms. There is necessary differentiation of space to facilitate the various responsibilities of the users, timeless symbolism elevating crucial philosophical principles, and good articulation with its architectural neighbors.

When we most recently looked at the building in Washington, we concluded that it is probably more exposed and less autonomous than originally intended, but this is not the building's fault. In creating this building, Gilbert met a key goal of successful architecture, to resolve a problem through design. The court was given a sense of institutional place and prominence it might not have attained in Judiciary Square, and the public was given a place to engage the Supreme Court not just in its judicial function but also as a historical and cultural institution, an object of protest, and as an icon for the Enlightenment heritage of courts as a repository of democratic practice.

Notes

NOTES TO CHAPTER 1

1. The Neoclassical Pentagon (1940) and the Brutalist-style FBI Building (1974) are among the newer, similarly high-profile structures. The high court's home is one of the last Neoclassical structures proximate to the National Mall, along with the National Portrait Gallery.

2. Adam Przeworski (1999, 24) observes that in "perusing innumerable definitions, one discovers that democracy has become an altar on which everyone hangs his or her favorite *ex voto*."

NOTES TO CHAPTER 4

1. Goodsell traces the literature related to public space in his (2003) work "The Concept of Public Space and Its Democratic Manifestations." See, in particular, his discussion of Hannah Arendt and Jürgen Habermas on the importance placed on openness of public space for healthy democratic politics (ibid., 362).

2. In drawing upon Aristotle's analogy, Brigham references page 99 of Ernest Barker's (1995) translation of *The Politics of Aristotle* published by Oxford University Press.

3. Similar doors lead into the U.S. Capitol Building. Maroon and Maroon (1996) suggest that the Columbus Doors of the Capitol "undoubtedly inspired" Gilbert, who worked with John Donnelly Jr. to design the doors (see p. 38).

4. As further evidence of the Supreme Court's conservative traditions, proposals to rename the Ladies' Dining Room as the "Spouses' Dining Room" after the appointment of Sandra Day O'Connor have been rejected (Maroon and Maroon 1996, 79).

NOTES TO CHAPTER 5

1. Perry cites Segal and Spaeth (1993) and Epstein and Knight (1998) as influential works serving to define the scholarship on judges as political actors and the judiciary as a political institution. The quoted text Perry introduces here is from Hinckley (1990, 4–7).

2. A curious reader might ask how a lens is different from a pattern. To differentiate, a lens is a theory or perspective through which the empirical world is observed. A pattern is an empirically observed physical feature of the built environment that can contain or reflect the values and perspectives articulated in a lens.

3. See the correspondence written by Rush to Elias Boudinot on July 9, 1788, in Rush ([1788] 1951, 1:475).

4. Mason provides the following source: American Bar Association (1879), *Report of the Second Annual Meeting*, Saratoga Springs, New York, August 1878, 190.

5. For a wonderful analysis of the contested meaning of Justice blindfolded, see Resnik and Curtis (2011, 62–105).

6. Beale (2004) provides an extensive overview of authorities that bolster this claim.

7. For example, though oral arguments are now recorded and made available to the public at large, cameras are strictly prohibited from the courtroom during sessions.

8. Perry (1999) takes this descriptive phrase from a critique of judicial robes launched by the federal judge Jerome Frank. He thought the dress painted an unrealistic view of the source of judicial wisdom as divine. Frank, according to Perry, felt this image conveyed to the public the message that the personal attitudes of judges were totally unrelated to judicial decision-making (see endnote 9 of Perry's analysis).

NOTES TO CHAPTER 6

1. The literature on the New Deal is voluminous. We direct readers to one of the earliest and most expansive works looking at the 1920s and the Roosevelt years, the Pulitzer Prize-winning *Age of Roosevelt* series by Arthur M. Schlesinger Jr.

2. The story of the creation of West Virginia is nicely told in Wittenberg, Sargus Jr., and Barrick, *Seceding from Secession: The Civil War, Politics, and the Creation of West Virginia.*

References

Alejandro, Roberto. 1993. *Hermeneutics, Citizenship, and the Public Sphere.* Albany: State University of New York Press.

Alexander, Christopher. 1979. *The Timeless Way of Building.* New York: Oxford University Press.

Alexander, Christopher, Sara Ishikawa, Murray Silverstein, with Max Jacobson, Ingrid Fiksdahl-King, and Shlomo Angel. 1977. *A Pattern Language: Towns, Buildings, Construction.* New York: Oxford University Press.

Alexander, Christopher, Hajo Neis, Artemis Anninou, and Ingrid King. 1987. *A New Theory of Urban Design.* New York: Oxford University Press.

Alexander, Christopher, Murray Silverstein, Shlomo Angel, Sara Ishikawa, and Denny Abrams. 1975. *The Oregon Experiment.* New York: Oxford University Press.

Allen, William C. 2001. *History of the United States Capitol: A Chronicle of Design, Construction, and Politics.* Washington, DC: Government Printing Office.

Ambrose, Stephen E. 2000. *Nothing Like It in the World: The Men Who Built the Transcontinental Railroad 1863–1869.* New York: Simon and Schuster.

Ameri, Amir H. 1997. "Housing Ideologies in the New England and Chesapeake Bay Colonies, c. 1650–1700." *Journal of the Society of Architectural Historians* 56 (1): 6–15.

American Bar Association. 1879. *Report of the Second Annual Meeting,* Saratoga Springs, New York, August 1878, 190. Philadelphia: George S. Harris and Sons.

The American Heritage Dictionary. 2001. 4th ed. (21st Century Reference). New York: Houghton Mifflin.

American Institute of Architects. 1903. *Proceedings of the 37th Annual Convention of the American Institute of Architects, October 15, 16, and 17, 1903.* Washington, D.C.: Gibson Brothers.

———. 1972. "Code for Architectural Design Competitions." AIA Document J331, December, p. 2.

Anthony, Kathryn H. 1987. "Private Reactions to Public Criticism: Students, Faculty, and Practicing Architects State Their Views on Design Juries in Architectural Education." *Journal of Architectural Education* 40 (3): 2–11.

Arendt, Hannah. 1958. *The Human Condition.* Chicago: University of Chicago Press.

———. 1972. *Crises of the Republic: Lying in Politics, Civil Disobedience, On Violence, Thoughts on Politics and Revolution.* New York: Harcourt Brace Jovanovich.

Arkes, Hadley. 2007. "Building Democracy." A review of *Architecture of Democracy: American Architecture and the Legacy of the Revolution*, by Allan Greenberg. Claremont Institute. *Claremont Review of Books* 7 (3). Accessed on May 7, 2012. https://claremontreviewofbooks.com/building-democracy/.

Baedeker, Karl, ed. 1885. *Egypt: Handbook for Travellers, Part First, Lower Egypt, with the Fayum and the Peninsula of Sinai.* Leipzig, Germany: Karl Baedeker.

Barker, Ernest, ed. and trans. 1995. *The Politics of Aristotle.* Oxford: Oxford University Press.

Barnhart, Robert K., ed. 1988. *The Barnhart Dictionary of Etymology.* Bronx, NY: H. W. Wilson.

Beale, Gregory K. 2004. *The Temple and the Church's Mission: A Biblical Theology of the Dwelling Place of God.* Downers Grove, IL: InterVarsity Press.

Belting, Hans. 1987. "Vasari and His Legacy: The History of Art as Process?" In *The End of the History of Art?*, 79–80. Translated by Christopher Wood. Chicago: University of Chicago Press.

Benjamin, Asher. (1806) 1816. *The American Builder's Companion.* Boston: R. P. and C. Williams.

Bergman, Paul, and Michael Asimow. 2013. *Reel Justice: The Courtroom Goes to the Movies.* Kansas City, MO: Andrews McMeel.

Blavatsky, Helena Petrovna. 1888. *La Doctrina Secreta, síntesis de ciencia, religión y filosofía.* Point Loma, CA: Theosophical University Press.

Blodgett, Geoffrey. 1985. "Cass Gilbert, Architect: Conservative at Bay." *Journal of American History* 72 (3): 615–36.

Brand, Stewart. 1994. *How Buildings Learn: What Happens After They're Built.* New York: Viking Penguin.

Brigham, John. 1987. *The Cult of the Court.* Philadelphia: Temple University Press.

———. 1994. "Exploring the Attic: Courts and Communities in Material Life." In *Courts, Tribunals, and New Approaches to Justice*, edited by Oliver Mendelsohn and Laurence Maher, 131–55. Melbourne: La Trobe University Press.

———. 2009. *Material Law: A Jurisprudence of What's Real.* Philadelphia, PA: Temple University Press.

Burke, Edmund. 1967. *The Correspondence of Edmund Burke.* Vol. 6. Edited by Alfred Cobban and Robert A. Smith. Chicago: University of Chicago Press.

Busey, Samuel Clagett. 1898. *Pictures of the City of Washington in the Past*. Washington, DC: William Ballantyne and Sons.

Byard, Paul Spencer. 2001. "Representing American Justice: The United States Supreme Court." In *Cass Gilbert, Life and Work: Architect of the Public Domain*, edited by Barbara Christen and Steven Flanders, 272–88. New York: W. W. Norton.

Calabresi, Steven G. 2006. "'A Shining City on a Hill': American Exceptionalism and the Supreme Court's Practice of Relying on Foreign Law." *Boston University Law Review* 86: 1334–1416.

Chantrell, Glynnis, ed. 2002. *The Oxford Dictionary of Word Histories*. New York: Oxford University Press.

Cheyne, Thomas Kelly, and John Sutherland Black, eds. 1902. *Encyclopaedia Biblica: A Critical Dictionary of the Literary, Political and Religious History, the Archaeology, Geography and Natural History of the Bible*. Toronto: George N. Morang.

Christen, Barbara S., and Steven Flanders. 2001. *Cass Gilbert, Life and Work: Architect of the Public Domain*. New York: W. W. Norton.

Congressional Record. 1940. Vol. 86. Proceedings and Debates of the 76th Congress, Third Session. Washington, DC: Government Printing Office.

"Courtroom Friezes: East and West Walls." Office of the Curator of the United States Supreme Court. Accessed March 29, 2012. https://www.supreme -court.gov/about/eastandwestwalls.pdf.

"Courtroom Friezes: South and North Walls." Office of the Curator of the United States Supreme Court. Accessed March 29, 2012. https://www.supreme -court.gov/about/northandsouthwalls.pdf.

Craig, Lois A. 1978. *The Federal Presence: Architecture, Politics, and Symbols in United States Government Building*. Cambridge, MA: MIT Press.

C-SPAN. 2011. "East and West Conference Rooms." Accessed December 22, 2011. http://supremecourt.c-span.org/Video/VirtualTour/SC_VT _EastWestConferenceRoom.aspx.

Donnelly, Marian Card. 1968. *The New England Meeting Houses of the Seventeenth Century*. Middletown, CT: Wesleyan University Press.

"Early American Imprints, Series I: Evans, 1639–1800." Archive of Americana. Readex: A Division of NewsBank. https://www.readex.com/products /early-american-imprints-series-i-evans-1639-1800.

Easton, David. 1957. "An Approach to the Analysis of Political Systems." *World Politics* 9 (3): 383–400.

———. 1965a. *A Framework for Political Analysis*. Englewood Cliffs, NJ: Prentice-Hall.

———. 1965b. *A Systems Analysis of Political Life*. New York: John Wiley.

Easton, Matthew George. (1897) 2007. *The Bible Dictionary: Your Biblical Reference Book*. London: Forgotten Books.

Edelman, Murray. 1985. *The Symbolic Uses of Politics*. 2nd ed. Champaign-Urbana: University of Illinois Press.

————. 1995. *From Art to Politics: How Artistic Creations Shape Political Conceptions*. Chicago: University of Chicago Press.

Ehrenberg, Victor. 1950. "Origins of Democracy." *Historia: Zeitschrift für Alte Geschichte* 1 (4): 515–48.

Encyclopaedia Britannica. 2012. Accessed May 7, 2012. http://www.britannica.com/EBchecked/topic/146847/curia.

Epstein, Lee, and Jack Knight. 1998. *The Choices Justices Make*. Washington, DC: CQ Press, Congressional Quarterly.

Erickson, Hal. 2009. *Encyclopedia of Television Law Shows: Factual and Fictional Series about Judges, Lawyers and the Courtroom, 1948–2008*. Jefferson, NC: McFarland.

"Exterior Portrait Medallions and The Great Hall Metopes." Office of the Curator of the Supreme Court Building of the United States. Accessed March 29, 2012. https://www.supremecourt.gov/about/medallionsandmetopes.pdf.

Fairchild, Erika. 1993. *Comparative Criminal Justice Systems*. Belmont, CA: Wadsworth.

Finnestad, Ragnhild B. 1997. "Temples of the Ptolemaic and Roman Periods: Ancient Traditions in New Contexts." In *Temples of Ancient Egypt*, edited by Byron E. Shafer, 185–237. Ithaca, NY: Cornell University Press.

Flanders, Steven. 2001. "Preface." In *Cass Gilbert, Life and Work: Architect of the Public Domain*, edited by Barbara Christen and Steven Flanders, 9–14. New York: W. W. Norton.

Foner, Eric. 2019. *The Second Founding: How the Civil War and Reconstruction Remade the Constitution*. New York: Simon and Schuster.

Francis, Jacinta, Billie Gillis-Corti, Lisa Wood, and Matthew Knuiman. 2012. "Creating a Sense of Community: The Role of Public Space." *Journal of Environmental Psychology* 34 (4): 401–9.

Francis, Mark. 1982. "Reflections on Community Design." Paper presented at the National Conference on Participatory Design in Low Income Communities, American Institute of Architects, Washington, DC.

Friedrich, Thomas. 2012. *Hitler's Berlin: Abused City*. New Haven, CT: Yale University Press.

Gall, George H. 1913. *Improvement of the Park System of the District of Columbia. I. Report of the Senate Committee on the District of Columbia. II. Report of the Park Commission*. Abridgment of Senate Report No. 166, 57th Congress, 1st sess. Washington, D.C.: Issue 16 of Senate document; Issue 6535 of U.S. congressional serial set.

Garfield, James A. 1880. "Obedience to the Law of the Foremost Duty of Congress." Speech delivered on March 17, 1880. Accessed March 27, 2012. http://archive.org/stream/obediencetolawof00garf/obediencetolawof00garf_djvu.txt.

Gargola, Daniel J. 1995. *Lands, Laws, and Gods: Magistrates and Ceremony in the Regulation of Public Lands in Republican Rome*. Chapel Hill: University of North Carolina Press.

Gay, Peter. 1968. "The Enlightenment." In *The Comparative Approach to American History*, edited by C. Vann Woodward, 34–46. New York: Oxford.

Gerring, John. 1998. *Party Ideologies in America, 1828–1996*. New York: Cambridge University Press.

Gibson, James L., Gregory A. Caldeira, and Vanessa A. Baird. 1998. "On the Legitimacy of National High Courts." *American Political Science Review* 92 (2): 343–58.

Gilbert, Cass. 1927. Cass Gilbert to Bacon, July 25, 1927. Box 12, Gilbert Papers, Library of Congress.

———. 1929. Diary, entry dated December 10, 1929. Box 13, Gilbert Papers, Library of Congress.

———. 1933. Cass Gilbert to George Squire, November 13, 1933. Box 14, Gilbert Papers, Library of Congress.

Gilbert, Frank. 2012. "Justice Brandeis's Opposition to the New Supreme Court Building in 1935." Interview with C-SPAN. Accessed March 27, 2012. http://supremecourt.c-span.org/Video/Historians/SC_HIST_FrankG_02.aspx.

Glancey, Jonathan. 2000. *The Story of Architecture*. London: Dorling Kindersley.

Glazer, Nathan, and Mark Lilla, eds. 1987. *The Public Face of Architecture: Civic Culture and Public Spaces*. London: Free Press.

Goodman, Nelson. 1985. "How Buildings Mean." *Critical Inquiry* 11 (4): 642–53.

Goodsell, Charles. 1987. "The City Council Chamber: From Distance to Intimacy." In *The Public Face of Architecture: Civic Culture and Public Spaces*, edited by Nathan Glazer and Mark Lilla, 192–208. London: Free Press.

———. 1988. *The Social Meaning of Civic Space: Studying Political Authority through Architecture*. Lawrence: University Press of Kansas.

———. 1998. "The Statehouse: Elite Space in Conflict." *Journal of Architectural and Planning Research* 15 (1): 6–23.

———. 2001. *The American Statehouse: Interpreting Democracy's Temples*. Lawrence: University Press of Kansas.

———. 2003. "The Concept of Public Space and Its Democratic Manifestations." *American Review of Public Administration* 33 (4): 361–83.

Grana, Sheryl J., and Jane C. Ollenburger. 1999. *The Social Context of Law*. Upper Saddle River, NJ: Prentice Hall.

Gray, Camilla. 1962. *The Great Experiment: Russian Art 1863–1922*. New York: Abrams.

Green, Cedric. 1979. "Playing Design Games." *Journal of Architectural Education* 33 (1): 22–26.

Greenberg, Allan. 1987. "Symbolism in Architecture: Courtrooms." In *The Public Face of Architecture: Civic Culture and Public Spaces*, edited by Nathan Glazer and Mark Lilla, 209–18. London: Free Press.

———. 2006. *Architecture of Democracy: American Architecture and the Legacy of the Revolution*. New York: Rizzoli.

Grossman, Elizabeth G. 1986. "Two Postwar Competitions: The Nebraska State Capitol and the Kansas City Liberty Memorial." *Journal of the Society of Architectural Historians* 45 (3): 244–69.

Grossman, Nerit. 2015/2019. "Just Looking: Justice as Seen in Hollywood Court-room Films." *Law, Culture, and the Humanities* 15: 62–105.

Guénoun, Solange, James H. Kavanagh, and Roxanne Lapidus. 2000. "Jacques Rancière: Literature, Politics, Aesthetics: Approaches to Democratic Disagreement." *SubStance* 29 (2): 3–24.

Habermas, Jürgen. 1964. "The Public Sphere: An Encyclopedia Article." Translated by Sara Lennox and Frank Lennox. *New German Critique* 3 (Autumn 1974): 49–55.

Hadingham, Evan. 2008. "Unlocking Mysteries of the Parthenon: Restoration of the 2,500-Year-Old Temple Is Yielding New Insights into the Engineering Feats of the Golden Age's Master Builders." *Smithsonian Magazine*. Accessed March 29, 2012. https://www.smithsonianmag.com/history/unlocking -mysteries-of-the-parthenon-16621015/.

Hallas, Maria, and Jimm Phillips. September 2011. "A Missed Target, 10 Years Later—the U.S. Capitol." *American Observer*. Accessed March 18, 2017. http://wp11.americanobserver.net/2011/09/a-missed-target-10-years -later-the-u-s-capitol/.

Hamilton, Alexander. 2003. "Federalist No. 78." In *The Federalist Papers*, edited by Clinton Rossiter, 463–471. New York, NY: Penguin Books.

Haran, Menahem. 1978. *Temples and Temple Service in Ancient Israel*. Oxford: Clarendon.

Harding, Warren G. 1920. "Americanism." Speech delivered on January 10, 1920. Accessed January 15, 2021. https://millercenter.org/the-presidency /presidential-speeches/january-20-1920-americanism.

Hartog, Hendrik. 1981. "Distancing Oneself from the Eighteenth Century: A Commentary on Changing Pictures of American Legal History." In *The Law in the American Revolution and the Revolution in the Law: A Collection of Review Essays on American Legal History*, edited by Hendrik Hartog, 229–57. New York: New York University Press.

Haviland, John. 1818. *The Builder's Assistant*. Philadelphia: John Bioren.

"Heightened Security Changes D.C. Atmosphere." 2004. *PBS Newshour* (August 6). Accessed March 18, 2017. http://www.pbs.org/newshour/bb/terrorism-july -dec04-security_8-6/.

Herrtage, Sydney J. H., and Henry B. Wheatley, with the Camden Society (Great Britain). (1882) 1987. *Catholicon Anglicum, an English-Latin Wordbook, Dated 1483*. Edited and with an introduction and notes by S. J. H. Herrtage [and] with a preface by H. B. Wheatley. London: N. Trübner.

Hibbing, John R., and Elizabeth Theiss-Morse. 1995. *Congress as Public Enemy: Public Attitudes toward American Political Institutions*. New York: Cambridge University Press.

Hinckley, Barbara. 1990. *The Symbolic Presidency: How Presidents Portray Themselves*. New York: Routledge.

Hodak, George. 2011. "February 2, 1790: Supreme Courts Holds Inaugural Session." *ABA Journal.* February 1. https://www.abajournal.com/magazine/article /february_2_1790_supreme_court_holds_inaugural_session.

Hoffer, Peter Charles. 1992. *Law and People in Colonial America.* Baltimore, MD: Johns Hopkins University Press.

"Homes of the Court." N.d. The Supreme Court Historical Society, History of the Court. Accessed March 27, 2012. http://supremecourthistory.org/history -of-the-court-homes-of-the-court/.

"House of Commons Rebuilding." 1943. House of Commons Debates, October 28, 1943, Vol. 393. http://hansard.millbanksystems.com/commons/1943/oct /28/house-of-commons-rebuilding.

Howe, Samuel. 1917. "A New York Court House: A Court Encloses an Ancient Temple or Church." *The Art World* 2 (6): 541–44.

Hubbard, William. 1987. "A Meaning for Monuments." In *The Public Face of Architecture: Civic Culture and Public Spaces,* edited by Nathan Glazer and Mark Lilla, 124–41. London: Free Press.

Hurwit, Jeffrey. 2007. "The Glorious Parthenon." Interview conducted by Gary Glassman and edited by Susan K. Lewis. Accessed March 26, 2012. http:// www.pbs.org/wgbh/nova/ancient/glorious-parthenon.html.

Ickes, Harold L. 1935. *Back to Work: The Story of PWA.* London: Forgotten Books.

"Illustrated Chronology of the Capitol Shootings." 1998. *Washington Post.* Accessed March 19, 2017. https://www.washingtonpost.com/wp-srv/national/longterm /shooting/stories/chrono072598.htm.

Jackson, Anthony. 1965. "The Politics of Architecture: English Architecture 1929–1951." *Journal of the Society of Architectural Historians* 24 (1): 97–107.

Jackson, J. B. 1987. "Forum Follows Function." In *The Public Face of Architecture: Civic Culture and Public Spaces,* edited by Nathan Glazer and Mark Lilla, 117–23. London: Free Press.

Jacobs, Dennis. 2001. "Postscript." In *Cass Gilbert, Life and Work: Architect of the Public Domain,* edited by Barbara Christen and Steven Flanders, 289–92. New York: W. W. Norton.

Jones, Jeffrey M. 2017. "Trust in Judicial Branch Up, Executive Branch Down." *Gallup* (September 20). Accessed December 6, 2019. https://news.gallup .com/poll/219674/trust-judicial-branch-executive-branch-down.aspx.

Jones, Kay Bea, and Stephanie Pilat, eds. 2020. *The Routledge Companion to Italian Fascist Architecture: Reception and Legacy.* New York: Routledge.

Judicial Conference of the United States. 2007. "U.S. Courts Design Guide." Accessed January 16, 2021. https://www.gsa.gov/cdnstatic/Courts_Design_Guide_07.pdf.

Kammen, Michael. 1992. "Temples of Justice: The Iconography of Judgment and American Culture." In *Origins of the Federal Judiciary: Essays of the Judiciary Act of 1789,* edited by Maeva Marcus, 248–80. New York: Oxford University Press.

———. 2006. *A Machine That Would Go of Itself: The Constitution in American Culture*. New Brunswick, NJ: Transaction Publishers.

Keffer, Kathleen A. 2011. "Choosing a Law to Live by Once the King Is Gone." *Regent University Law Review* 24 (1): 147–68.

Kimball, Thomas. 1920. "The Opening Address of President Kimball at the Inter-Professional Conference in Detroit." *Journal A.I.A.* 8: 6.

"King William County Courthouse." 2021. Virginia Department of Historic Resources. Accessed January 15, 2021. https://www.dhr.virginia.gov/historic-registers /050-0038/#:~:text=King%20William%20County's%20courthouse%20is ,oldest%20courthouse%20in%20continuous%20use.

Klein, Ernest. 1966. *A Comprehensive Etymological Dictionary of the English Language: Volume I, A–K*. New York: Elsevier.

Kohler, Sue, and Pamela Scott, eds. 2006. *Designing the Nation's Capital: The 1901 Plan for Washington, D.C.* Washington, D.C.: U.S. Commission of Fine Arts. https://www.nps.gov/parkhistory/online_books/ncr/designing-capital/plates .html.

Labaree, Benjamin W. 1962. "New England Town Meeting." *American Archivist* 25 (2): 165–72.

Lafever, Minard. 1835. *Beauties of Modern Architecture*. New York: D. Appleton.

Lamb, Martha Joanna. 1881. *History of the City of New York*. Vol. 2. New York: A. S. Barnes.

Laster, Kathy, Krista Breckweg, and John King. 2000. *The Drama of the Courtroom*. Alexandria, NSW, Australia: Federation Press.

Lipstadt, Hélène 1989a. "The Experimental Tradition." In *The Experimental Tradition: Essays on Competitions in Architecture*, edited by Hélène Lipstadt, 9–19. New York: Princeton Architectural Press.

———, ed. 1989b. *The Experimental Tradition: Essays on Competitions in Architecture*. New York: Princeton Architectural Press.

Lockyer, J. Norman. 1894. *The Dawn of Astronomy: A Study of Temple Worship and Mythology of the Ancient Egyptians*. New York: MacMillan.

Lounsbury, Carl. 2006. "God Is in the Details: The Transformation of Ecclesiastical Architecture in Early Nineteenth-Century America." *Perspectives in Vernacular Architecture* 13 (1): 1–21.

Lubetkin, Berthold. 1932. "Architectural Thought Since the Revolution." *Architectural Review* 71: 201.

Lynch, Kevin. 1960. *The Image of the City*. Cambridge, MA: MIT Press.

Lyndon, Donlyn. 1987. "Public Buildings: Symbols Qualified by Experience." In *The Public Face of Architecture: Civic Culture and Public Spaces*, edited by Nathan Glazer and Mark Lilla, 155–76. London: Free Press.

Machura, Stefan. 2007. "Ansehensverlust der Justiz? Licht und Schatten des Gerichts-showkonsums." In *Im Namen des Fernsehvolkes. Neue Formate für Orientierung und Bewertung*, edited by K. Döveling, L. Mikow, and J-U Nieland, 93–101. Konstanz, Germany: UVK.

Mann, Bruce H. 1984. "The Formalization of Informal Law: Arbitration before the American Revolution." *New York University Law Review* 59 (3): 443–81.

———. 1986. "Law, Legalism, and Community before the American Revolution." *Michigan Law Review* 84 (7): 1415–39.

Markus, Thomas A. 1993. *Buildings and Power: Freedom and Control in the Origin of Modern Building Types.* London: Routledge.

Maroon, Fred J., and Suzy Maroon. 1996. *The Supreme Court of the United States.* West Palm Beach: Lickle.

Mason, Alpheus Thomas. 1991. *The Supreme Court: From Taft to Burger.* 3rd ed. Baton Rouge: Louisiana State University Press.

Massachusetts, Massachusetts General Court. 1814. *The Charters and General Laws of the Colony and Province of Massachusetts Bay.* Boston: T. B. Wait.

McDonough, Tom. 2001. "The Surface as Stake: A Postscript to Timothy M. Rohan's 'Rendering the Surface.'" *Grey Room* 5: 102–11.

McNamara, Martha J. 2004. *From Tavern to Courthouse: Architecture and Ritual in American Law, 1658–1860.* Baltimore, MD: Johns Hopkins University Press.

Meyer, Jeffrey F. 2001. *Myths in Stone: Religious Dimensions of Washington, D.C.* Berkeley: University of California Press.

Millard, Catherine. 1991. *The Rewriting of America's History.* New York: Christian.

Mitchell, Katharyne. 1997. "Conflicting Geographies of Democracy and the Public Sphere in Vancouver B.C." *Transactions of the Institute of British Geographers* 22 (2): 162–79.

Montesquieu, Charles de Secondat. 1968. *Considerations on the Causes of the Greatness of the Romans and Their Decline.* Translated by David Lowenthal. Ithaca, NY: Cornell University Press.

Moore, Charles, ed. 1902. "The Improvement of the Park System of the District of Columbia." Washington, DC: Government Printing Office. Accessed March 26, 2012. https://www.loc.gov/item/02026044/.

Morgan, Gwenda. 1986. "Review: Community and Authority in the Eighteenth-Century South: Tidewater, Southside and Backcountry." *Journal of American Studies* 20 (3): 435–48.

Morris, William A. 1929. "The Lesser Curia Regis under the First Two Norman Kings of England." *American Historical Review* 34 (4): 772–78.

Mullan, David George. 2000. *Scottish Puritanism, 1590–1638.* Oxford: Oxford University Press.

National Register of Historic Places. 1988. Independence National Historic Park, Philadelphia County, Pennsylvania, National Register #66000683.

Neils, Jenifer. 1999. "Reconfiguring the Gods on the Parthenon Frieze." *Art Bulletin* 81 (1): 6–20.

Ober, Josiah. 1996. *The Athenian Revolution: Essays on Ancient Greek Democracy and Political Theory.* Princeton, NJ: Princeton University Press.

Official Congressional Directory, 105th Congress 1997–1998. 1997. Washington, D.C.: Government Printing Office.

"The Old Senate Chamber, 1810–1859." United States Senate. Accessed January 16, 2021. https://www.senate.gov/artandhistory/art/resources/pdf/Old_Senate _Chamber.pdf.

Owusu, Heike. 2000. *Egyptian Symbols.* Toronto: Sterling.

Parkinson, John R. 2012. *Democracy and Public Space: The Physical Sites of Democratic Performance.* New York: Oxford University Press.

Perry, Barbara A. 1999. *The Priestly Tribe: The Supreme Court's Image in the American Mind.* New York: Praeger.

———. 2001. "The Israeli and United States Supreme Courts: A Comparative Reflection on Their Symbols, Images, and Functions." *Review of Politics* 63 (2): 317–40.

———. 2002. "'The Cult of the Robe': The U.S. Supreme Court in the American Mind." *Social Education* 66 (1): 30–33.

Phillips, Todd S., and Michael A. Griebel. 2003. *Building Type Basics for Justice Facilities.* Hoboken, NJ: John Wiley and Sons.

Przeworski, Adam. 1999. "Minimalist Conception of Democracy: A Defense." In *Democracy's Value,* edited by Ian Shapiro and Casiano Hacker-Cordón, 23–55. Cambridge: Cambridge University Press.

Rapoport, Amos. 1969. *House, Form, and Culture.* Englewood Cliffs, NJ: Prentice Hall.

"Regulations and Program for the Ames City Hall Competition." 1967. AIA Archives RG 802, p. 13. Published results in "Commission by Competition." *Iowa Architect,* n.d.

Resnik, Judith, and Dennis Curtis. 2011. *Representing Justice: Invention, Controversy, and Rights in City-States and Democratic Courtrooms.* New Haven, CT: Yale University Press.

———. 2013. "Inventing Democratic Courts: A New and Iconic Supreme Court." *Journal of Supreme Court History* 38 (2): 207–79.

Richards, J. M. 1937. "The Condition of Architecture and the Principle of Anonymity." In *Circle: International Survey of Constructive Art,* edited by Leslie Martin, Ben Nicholson, and Naum Gabo, 184–89. London: Faber and Faber.

Richardson, Elliot L. 1951. "Freedom of Expression and the Function of Courts." *Harvard Law Review* 65 (1): 1–54.

Rodgers, Paul. 2011. *United States Constitutional Law: An Introduction.* Jefferson, NC: McFarland.

Roeber, A. G. 1980. "Authority, Law, and Custom: The Rituals of Court Day in Tidewater Virginia, 1720–1750." *William and Mary Quarterly* 37 (1): 29–52.

———. 1981. *Faithful Magistrates and Republican Lawyers: Creators of Virginia Legal Culture, 1680–1810.* Chapel Hill: University of North Carolina Press.

Rosenberg, Norman. 1994. "Hollywood on Trials: Courts and Films, 1930–1960." *Law and History Review* 12: 341–67.

Ross, Richard J. 1993. "The Legal Past of Early New England: Notes for the Study of Law, Legal Culture, and Intellectual History." *William and Mary Quarterly* 50 (1): 28–41.

Rush, Benjamin. (1788) 1951. "Letter to Elias Boudinot, July 9, 1788." In *Letters of Benjamin Rush*, edited by L. H. Butterfield. Princeton, NJ: American Philosophical Society.

Rush, George E. 1994. *The Dictionary of Criminal Justice*. 4th ed. Guilford, CT: Dushkin.

Ryan, Edward L. 1933. "The State Court House." *Virginia Magazine of History and Biography* 41 (4): 280–88.

Ryken, Leland. 1990. *Worldly Saints: The Puritans as They Really Were*. Grand Rapids, MI: Zondervan Publishing House.

Ryken, Leland, James C. Wilhoit, and Tremper Longman III, eds. 1998. *Dictionary of Biblical Imagery: An Encyclopedic Exploration of the Images, Symbols, Motifs, Metaphors, Figures of Speech and Literary Patterns of the Bible*. Downers Grove, IL: InterVarsity Press.

Ryland, Elizabeth Hawes. 1940. "King William County and Its Court House." *William and Mary Quarterly* 20 (1): 99–112.

Sauter, Willmar. 2000. *The Theatrical Event: Dynamics of Performance and Perception*. Iowa City: University of Iowa Press.

Schlesinger, Arthur M. 1957. *The Age of Roosevelt*. 3 vols. Boston: Houghton Mifflin.

Schluntz, Roger L. 1982. "Design Competitions: For Whose Benefit Now?" *Journal of Architectural Education* 35 (4): 2–9.

Scobie, Alex. 1990. *Hitler's State Architecture: The Impact of Classical Antiquity*. University Park: Pennsylvania State University Press.

Scott, Felicity D. 2003. "Involuntary Prisoners of Architecture." *October* 106 (Fall): 75–101.

Segal, Jeffrey A., and Harold J. Spaeth. 1993. *The Supreme Court and the Attitudinal Model*. New York: Cambridge University Press.

Shaw, Albert, ed. 1900. *American Monthly Review of Reviews: An International Magazine*. Vol. 22. New York: Review of Reviews Corp.

Simpson, John A., and Edmund S. C. Weiner. 1989. *The Oxford English Dictionary: Volume VII Hat-Intervacuum*. 2nd ed. Oxford: Clarendon Press.

Slauter, Eric. 2009. *The State as a Work of Art: The Cultural Origins of the Constitution*. Chicago: University of Chicago Press.

Smith, Jason Scott. 2006. *Building New Deal Liberalism: The Political Economy of Public Works, 1933–1956*. New York: Cambridge University Press.

Smith, Jeffrey A. 1990. *Franklin and Bache: Envisioning the Enlightened Republic*. New York: Oxford.

Smith, Margaret B. 1906. *The First Forty Years of Washington Society*. New York: Charles Scribner's Sons.

Sommer, Robert. 1983. *Social Design: Creating Buildings with People in Mind*. Englewood Cliffs, NJ: Prentice-Hall.

Spreiregen, Paul D. 1979. *Design Competitions*. New York: McGraw-Hill.

Stern, Robert A. M. 2001. "Introduction." In *Cass Gilbert, Life and Work: Architect of the Public Domain*, edited by Barbara Christen and Steven Flanders, 15–24. New York: W. W. Norton.

Story, Joseph. 1851. *Life and Letters of Joseph Story, Associate Justice of the Supreme Court of the United States, and Dane Professor of Law at Harvard University*. 2 vols. Edited by William W. Story. Boston: Little and Brown.

Sullivan, Elaine. 2008. "Introduction to the Temple of Karnak." *Digital Karnak*. Accessed March 26, 2012. http://dlib.etc.ucla.edu/projects/Karnak.

Sumner, William G. 1906. *Folkways: A Study of the Sociological Importance of Usages, Manners, Customs, Mores, and Morals*. Boston: Ginn.

Sweeney, Kevin M. 1993. "Meetinghouses, Town Houses, and Churches: Changing Perceptions of Sacred and Secular Space in Southern New England, 1720–1850." *Winterthur Portfolio* 28 (1): 59–93.

Tocqueville, Alexis. 1840a. "Chapter X: Why the Americans Are More Addicted to Practical rather Than Theoretical Science." In *Democracy in America*, vol. 2. http://xroads.virginia.edu/~HYPER/DETOC/ch1_10.htm.

———. 1840b. "Chapter XI: In What Spirit the Americans Cultivate the Arts." In *Democracy in America*, vol. 2. http://xroads.virginia.edu/~HYPER/DETOC/ch1_11.htm.

Trumbull, James Russell. 1902. *History of Northampton, Massachusetts; from Its Settlement in 1654*. Northampton, MA: Press of Gazette.

United States Courts. 2011. Educational Resources: U.S. Supreme Court Procedures. Accessed December 28, 2011; no longer available. http://www.uscourts.gov/EducationalResources/ConstitutionResources/SeparationOfPowers/USSupremeCourtProcedures.aspx.

Upton, Dell. 1997. *Holy Things and Profane: Anglican Parish Churches in Colonial Virginia*. New Haven, CT: Yale University Press.

Urofsky, Melvin I. 2005. "The Taft Court (1921–1930): Groping for Modernity." In *The United States Supreme Court: The Pursuit of Justice*, edited by Christopher Tomlins, 199–220. Boston: Houghton Mifflin.

U.S. Commission of Fine Arts. N.d. "History of the Commission of Fine Arts." Accessed February 15, 2021. https://www.cfa.gov/about-cfa/history.

U.S. Courts Design Guide. 1991. United States: Administrative Office of the U.S. Courts, Space and Facilities Division. Washington, DC.

U.S. National Park Service. 1993. Historic American Buildings Survey (HABS). *Judiciary Square (Reservation No. 7)*. HABS DC-690. Washington, D.C.: Library of Congress Prints and Photographs Division.

U.S. Supreme Court. 2003a. "Courtroom Friezes: South and North Walls." Accessed January 15, 2021. https://www.supremecourt.gov/about/northandsouthwalls.pdf.

———. 2003b. "Figures of Justice." Accessed January 15, 2012. https://www.supremecourt.gov/about/figuresofjustice.pdf.

———. 2009. "The West Pediment: Information Sheet." Accessed January 15, 2021. https://www.supremecourt.gov/about/WestPediment8-10-2009_Final.pdf.

———. 2010a. "Courtroom Friezes: East and West Walls." Accessed January 15, 2021. https://www.supremecourt.gov/about/eastandwestwalls.pdf.

———. 2010b. "Elena Kagan's Oath Ceremony." U.S. Supreme Court press release, August 5. Accessed January 15, 2021. https://www.supremecourt.gov/public info/press/pressreleases/pr_08-05-10.

———. 2010c. "Rules of the Supreme Court of the United States." Accessed January 15, 2021. https://www.supremecourt.gov/pdfs/rules/rules_2010.pdf.

———. 2010d. "Statues of *Contemplation of Justice* and *Authority of Law*." Accessed January 15, 2021. https://www.supremecourt.gov/about/FraserStatuesInfo Sheet.pdf.

———. 2010e. "Supreme Court Visitor Entrance." U.S. Supreme Court press release, May 3. Accessed January 15, 2021. https://www.supremecourt.gov/public info/press/pressreleases/pr_05-03-10.

———. 2015. "Symbols of Law." Accessed January 15, 2021. https://www.supreme court.gov/about/SymbolsofLawInfoSheet%209-28-2015_Final.pdf.

———. 2018. "The Bronze Doors." Accessed January 15, 2021. https://www.supreme court.gov/about/BronzeDoors_5-7-2018_Final.pdf.

———. 2019a. "Guide for Counsel in Cases to be Argued before the Supreme Court of the United States." Accessed January 15, 2021. https://www.supreme court.gov/casehand/Guide%20for%20Counsel%202019_rev10_3_19.pdf.

———. 2019b. "Reliefs on the Exterior Medallions and the Great Hall Frieze." Accessed January 15, 2021. https://www.supremecourt.gov/about/medallions andmetopes081419.pdf.

———. 2021a. "The Court and Its Traditions." Accessed January 15, 2021. http://www.supremecourt.gov/about/traditions.aspx.

———. 2021b. "The Court Building." Accessed January 15, 2021. http://www.supremecourt.gov/about/courtbuilding.aspx.

———. 2021c. "Frequently Asked Questions: Locating Court Documents and Information." Accessed January 15, 2021. https://www.supremecourt.gov/about/faq_documents.aspx.

———. 2021d. "Visitor's Guide to the Supreme Court." Accessed January 15, 2021. https://www.supremecourt.gov/visiting/visitorsguide-supremecourt.aspx.

———. 2021e. "What Can I See and Do?" Accessed January 15, 2021. https://www.supremecourt.gov/visiting/whatcaniseeanddo.aspx.

Vago, Steven. 1997. *Law and Society*. 5th ed. Upper Saddle River, NJ: Prentice Hall.

Vale, Lawrence J. 1992. *Architecture, Power, and National Identity*. New Haven, CT: Yale University Press.

Vanderkam, James C. 1991. "Joshua the High Priest and the Interpretation of Zechariah 3." *The Catholic Biblical Quarterly* 53 (4): 553–70.

Vishnia, Rachel Feig. 1996. *State, Society and Popular Leaders in Mid-Republican Rome 241–167 B.C.* London: Routledge.

Walsh, James P. 1980. "Holy Time and Sacred Space in Puritan New England." *American Quarterly* 32 (1): 79–95.

Walton, John H. 2001. *Genesis.* Grand Rapids, MI: Zondervan.

Ware, William R. 1899. "American Architect." *American Architect and Building News* 66: 107–9.

Warren, Earl. 1958. "Chief Justice William Howard Taft." *Yale Law Journal* 67 (3): 353–62.

Waterman, Thomas T. 1936. "The Old Court House Buildings, Stafford Court House, Virginia." *William and Mary Quarterly* 16 (2): 247.

Weber, Max. (1905) 1992. *The Protestant Ethic and the Spirit of Capitalism.* Translated by Talcott Parsons and Anthony Giddens. New York: Routledge.

———. (1914) 1954. *Max Weber on Law in Economy and Society.* Edited by Max Rheinstein. Translated by Edward A. Shils and Max Rheinstein. Cambridge, MA: Harvard University Press.

———. (1918) 2004. *The Vocation Lectures.* Edited by David Owen and Tracy B. Strong. Translated by Rodney Livingstone. Indianapolis: Hacket.

Wiseman, Carter. 1998. *Shaping a Nation: Twentieth-Century American Architecture and Its Makers.* New York: W. W. Norton.

Wittenberg, Eric J., Edmund A. Sargus Jr., and Penny L. Barrick. 2020. *Seceding from Secession: The Civil War, Politics, and the Creation of West Virginia.* New York: Savas Beatie.

Wood, Ellen Meiksins. 1988. *Peasant-Citizen and Slave: The Foundations of Athenian Democracy.* London: Verso.

Wood, Joseph S. 1986. "The New England Village as an American Vernacular Form." *Perspectives in Vernacular Architecture* 2: 54–63.

Woodward, Bob, and Scott Armstrong. 1979. *The Brethren: Inside the Supreme Court.* New York: Simon and Schuster.

Wright, Frank Lloyd. 1977. *An Autobiography: Frank Lloyd Wright.* New York: Horizon Press.

Yeroulanou, Marina. 1998. "Metopes and Architecture: The Hephaisteion and the Parthenon." *Annual of the British School at Athens* 93: 401–25.

Young, Iris Marion. 2000. *Inclusion and Democracy.* Oxford: Oxford University Press.

Young, James Sterling. 1966. *The Washington Community: 1800–1828.* New York: Columbia University Press.

Yurco, Frank J. 1990. "3,200-Year-Old Picture of Israelites Found in Egypt." *Biblical Archaeology Review* 16 (5). Accessed March 29, 2010. http://cojs.org/3200 -year-old-picture-of-israelites-found-in-egypt/.

Index

Page numbers in *italic type* refer to illustrative matter.

www.ingramcontent.com/pod-product-compliance
Lightning Source LLC
Chambersburg PA
CBHW020703270326
41928CB00005B/243